"We are blessed with scholarly commentari  as with more popular surveys. Rarer are thos of the text with the research of the former of the latter. One feature distinguishing *Mark by the Book* is the rubric applied to each story: reading it downward (Christ-centered focus), sideways (parallel Gospel accounts), backward (Old Testament prophecy), and forward (future fulfillment). This approach exposes the meaning in each pericope with powerful effect and remarkable insight. I highly recommend this exploration of Mark."

—**Michael Horton**, J. Gresham Machen Professor of Systematic Theology and Apologetics, Westminster Seminary California

"What a wonderful idea—a commentary for redemptive-historical preaching! Here we have a skillful unfolding of the message of Mark, first by close examination of the text, not verse-by-verse, but by looking intently at the Gospel's crucial, life-changing stories—stories that reveal to us the character, person, and deeds of Jesus. Smuts then compares Mark's telling with other Gospels to underscore Mark's special interests, takes note of how Jesus fulfills the hopes of Israel flowing from the Old Testament, and finally shows us how Jesus affects the future, the rest of the New Testament, and the church. Dr. Smuts has clearly immersed himself in Mark, not as an isolated text but as part of God's whole Bible, addressed to God's whole people, and here is the fruit of his study: informed, accessible, enthusiastic, and pastoral."

—**Dan G. McCartney**, Professor of New Testament Interpretation, Redeemer Seminary, Dallas

"Premised on the redemptive-historical character of biblical revelation, Smuts's studies in Mark's Gospel provide instructive examples of his 'multidirectional' hermeneutic that also demonstrate the potential of his approach for a sound understanding of the other Gospels. Without necessarily agreeing with the author's exegetical conclusions at every point, not only his intended audience of college students but others—seminarians, pastors, college and seminary teachers, and other interested persons—will benefit from this carefully researched and clearly conceived and written volume."

—**Richard B. Gaffin Jr.**, Professor of Biblical and Systematic Theology, Emeritus, Westminster Theological Seminary, Philadelphia

"I commend *Mark by the Book* for four reasons. First, experience: it is the product of years of teaching students. Second, focus: it is crystal clear, insightful, and Christ centered. Third, practicality: it works. The author has successfully used it to train students how to interpret Scripture better. Fourth, fruit: the result is better handling of God's Word, more love for Jesus, and a greater zeal to spread the good news—four very good things!"

—**Robert A. Peterson**, Professor of Systematic Theology, Covenant Theological Seminary, St. Louis

MARK
BY THE
BOOK

MARK
BY THE
BOOK

A NEW MULTIDIRECTIONAL
METHOD FOR UNDERSTANDING
THE SYNOPTIC GOSPELS

P. W. SMUTS

PUBLISHING
P.O. BOX 817 • PHILLIPSBURG • NEW JERSEY 08865-0817

ISBN 978-1-59638-440-8 (pbk.)
ISBN: 978-1-59638-758-4 (ePub)
ISBN: 978-1-59638-759-1 (Mobi)

Printed in the United States of America

Library of Congress Cataloging-in-Publication Data

Smuts, Peter W., 1958-
 Mark by the book : a new multidirectional method for
understanding the Synoptic Gospels / Peter W. Smuts.
   p. cm.
 Includes bibliographical references (p.   ) and indexes.
 ISBN 978-1-59638-440-8 (pbk.)
 1. Bible. N.T. Mark--Criticism, interpretation, etc. I. Title.
 BS2585.52.S68 2013
 226.3'06--dc23
                    2012027516

I dedicate this book to the wife of my youth, Dagmar, my best friend, a true "helpmeet," a fellow disciple of the Lord Jesus Christ, and an heir with me of the gracious gift of life.

CONTENTS

FOREWORD

SERIOUS STUDY of the four Gospels is a rich and rewarding enterprise. In these documents—attributed to Matthew, Mark, Luke, and John from the earliest centuries of the church—the Spirit of God gives us a three-dimensional portrait of the most appealing and alarming, comforting and confrontational, majestic and meek and mystifying person ever to walk the earth: "Jesus Christ, the Son of God," as Mark introduces him (Mark 1:1).

Serious study of the Gospels is not only spiritually enriching, but also a daunting challenge. The person of Jesus reaches out from the page to take hold of us in disconcerting ways. He does not let us distance ourselves as aloof readers or scholars, but insists on addressing us as fallen and alienated image-bearers of God, in need of the redemption that he came to earth to achieve, at the highest cost to himself. Moreover, in order for us to grasp the meaning of the accounts that make up any of the four versions of the good news, we need to pay attention to the setting of any passage within several contexts simultaneously. Of course, for any text anywhere in Scripture, our interpretation must consider its various contexts. We will hear its message most truly and most fully when we notice its location in its own book and historical situation, and then in the broader flow of the Bible's unfolding history of redemption and revelation. But for the Gospels, even more contexts demand our attention, if we are going to hear all that the Spirit of truth says in his testimony to the incarnate Son and Servant of God through these inspired good-news-tellers, Matthew, Mark, Luke, and John.

Learning to read the Gospels is somewhat like learning to ride a bike. To make progress, or even to survive without bruised elbows and skinned knees, you need to pay attention to many things at once:

pedaling, gripping the handlebars, steering, keeping your balance, lean-
ing on the turns (but not too far), avoiding obstacles ahead, staying out
of the path of approaching vehicles behind, and keeping an eye out for
cross-traffic from the side. Similarly, as Dr. P. W. Smuts shows, to read
the Gospels well and to savor the richness of their revelation of Jesus
the Christ, we must pay attention in four directions at once, or at least
in close and intentional succession. In the introduction to a multidirectional hermeneutic for exploring the Gospels, Dr. Smuts explains why
and how we need to read each passage *downward* (seeing its depth in the
context of the evangelist's whole document), *sideways* (comparing it with
parallel accounts, particularly in the other two Synoptic Gospels), *backward* (discerning allusions to previous revelation in the Old Testament),
and *forward* (tracing motifs in Jesus' ministry as they are developed in
the rest of the New Testament, for the church this side of the cross, the
resurrection, and the descent of the Spirit).

Just as a young child taking her "maiden voyage" on a two-wheeler
takes comfort and courage from knowing that Dad is trotting alongside,
his hand stabilizing the bike and its rider and his voice of experience
offering coaching and encouragement, so in *Mark by the Book* a sea-
soned New Testament scholar and teacher runs with us through Mark's
compact, yet fully packed witness to the good news. Dr. Smuts teaches
us how to read the Synoptic Gospels for all they are worth by showing
us how it is done. His blend of coaching and modeling makes sound
hermeneutical theory concrete in practice. But he does more than this.
Each chapter is not merely a hermeneutics lesson or lab. An aroma of
worship and a summons to trust in the suffering and risen Messiah
pervade the exposition, even as we watch multidirectional reading performed soundly and soberly.

Another feature that distinguishes *Mark by the Book* from some
approaches to the Synoptics, in both evangelical and historical-critical
circles, is the way in which Dr. Smuts's confidence in the divinely imparted
theological *unity* of the whole biblical canon—Old Testament and New
Testament—enriches his backward and forward readings. Fully mindful
of the historical contrasts that distinguish the Scriptures conveyed to
Israel in the age of anticipation from the far fuller, semi-eschatological
revelation that accompanied the coming of Christ, Dr. Smuts shows—
through the numerous Old Testament allusions embedded in Mark's

Gospel—that the same God of truth who spoke of old through prophets has now spoken at last in the Son (Heb. 1:1–4). Promise and fulfillment are related to each other by both continuity and progress. Dr. Smuts's forward readings likewise remind us that the teaching and events that Mark conveys to the post-Pentecost church actually occurred before Pentecost, in Jesus' humble and powerful kingdom-inaugurating ministry, which led to his death and resurrection. The rest of the New Testament—both the continuing narrative of the book of Acts and the Epistles' doctrinal and ethical instruction—provides the perspective that we need to "translate," for example, Jesus' heart-searching challenge to a rich young man into the Spirit's word to the whole church throughout time and around the world (Mark 10:17–31). As with the movement from Old Testament anticipation to the dawn of God's kingdom in Christ's earthly ministry, so also as particular passages in Mark are read in the wider and later horizon of the whole New Testament, we see a beautiful blend of continuity and elaboration in the fullness of God's Word that now addresses the church.

With pleasure I invite you to learn a wise and full-orbed approach to interpreting the Synoptic Gospels by following Dr. Smuts's lead as he reads Mark "by the Book"—the *whole Book* that God's Spirit has breathed out in his witness to Jesus the Son. Listen to the voice of the second evangelist in his quartet with the others, pick up the echoes of God's earlier words through Israel's prophets, and attend to the Spirit's commentary in Acts and the Epistles. As your reading skills grow, may your trust in Jesus, the Servant-King to whom Mark testifies, grow as well.

Dennis E. Johnson, PhD
Professor of Practical Theology
Westminster Seminary California

ACKNOWLEDGMENTS

I AM CONSCIOUS that in writing this book, my first, I stand on the shoulders of many others. I am grateful to the Lord God for his providential guidance that has brought me into contact with teachers and pastors—both in the present and from a bygone era—and colleagues and friends, who have inspired me to love and serve the Lord Jesus Christ, the subject matter of this book. I am reminded of the words of J. C. Ryle, a nineteenth-century churchman, who wrote as follows in his classic work *Holiness*:

> It would be well if professing Christians in modern days studied the four Gospels more than they do. No doubt all Scripture is profitable. It is not wise to exalt one part of the Bible at the expense of another. But I think it should be good for some who are very familiar with the Epistles, if they knew a little more about Matthew, Mark, Luke, and John. Now why do I say this? I say it because I want professing Christians to know more about Christ. It is well to be acquainted with all the doctrines and principles of Christianity. It is better to be acquainted with Christ Himself. It is well to be familiar with faith, and grace, and justification, and sanctification. They are all matters "pertaining to the King." But it is far better to be familiar with Jesus Himself, to see the King's own face, and to behold His beauty. This is one secret of eminent holiness. He that would be conformed to Christ's image, and become a Christ-like man, must be constantly studying Christ Himself.[1]

It would be a worthy outcome if this book, in any measure, inspired the reader to constantly study Christ himself.

---

1. J. C. Ryle, *Holiness* (Welwyn, UK: Evangelical Press, 1979), 191.

I want to thank the Board of the Bible Institute of South Africa for granting me a sabbatical during which a substantial portion of this book was completed. I also want to acknowledge the prayers of friends, on both sides of the Atlantic, that have sustained and encouraged me during the writing process. A special word of thanks must go to Robert Peterson, whose guidance and assistance, particularly in the early stages of this writing project, were of enormous help in bringing this book to publication.

January 2012
Cape Town

INTRODUCTION TO A MULTIDIRECTIONAL GOSPEL HERMENEUTIC

THE SYNOPTIC GOSPELS play an important role in the Christian faith. These Gospels are all about Jesus, the cornerstone of the Christian faith. It is therefore important that the Christian reader have a clear understanding of this part of the Bible. But the interpreter of the Gospels is faced with several challenges that include the relationship between the Old Testament and the Gospels, the relationship between the various Gospels, and the relationship between the Christian and the Gospels. In the case of the Old Testament, how does Jesus fulfill these Scriptures? In the case of the other Gospels, should the goal be to harmonize the Gospels or preserve their distinctives? In the case of the believer, can the teaching of the Gospels simply be applied to the Christian? For many Christians, the approach to these questions can be uncritical, or hit and miss; no model or set of principles is in place to address them. Commentaries, generally speaking, are not much help. The reader is left to guess at the principles that govern a commentator's interpretation or exegesis of the text. Books that describe the process of interpreting the Gospels sometimes discuss this matter under the general heading of interpreting narrative literature; they do not always take into account some of the distinctives of interpreting the Gospels. Even books that do focus exclusively on Gospel exegesis can be overtechnical and theoretical, with little practical application of the principles taught. The reader of the Gospels is all too often left to his or her own devices. Consequently, the Gospels are easily misinterpreted and misapplied in the modern context. The purpose of this book is to address this problem by describing and applying a straightforward approach to the interpretation of the Synoptic Gospels that can benefit any interpreter of these Scriptures.

A traditional evangelical model of biblical interpretation draws a distinction between exegesis and hermeneutics. The goal of exegesis is to determine what the biblical text *meant* in its original historical context, while the goal of hermeneutics is to determine what the biblical text *means* for the reader today. To achieve this goal, as a first step, interpreters must place themselves in the shoes of the original readers, so to speak, as they analyze the details of the text in its immediate literary context, sometimes referred to as the *co-text*. This places the focus firmly on the details of the text. In the case of narrative material such as the Gospels, these details include the setting, characters, story line, and flow of the text, which the interpreter should factor in to determine the author's intended meaning in the historical context. On occasion, an introductory or concluding statement in a unit of text will clue the reader to the author's intended meaning. Accurate exegesis will adequately explain all the details of the text.

In the case of the Synoptic Gospels, we argue that this traditional model of interpretation should be expanded to include an approach that grounds the Gospels in the entire canon of Scripture. Simply put, the proper literary context of the text of the Gospels is the whole Bible. This perspective on the Gospels reflects the progressive nature and organic unity of biblical revelation. Old Testament quotations, allusions, or motifs are scattered throughout the Gospels, alerting the reader to the need to factor in the broader Old Testament or redemptive-historical context of the text. Moreover, in the case of so-called Gospel double or triple traditions (i.e., parallel accounts in two or three of the Synoptic Gospels), a comparative reading of the parallel accounts can help the reader to better discern the purpose of a particular Gospel account. A consideration of the rest of the New Testament writings will enable the Christian reader to identify any subsequent teaching or developments that may qualify the contemporary application of the Gospels on a particular motif or theme. Consequently, the ideal reader of the Gospels is one who interprets them in the broader flow of redemptive history—what precedes and what follows—thereby detecting connections, contrasts, and developments found elsewhere in Scripture that relate directly to the interpretation and application of the text being interpreted. This, in a nutshell, is the model that we will apply to the interpretation of the Gospels. We have dubbed this model a *multidirectional* approach to the interpretation of the Gospels to reflect the dynamics of reading the Gospels from the various perspectives—downward, sideways, backward, and forward—alluded to above.

A brief historical perspective on this matter may be helpful at this point. With the advent of redaction criticism during the last century that construed the Gospel writers as theologians, rather than "cut-and-paste" editors of traditions, it became the practice, even among evangelicals, to seek to establish the distinctive theology of each of the Gospels. The goal was to preserve the theological distinctives of each Gospel rather than to attempt to harmonize the different accounts. So it became commonplace to speak of Matthean or Markan or Lukan theology, each with its own distinctive portrait of Jesus.[1] The publication of various synopses of the canonical Gospels presented parallel material side by side to facilitate a comparative reading of the Gospels as a strategy to identify the particular distinctive(s) of each synoptic account.

We recognize that the Synoptic Gospel writers did each compose their narratives with a distinct purpose in mind. Luke is the most explicit in this regard (Luke 1:4; cf. John 20:31). In the case of Matthew and Mark, whose Gospels contain no explicit purpose statements, the sense of purpose can be detected in the narrative details of each Gospel, and should guide the interpretation of these writings. There is no doubt that a comparative or *sideways* reading of the Gospels can be of considerable help when attempting to discern the particular purpose of any Gospel text. Agreements and differences in the wording and arrangement between parallel materials will alert the reader to the distinctives of each Gospel.[2] The meaning of any text should be grounded in all the

---

1. In the Gospels, you have Jesus on the move. Therefore, in this digital age, it is probably more accurate to think of the Gospels as edited video clips of Jesus' life, with each Gospel writer selecting the same or different camera angles of the same incidents, or selecting different video material to narrate his distinctive record of the life and ministry of Jesus.

2. The redaction critic may ask how one Gospel writer changed or adapted a parallel tradition as a clue to determining the theological perspective of a particular Gospel text. This question

narrative details, however, not just in those details that are unique to it. The goal of a sideways reading is to view all the details of the text in the light shed by the other Gospel writers. Parallel accounts should not be blended so as to distort the meaning of a particular Gospel text.[3] The literary integrity of each Gospel should be preserved. The immediate literary context of any Gospel text should therefore remain primary in any hermeneutical endeavor, a process that we refer to as a *downward* reading of the Gospel, reflecting the motion of interpreting the text in light of what precedes and what follows it.

This sideways and downward Gospel reading strategy should, in our opinion, be expanded to include a so-called *backward* reading of the Gospels that factors in their Old Testament background. The fingerprints of the Old Testament are all over the pages of the Gospels. One writer highlights the foundational role of the Old Testament in the Gospels as follows:

> It is difficult to overemphasize the importance of the function of the OT in the Gospels. It is readily apparent that the Jewish Scriptures were foundational to many of Jesus' teachings and probably to his self-understanding as well. Specific OT passages and themes lie behind many of the parables and often lie at the center of debate between

---

usually assumes a particular chronological sequence for the composition of the Gospels based on an analysis of the possible literary interdependence between them. The exact nature of any literary interdependence remains a point of contention, referred to as the *synoptic problem* by modern scholarship. Today many scholars would argue for Markan priority, that is, that Mark was the first to write his Gospel. A few scholars, however, continue to insist that Matthew was the first to pen his Gospel. The facts are such that it is unwise to be dogmatic about any of the proposed solutions to this problem. Consequently, it becomes precarious to base an interpretation of a Gospel text on any particular composition sequence or source-critical theory. In our opinion, however, this state of affairs does not undermine the legitimacy of a sideways reading of the text, as long as the reader uses a parallel tradition to illuminate the significance of the details of a Gospel text without importing details that are foreign to that particular Gospel. The Gospels scholar Robert Stein contends that even if Mark's Gospel, the focus of our study, was the first to be composed, the reader of this Gospel is still given clues to Mark's particular theological perspective in the so-called Markan seams, insertions, summaries, arrangement of material, introduction, choice of vocabulary, Christological titles, modifications, selection and omission of material, and conclusion. Our proposed sideways reading of the Gospel will help the reader to identify the presence and significance of some of these details in the text. Robert H. Stein, "Interpreting the Synoptic Gospels," in *Interpreting the New Testament: Essays on Methods and Issues*, ed. David Alan Black and David S. Dockery (Nashville: Broadman & Holman, 2001), 349–51.

3. We will not attempt to reconcile all the differences between the parallel accounts; other resources address this issue. E.g., Craig Blomberg, *The Historical Reliability of the Gospels* (Downers Grove, IL: InterVarsity Press, 1987). Rather, our focus will be on interpreting the details of the text.

Jesus and his opponents. The relationship of Jesus to the OT was not lost on the Evangelists. They sought in various ways to show how Jesus understood Scripture, fulfilled Scripture and was clarified by Scripture. In fact there is no significant idea developed in the Gospels that does not in some way reflect or depend on the OT.[4]

The Gospel writers assumed a knowledge of the Old Testament Scriptures on the part of their readers when they composed their narratives. Consequently, any interpreter who ignores this broader literary context runs the risk of misconstruing the meaning of the Gospels. The reader of the Gospels will be prompted to engage with the Old Testament by the presence of Old Testament quotations, by the recognition of Old Testament allusions or motifs, or through word studies that reveal an Old Testament pedigree. This exercise is not without its difficulties. Much exegetical insight may be gained, however, if the reader simply takes the step to access and reflect on the literary context of the Old Testament quotation, allusion, or word occurrence, to ascertain how it may affect the meaning of the Gospel narrative in which it occurs.[5] Our backward analysis of Mark 1:1–8, in chapter 2, will provide some additional guidelines regarding this component of the exegetical process.

Finally, we argue that it is also necessary to employ a so-called *forward* reading of the Gospels. Although Jesus Christ is the One who fulfills the Old Testament Scriptures (Matt. 5:17), this should not be

---

4. C. A. Evans, "Old Testament in the Gospels," in *Dictionary of Jesus and the Gospels* (Downers Grove, IL: InterVarsity Press, 1992), 579.

5. According to Craig Evans, "to assess properly the function of the OT in the NT, the following questions must be raised: (1) What OT text(s) is (are) being cited? . . . (2) Which text-type is being cited (Hebrew, Greek, Aramaic)? . . . How does the version that the NT has followed contribute to the meaning of the quotation? (3) Is the OT quotation part of a wider tradition or theology in the OT? If it is, the quotation may be alluding to a context much wider than the specific passage from which it has been taken. (4) How did various Jewish and Christian groups and interpreters understand the passage? . . . (5) In what ways does the NT citation agree or disagree with the interpretations found in the versions and other ancient exegeses? Has the Jesus/Christian tradition distinctively shaped the OT quotation and its interpretation, or does the NT exegesis reflect interpretation current in pre-Christian Judaism? (6) How does the function of the quotation compare to the function of other quotations in the NT writings under consideration? Has a different text-type been used? Has the OT been followed more closely or less so? (7) Finally, how does the quotation contribute to the argument of the NT passage in which it is found?" *Ancient Texts for New Testament Studies* (Peabody, MA: Hendrickson, 2005), 6–7. Some of these legitimate questions that Evans raises demand a level of expertise that eludes all but a few in the field. By focusing on questions 1, 3, and 7 of Evans's list, our approach to the Old Testament background is designed to make it accessible to the average reader of the Bible.

misunderstood to mean that the canonical Gospels, which record his ministry, represent the pinnacle or completion of redemptive revelation. Rather, the Gospels reflect a time of transition in redemptive history that bridges the old and new covenants. The Gospels deal with the inauguration of God's kingdom that leads into the church age, signaled by the outpouring of the Spirit at Pentecost (Acts 2:1–21). This subsequent church age, sometimes referred to as "the last days" (e.g., Acts 2:17, quoting Joel 2:28), ushers in the end of the age and the consummation of God's kingdom. The church's infancy is recorded in the Acts of the Apostles, its struggles addressed in the New Testament Epistles, and its glorious climax spelled out in the Apocalypse of John. The point is that the Gospels and the rest of New Testament revelation represent two different periods in redemptive history.[6] The Christian reader lives in this church age, and not in the redemptive-historical era of the Gospels. Accordingly, we argue, the interpreter of the Gospels cannot insist on a simple and straightforward application of the Gospels in the church age; the progress of redemptive history may have brought changes or introduced elements of discontinuity.

Jesus' instruction to the man healed of his leprosy illustrates the point: "See that you don't tell this to anyone. But go, show yourself to the priest and offer the sacrifices that Moses commanded for your cleansing, as a testimony to them" (Mark 1:44). This command cannot simply be applied to the believer today; it cannot be obeyed as it stands, whether by a Jewish or Gentile believer in the church today. Consequently, the Christian is compelled to ask how developments in the subsequent New Testament–era canonical writings may qualify or modify Jesus' teaching for the churchgoer.[7] We call this process a forward reading of the

6. We cannot date the New Testament writings with any degree of precision. But even if the Synoptic Gospels were written later than some of the New Testament Epistles, this does not alter the fact that they reflect an earlier and different stage in redemptive history. Contrary to some critical scholarship, we are assuming at this point that the Gospels reflect the life of the historical Jesus rather than later developments within the early church.

7. A text such as 2 Timothy 3:16–17 makes the point that all Scripture has applicatory relevance to the believer in the church age. So truths or principles may be gleaned from earlier stages of redemptive history to inform the Christian believer's behavior today (see Heb. 11:1–40; 12:16–17). But this should not be misunderstood to mean that all Scripture can simply be applied without modification to the believer today. For example, the Christian no longer offers Old Testament animal sacrifices because of the once-for-all sacrifice of Jesus on the cross. The flow of the story of salvation makes this obvious, a point reinforced by the teaching of the letter to the Hebrews (Heb. 9:26). Yet the principle of sacrifice still applies to the Christian, a truth taught by an oft-

Gospels. This step applies even when we may deem obedience to a particular command of Jesus possible. So, for example, a straightforward application of Jesus' command to the so-called rich young ruler would require that every seeker "go, sell everything you have and give to the poor" (Mark 10:21). A forward reading of the Gospels, however, reveals that this command is not applied to other seekers or disciples in the early church, although the voluntary practice of selling one's possessions and helping the needy is evident on occasion (e.g., Acts 2:45; 4:34–35). Consequently, the church has traditionally viewed Jesus' command to this rich young ruler as specific to this encounter, but not prescriptive for every Christian—rightly so, in our opinion. Thus, we may properly speak of the need to engage in this kind of forward reading of the Gospels.[8] On occasion, this hermeneutic may well affirm that at many points the teaching of the Gospels can simply be applied to the Christian without qualification or modification. Nevertheless, this step will function as an important safeguard to ensure the valid application of gospel truth to the Christian.[9]

We have argued above for a multidirectional hermeneutic to accurately interpret the Synoptic Gospels and apply them to the

---

quoted verse in the New Testament (Rom. 12:1). We are simply arguing that the same principle, as a matter of course, should be applied to the interpretation and application of the Gospels to ensure a valid application of the truths taught.

8. McCartney and Clayton, in harmony with our proposed forward reading of the text, recommend the following steps to safeguard accurate application of the biblical text: establish how the biblical text transcends its original historical setting; identify the ways in which earlier events and institutions point to the later and fuller fulfillment; observe the context of the canon as a whole, or application of the so-called analogy of faith; and finally, identify how changes in the redemptive-historical situation may have affected the text's applicability in the present situation. Dan McCartney and Charles Clayton, *Let the Reader Understand: A Guide to Interpreting and Applying the Bible* (Wheaton, IL: Bridgepoint, 1994), 151. In a similar vein, authors Klein, Blomberg, and Hubbard list a series of ten questions to determine whether the specific elements of a biblical passage can be applied unchanged to the Christian today. Most relevant for our purposes are the following two questions, which essentially affirm our forward reading of the Gospels: Does subsequent revelation limit the application of a particular passage even if the book in which it appears does not? Is the specific teaching "contradicted" elsewhere in ways that show that it was limited to exceptional situations? William W. Klein, Craig Blomberg, and Robert L. Hubbard Jr., *Introduction to Biblical Interpretation* (Nashville: Thomas Nelson, 2004), 488–89.

9. As a general rule of biblical application, the Christian reader may helpfully ask as a safeguard, "What does the whole Bible teach on this matter?" before applying any text. This step will help to reduce the erroneous application of biblical truth by ensuring that the reader has the whole picture of what the Bible teaches on a particular point. Of course, in applying this maxim, the Christian reads not from the perspective of the Old Testament believer, but from that of the New Testament saint.

Christian reader—a downward, sideways, backward, and forward reading of any Synoptic Gospel text. A downward reading of the text focuses on the text within the context of the particular Gospel; a sideways reading focuses on all the Gospel parallel traditions. A backward reading focuses on the Old Testament background, while a forward reading focuses on a motif in the rest of the New Testament. The dynamics of this Gospel hermeneutic may be graphically represented as follows: **Text** ←→ Gospel ←→ Gospels ←→ Old Testament ←→ New Testament = accurate interpretation and application of the text to the Christian reader today!

Clearly, this model compels the reader to reflect on the Gospels against the broader sweep of redemptive history taught in the entire Bible. All of this may be neatly summarized in the principle: "The better you know the whole Bible, the better you will be able to interpret any part of the Bible!" While not limited to the interpretation of the Gospels, this principle has particular relevance to this type of literature. In this book, this multidirectional hermeneutic will be applied to Mark's Gospel. The dynamic of this hermeneutic leads most naturally to the title of the book—*Mark by the Book*!

WHY MARK'S GOSPEL?

The value of this multidirectional model of interpretation is that it can be applied with benefit to the interpretation of any of the Synoptic Gospels.[10] But why, then, focus on Mark's Gospel? There are a number of reasons for this; let me mention just two of them. First, approximately 90 percent of Mark's Gospel is reproduced in Matthew's Gospel, and over 50 percent in Luke's Gospel, facilitating a sideways reading of Mark's narrative. Second, although Mark's Gospel has relatively few Old Testament quotations compared to Matthew's Gospel, a backward reading of Mark's narrative will reveal a surprising number of Old Testament allusions, with the consequent need to factor in these Scriptures when interpreting this particular Gospel. Simply put, even Mark's Gospel can benefit from a backward reading.

10. On occasion, of course, not all steps of this proposed model will apply—where, for example, no parallel traditions or Old Testament quotations or allusions are present in a particular Gospel text.

THE PURPOSE OF THE BOOK

The purpose of this book is to demonstrate to the Christian reader both the validity and the significant benefits of consistently applying this multidirectional model of interpretation to the Gospels. The reader expecting a complete commentary on Mark's Gospel will be disappointed. Our goal is not to write a commentary per se, or to insist on a particular interpretation of this Gospel; the focus of our study will rather be on the "how-to" of interpreting the Gospels. It should be obvious that this model is not dependent on any particular interpretation of the Gospel; the reader can disagree with our exegesis on a particular text without this invalidating the model as an approach to interpreting the Gospels. Indeed, in our opinion, there is nothing controversial about this model; rather, it is a repackaging into a single model of various accepted principles of how to interpret the Gospels that are not always held together, or consistently applied, when the Synoptic Gospels are interpreted.

THE PLAN AND STYLE OF THE BOOK

We will apply this multidirectional hermeneutic to a select number of passages from Mark's Gospel to illustrate the various steps of this model of interpretation. It is important that these passages be drawn from the entire Gospel to underscore the validity of this model as a Gospel hermeneutic. To achieve this goal, we have selected passages from each chapter of Mark's Gospel. The sequence in applying the steps of the model will be logical, rather than redemptive-theological—that is, first the downward, then the sideways, followed by the backward and forward readings of the text. In our analysis of each of these texts, the intention is to demonstrate the necessity and value of applying this model to the interpretation of the Synoptic Gospels, rather than to provide an exhaustive commentary on the details of the text.

The style of the book is accessible, rather than scholarly. It is designed for the college layperson, rather than the seminarian.

THE SOURCES FOR THE BOOK

As the title of this book suggests, the focus of this hermeneutical model is on the Bible as the primary resource for interpreting the Gospels.

The goal is to encourage the reader to pay close attention to the details of the text in a broader canonical context, to demonstrate that the Bible is essentially self-interpreting. This is not to deny the role or value of research into the secondary literature. In fact, the use of secondary literature is always recommended as a means to confirm or correct one's interpretation of the text, if not also to enrich one's understanding of it.

A number of excellent commentaries on Mark's Gospel can be consulted with benefit, ranging from the popular to the more scholarly commentators, such as James R. Edwards,[11] R. T. France,[12] David E. Garland,[13] Robert H. Gundry,[14] William Lane,[15] and Robert H. Stein.[16] I want to acknowledge my indebtedness to these commentators in particular.

Other useful sources that may help with the implementation of our hermeneutical model include a *Synopsis of the Four Gospels*[17] that is designed to facilitate a sideways reading of the text. The recently published *Commentary on the New Testament Use of the Old Testament*[18] is a comprehensive, helpful, albeit technical, resource that will facilitate a backward reading of the text. A comprehensive or complete concordance, such as *The NIV Complete Concordance*,[19] will provide useful information for a forward reading of the text, supplemented by the cross-references contained in the well-known *Treasury of Scripture Knowledge*.[20] Indeed, a Bible with a good cross-referencing system will provide the Gospel reader with the basic information needed to implement our model of interpretation. In addition, a number of electronic Bible programs (for example, *BibleWorks*, *Logos*) incorporate useful

11. James R. Edwards, *The Gospel according to Mark*, Pillar New Testament Commentary (Grand Rapids: Eerdmans, 2002).

12. R. T. France, *The Gospel of Mark*, New International Greek Testament Commentary (Grand Rapids: Eerdmans, 2002).

13. David E. Garland, *Mark*, NIV Application Commentary (Grand Rapids: Zondervan, 1996).

14. Robert H. Gundry, *Mark: A Commentary on His Apology for the Cross* (Grand Rapids: Eerdmans, 1993).

15. William Lane, *The Gospel of Mark*, New International Commentary on the New Testament (Grand Rapids: Eerdmans, 1974).

16. Robert H. Stein, *Mark*, Baker Exegetical Commentary on the New Testament (Grand Rapids: Baker Academic, 2008).

17. Kurt Aland, ed., *Synopsis of the Four Gospels* (Stuttgart: German Bible Society, 1987).

18. G. K. Beale and D. A. Carson, eds., *Commentary on the New Testament Use of the Old Testament* (Grand Rapids: Baker Academic, 2007).

19. Edward W. Goodrick and John R. Kohlenberger III, *The NIV Complete Concordance* (Grand Rapids: Zondervan, 1981).

20. R. A. Torrey, *The Treasury of Scripture Knowledge* (Peabody, MA: Hendrickson, 1990).

features and resources that can help the interpreter with this hermeneutical enterprise.

While the primary *resource* for this model of interpretation is the Bible as a whole, the primary *inspiration* of this approach is the person and work of the Lord Jesus Christ. This hermeneutical model not only underscores the centrality of Christ in the redemptive purposes of God, but also highlights both his Old Testament roots and his contemporary relevance for the Christian believer. May he receive all the honor and glory!

1

AN INTRODUCTION TO MARK'S GOSPEL

JESUS DID NOT put pen to papyrus to record his ministry and teaching. He entrusted this task to his disciples and ensured that they would succeed in the endeavor (e.g., John 14:26). The four canonical Gospels—Matthew, Mark, Luke, and John—bear eloquent testimony to this truth. Our focus will be on Mark's Gospel. As a first step, it is worthwhile to ask a number of basic questions relating to Mark's Gospel. These so-called questions of special introduction—the *who, what, when,* and *why* of this Gospel—will not only help to anchor Mark's Gospel in history, but also give us a handle to help us interpret it.

We know very little about Mark, other than the few references to him in the New Testament (see Acts 12:12, 25; 13:5, 13; 15:36–39; Col. 4:10–11; 2 Tim. 4:11; Philem. 24; 1 Peter 5:13). He was not one of the Twelve who followed Jesus, although the New Testament links him to the apostle Paul and Barnabas (Acts 12:25; cf. 15:36–40), and tradition links him to the apostle Peter. Significantly, an oft-quoted early tradition states that Mark's Gospel is based on Peter's recollection of Jesus' words and deeds that Mark, as "Peter's interpreter," wrote down "accurately though not in order."[1] This apostolic connection bolsters our

---

1. A report by the church historian Eusebius quotes a lost document written by Papias (about A.D. 140), who in turn cites the apostle John as authority for the following information about this Gospel: "Mark, who became Peter's interpreter, wrote accurately, though not in order, all that he remembers of the things said or done by the Lord. For he had neither heard the Lord nor

I

confidence in the historical accuracy of Mark's Gospel and explains in part the wide circulation and acceptance that this Gospel has always enjoyed in the church.

Some scholars contend that Mark was the first to write a Gospel, but this contention is disputed.[2] What is certain is that the Gospels of Matthew, Mark, and Luke paint similar portraits of Jesus. Their similarities become most apparent when they are compared with John's Gospel, which is quite different in character. Thus, they are usually referred to as the *Synoptic Gospels* because they literally "see together" Jesus' ministry and teaching. Yet in a historical context where, Luke tells us, many accounts of Jesus' words and deeds were circulating (Luke 1:1), not all necessarily accurate, these three Gospels also provide multiple witnesses to the life of Jesus that function as a yardstick to help non-eyewitnesses such as us distinguish the true portrait of Jesus from the false (cf. Deut. 19:15).

Mark's Gospel has been described as a "Passion narrative with an extended introduction,"[3] reflecting the disproportionate amount of narrative space devoted to the last week of Jesus' life. Simply put, the cross looms large in Mark's portrait of Jesus; he cannot be understood apart from his suffering and death at Calvary. Mark writes a fast-paced account of Jesus' ministry. This is reinforced by his narrative style, which one commentator summarizes as follows:

> Mark is the briefest, and in some ways the most attractive, of the four Gospels. Its sparse, unpretentious prose provides uniquely vivid images of Jesus as a Man of action. Mark's narratives are marked by the frequent use of "immediately," which carry us along from scene to scene up to the culminating act of Jesus' courage in

---

been one of His followers, but afterwards, as I said, he had followed Peter, who used to compose his discourses with a view to the needs of his hearers, but not as though he were drawing up a connected account of the Lord's sayings. So Mark made no mistake thus recording some things just as he remembered them. For he was careful of this one thing, to omit none of the things he had heard [from Peter] and to make no untrue statements therein." *Ecclesiastical History* 3.39.15, quoted in Lawrence O. Richards, *The Bible Reader's Companion*, electronic ed. (Wheaton, IL: Victor Books, 1991), 630.

2. This dispute is evident in discussions regarding the solution to the so-called synoptic problem.

3. Martin Kähler, quoted in Craig L. Blomberg, *Jesus and the Gospels* (Leicester, UK: Apollos, 1997), 116. Kähler's comment refers to the structure of all the Gospels, but is most commonly quoted with reference to Mark's Gospel.

boldly facing the cross. His use of the present tense draws us into the scenes he sketches and helps us see events as the writer does, as an eyewitness.[4]

We cannot be certain when Mark recorded his Gospel, but most contemporary commentators argue for a date in the middle to late A.D. 60s.[5] An early tradition places Mark in Rome when he composed his Gospel. It is commonly argued that Mark's Gospel was also written to the predominantly Gentile church in Rome. The following evidence in his Gospel is sometimes harnessed to support this view:

- Its frequent transliteration (instead of translation) of Latin words (e.g., Mark 12:15; 15:16).
- Its scarcity of Old Testament quotations, and its omission of parables meaningful mainly to Jews (e.g., Good Samaritan; Pharisee and tax collector).
- Its explanations of Jewish words (3:17; 5:41; 7:11, 34; 14:36) and customs (7:3; 14:12; 15:42).

In our opinion, however, it is speculative to limit Mark's target audience to Rome. At best, these features suggest an audience that includes these readers. In fact, the many geographical references and Old Testament quotations and allusions that introduce Mark's Gospel (e.g., Mark 1:1-13, 40-44) could just as easily suggest a possible Jewish Palestinian audience, rather than a Gentile Roman set of readers. We are on firmer ground if we simply conclude that Mark wrote his Gospel for wide circulation, and that his intended audience included both Jewish and Gentile readers. Moreover, it should also be pointed out that undue emphasis on Mark's intended audience can deflect the Gospel reader from a proper focus on the person of Jesus Christ. It should always be remembered that the Gospels, "rightly divided," are primarily portraits of Jesus Christ (e.g., 1:1), and not windows into the problems faced by the early church, as some argue. For that matter, the Gospels were not written to solve our problems, although they do on occasion provide explicit guidance

---

4. Richards, *The Bible Reader's Companion*, 630.

5. See, for example, the discussion in D. A. Carson and Douglas J. Moo, *An Introduction to the New Testament*, 2nd ed. (Leicester, UK: Apollos, 2005), 179–82.

for Christian living (e.g., 8:31–38; 9:33–37; 10:32–45). The challenge, as the Christian reader interprets and applies the Gospels, is not to lose a proper focus on Jesus Christ.

We are now ready to commence our study of Mark's Gospel. In our analysis of this Gospel, we will implement our multidirectional model of interpretation, beginning with a downward reading of the text followed by a sideways, backward, and forward reading, with a concluding summary section.

2

JESUS IS INTRODUCED

Mark 1:1–8: The beginning of the gospel about Jesus Christ, the Son of God.

It is written in Isaiah the prophet:

"I will send my messenger ahead of you,
    who will prepare your way"—
"a voice of one calling in the desert, 'Prepare the way for the Lord,
    make straight paths for him.'"

And so John came, baptizing in the desert region and preaching a baptism of repentance for the forgiveness of sins. The whole Judean countryside and all the people of Jerusalem went out to him. Confessing their sins, they were baptized by him in the Jordan River. John wore clothing made of camel's hair, with a leather belt around his waist, and he ate locusts and wild honey. And this was his message: "After me will come one more powerful than I, the thongs of whose sandals I am not worthy to stoop down and untie. I baptize you with water, but he will baptize you with the Holy Spirit."

A DOWNWARD READING

Mark's Gospel is about Jesus! We may rightly conclude this from the opening verse, in which Mark shines a spotlight firmly and squarely on Jesus (Mark 1:1). According to Mark, this Jesus is worthy of our full attention. His credentials are impressive, even if perhaps a little obscure

5

to some modern readers. Mark identifies Jesus as the "Christ, the Son of God" (1:1; cf. 1:11; 5:7; 9:7; 15:39). The prophet Isaiah calls him "Lord" (quoted in 1:3), and John the Baptist, God's messenger, sent to prepare the way for Jesus, deems himself unworthy to even stoop down and untie the thongs of his sandals (1:2-7). Jesus merits such adulation.

Mark classifies his narrative as a "gospel"—or "Good News," as some translations of the Bible render it (Mark 1:1a, cf., e.g., NLT). Here is a story with a happy ending, although, as the reader will discover, it takes one or two unexpected twists and turns along the way. It is imperative, however, that we do not simply skip to the conclusion of the story to see how it all ends, even for those who think they know this Jesus. As Mark's account of Jesus unfolds, invariably faulty or inadequate perceptions of Jesus will be exposed, and the reader's understanding of and admiration for Jesus will be enhanced.

Mark takes us back to the "beginning of the gospel about Jesus Christ" (Mark 1:1). For Mark, it begins with the prophet Isaiah. Remarkably, this prophet predicts the coming of Jesus centuries in advance. Indeed, his coming is so important that Isaiah even speaks of a forerunner, one who will "prepare the way for the Lord" Jesus (v. 3). This mantle falls on John the Baptist (Mark 1:4). But the prophecy, rightly understood, is really about Jesus: "I [God] will send my messenger [John] ahead of you [Jesus], who will prepare your [Jesus'] way—a voice of one calling in the desert, 'Prepare the way for the Lord [Jesus], make straight paths for him [Jesus].'" John prepares the way for Jesus with a ministry of baptism (v. 4) and a message of One to come "more powerful" than he (vv. 7-8). Clearly, Mark's intent in all of this is to place the focus squarely on Jesus, and to magnify his person.

The geographical setting of these events is given some prominence in this text. All the action takes place in the desert, or wilderness, region (cf. Mark 1:3-4, 12-13). John the Baptist attracts throngs from "the whole Judean countryside and all the people of Jerusalem" (v. 5), suggesting an essentially Jewish audience. John comes baptizing and preaching a baptism of repentance for the forgiveness of sins (v. 4). All those who confess their sins, that is, who repent, are baptized in the Jordan River (v. 5).

The origin of John's baptism is obscure. The water imagery associated with his baptism suggests a symbolic cleansing or purification from sin. This purification symbolism is evident in the religious-historical context, where the *baptism* word group is used to refer to the widespread Jewish tradition of the ceremonial washing of hands, cups, pitchers, and kettles before eating and drinking with them (Mark 7:4). Some commentators link John's baptism to the later Jewish initiatory rite of proselyte baptism whereby Gentile converts were symbolically cleansed from their moral and cultic impurity after conversion.[1] The account of the cleansing of the diseased Naaman, the Syrian general, in the pages of the Old Testament is sometimes cited as a possible precursor to this practice (2 Kings 5:10–14). If John's baptism developed from this practice, it is noteworthy that this baptism is now also applied to his Jewish audience. In effect, there is now no difference between Jew and Gentile; both are in need of cleansing from sin, and the pathway for the forgiveness of sins is the same for all!

In his preaching, John signals a significant new era in redemptive history. John baptizes with water, but Jesus will baptize with the Holy Spirit (Mark 1:8). There is something qualitatively different about their baptisms. John's water baptism merely symbolizes the cleansing from sin that Jesus' Holy Spirit baptism in reality effects! Jesus ushers in the era of the Holy Spirit! This first summary statement of Jesus' ministry sets the agenda for Jesus in Mark's Gospel; it not only introduces the work of the Holy Spirit, but also highlights for the reader the priority of the "forgiveness of sins" motif in Jesus' ministry (e.g., 2:1–12). The person and work of Jesus represent "good news" indeed (cf. 1:1, 15). It is for all these reasons that John the Baptist points others to him!

A SIDEWAYS READING

Those familiar with the other Synoptic Gospels will immediately recognize that Mark begins his Gospel differently from Matthew's and Luke's accounts. Mark's Gospel opens with the events that herald the beginning of Jesus' public ministry. Conspicuous by its absence is the Markan equivalent of Jesus' genealogy and so-called birth narrative found at the beginning of Matthew and, in reverse order, in Luke (Matt. 1–2; Luke 2–3). It is sometimes suggested that Mark's omission at this point is governed by the fact that he is seeking to portray Jesus

1. See, for example, Robert H. Stein, *Mark*, Baker Exegetical Commentary on the New Testament (Grand Rapids: Baker Academic, 2008), 44.

primarily as a servant (e.g., Mark 10:45). Consequently, Jesus' impressive lineage, which Matthew sketches at the outset of his Gospel (see Matt. 1:1–17), would be inappropriate. Assuming for the moment that Mark had access to this genealogical information, his omission at this point may simply be governed by the fact that he is writing for a broader audience who might not grasp the significance of Jesus' Jewish lineage; it could read merely as a list of rather obscure names.[2] And what may we deduce from the lack of a birth narrative? A close reading of the birth narratives in Matthew's and Luke's Gospels reveals that their purpose, like that of the genealogies, revolves around establishing the divine credentials of Jesus (Matt. 1:21; Luke 1:32–33). But this lack in Mark's Gospel hardly detracts from the impressive portrait that Mark paints of Jesus at the outset of his Gospel. Our downward reading of Mark's opening verses has highlighted a portrayal of Jesus that is equally as exalted and impressive as that found in Matthew's or Luke's Gospel; it is simply conveyed through multiple testimonies, rather than genealogy or angelic announcement.

Mark's depiction of John the Baptist, however, has parallels with the other Synoptic Gospels. Mark's account of John's preaching is more concise than the other synoptic accounts (cf. Mark 1:2–8; Matt. 3:1–12; Luke 3:1–17); he has no harangue against the Jewish religious leaders and crowds—"You brood of vipers!"—recorded in both Matthew's and Luke's Gospels (Matt. 3:7–10; Luke 3:7–9). This may reflect Mark's focus on a predominantly Gentile audience, although the same may be said about Luke, who does include these details. The effect, however, is to keep the focus on Jesus, and the lack of this "judgment" motif, so pronounced in these parallel accounts, reinforces the picture of good news that Mark is portraying of Jesus' ministry. It is significant, then, that Mark, unlike Matthew and Luke, makes no reference to the judgment imagery of fire in John's description of the ministry of Jesus: "He will baptize you with the Holy Spirit [and with fire]" (Mark 1:8; cf. Matt. 3:11; Luke 3:16). This, after all, says Mark, is the "beginning of the gospel" or the "good news" about Jesus Christ (Mark 1:1).

2. It can be misleading to use the language of "omission" or "noninclusion" when discussing Mark's editorial activity; it implies that he had access to particular material or traditions that he purposefully chose to leave out. It is better in light of the debate surrounding the synoptic problem to speak of Mark's "lacking" certain details found in the other Synoptic Gospels, or at least understanding references to "omissions" in this sense.

A BACKWARD READING

Mark points the reader back to the Old Testament Scriptures through the inclusion of certain key words, and an Old Testament quotation, that link his narrative to these Scriptures and show the reader the continuity that exists between the Old Testament and the story of Jesus that Mark is about to tell. It is apparent that Mark assumes that his readers have some knowledge of the Old Testament Scriptures. Consequently, readers of the Gospels who are unfamiliar with the Old Testament should develop a basic reading strategy to access these Scriptures, lest they miss the meaning of the text.

First, a word of caution. One way to access the Old Testament background is to identify key words that have links to these Scriptures. For the novice, good commentaries will help you identify these words, while a concordance will enable you to track down all the relevant occurrences. Rather than limit yourself to these so-called word studies, however, it is better to think in terms of "concept" or "thematic" studies. Failure to do so can skew the biblical evidence and distort your research on a particular theme. So, for example, a concordance search in the Old Testament on the occurrence of the phrase "kingdom of God" will deliver no hits. This result should not be misinterpreted to mean that the "kingdom of God" is not an Old Testament concept. After all, when Jesus preaches forthrightly, and without elaboration, on "the kingdom of God" at the outset of his earthly ministry, the response of his Jewish hearers is not one of bewilderment or confusion; the concept of God's kingdom was well known to them (e.g., Mark 1:15) and can be detected in such Old Testament concepts as the "rule" and "authority" of God over his people. A more fruitful approach, therefore, is to identify the concept or theme involved and then seek related words or phrases that describe or qualify this concept.

Second, a word of exhortation. In the case of an Old Testament quotation that occurs in one of the Gospels, it is important not only to identify the Old Testament source of the quotation, but also to access the Old Testament literary context, or *co-text*, of the quotation for additional clues about the New Testament author's intended meaning.[3] One

3. Well-known English Bible translations such as the NIV, ESV, KJV, and NASB will usually identify the source of Old Testament quotations in footnote citations. The reader can be guided by this information.

should think of the quotation as shorthand reference back to the Old Testament source and its broader literary context. Remember that the New Testament writers did not have the luxury of citing the chapter and verse divisions found in our more modern Bible translations; they were added much later in the history of the church. The exhortation, then, is to take the time to reflect on the Old Testament context. The same can be said of word or thematic studies. For example, although the phrase "Son of God" does not occur in the Old Testament, a contextual analysis of the references to "son" will reveal the presence of the concept—for example, when God speaks of "my son" (e.g., 2 Sam. 7:14; Ps. 2:7).

Our backward reading of this text will not be exhaustive. Rather, our focus will be on aspects of the analysis that demonstrate the value of this step in the exegetical process. We begin with a cluster of words in Mark 1:1, all of which reveal Old Testament pedigrees: "The beginning of the gospel about Jesus Christ, the Son of God." The reference to "the *beginning* of the gospel" brings to mind a possible allusion to the creation account in Genesis 1:1: "In the beginning God created the heavens and the earth." If Mark intends this allusion, it elevates the significance of this gospel to that of a parallel creation event! That is remarkable, and certainly captures the reader's attention. But one should not be dogmatic about this connection because in what follows Mark proceeds to quote from Isaiah, not Genesis, and John's Jewish audience and wilderness setting suggest that a "new exodus" rather than a "new creation" image would be more appropriate (see Mark 1:4–5). Nevertheless, the Genesis allusion is worth pondering.

But what about this "gospel about Jesus Christ" (Mark 1:1), or "Good News about Jesus the Messiah" (NLT)? Mark quotes the prophet Isaiah, revealing that this "gospel" has its roots in the Old Testament prophetic Scriptures (Mark 1:2–3). According to Isaiah, the good news begins with a messenger and culminates with the coming of "the LORD" (Isa. 40:3), a conclusion affirmed by Isaiah in what follows in his Old Testament prophecy: "Get you up to a high mountain, O Zion, herald of good news; lift up your voice with strength, O Jerusalem, herald of good news; lift it up, fear not; say to the cities of Judah, 'Behold your God!'" (Isa. 40:9 ESV). The good news of the gospel is about the coming of "the Lord," a reference in the Old Testament context to the Lord "God" (cf. Isa. 40:3b, 9b), and a reference in the Markan context to Jesus. The implication is obvious:

Jesus is none other than God in the flesh! This truth is at the heart of the good news of Jesus Christ.

Before we continue with our backward reading of this text, it is necessary to pause for a moment to make an important observation. Modern Western Christians can fall into the trap of reading the Gospel narratives through so-called Western spectacles that tend to filter out the significance of certain details in the text. Their historical context desensitizes them to these details, with the net result that they miss the author's intended meaning. The challenge is to remember the original first-century Jewish historical setting of our text and its Old Testament background. This brings us to a case in point. When Mark introduces Jesus to the reader as "Jesus Christ" (Mark 1:1), many modern Western readers assume that *Christ* is a last name, like *Smith*. But this designation has deep Old Testament roots. It is a title of sorts; Jesus is "the Christ," the Greek rendition of the Hebrew word *Messiah*, meaning "anointed one" (cf. Matt. 1:17; Mark 8:29; John 20:31). The actual Hebrew word *Messiah* occurs only twice in the Old Testament Scriptures, in a rather cryptic prophetic vision recorded in Daniel 9:24–27, which many believe is fulfilled in the incarnation of Jesus and his death on the cross; he is the "anointed one" that Daniel refers to. Some commentators also draw a link between Jesus as God's Anointed One and the anointing of prophets, priests, and kings in Old Testament Israel to signify the diverse nature of Jesus' earthly calling (cf. Lev. 4:3; 2 Sam. 19:21; 1 Kings 19:16).[4] While this is true, the concept of "Messiah" appears to be broader in its scope, and includes a number of strands of prophecy that predict the intervention of God, or a Messiah-figure, to deliver his people from their enemies (cf. Gen. 3:15; Isa. 35:1–10; 40:10; 42:1; Mal. 3:1). According to one source, more than four hundred Old Testament passages are taken by ancient Jewish teachers to speak of the Messiah. The sheer number of these prophecies created a messianic expectation in the minds and hearts of God's people, but it also accounts for the messianic confusion that we encounter in the pages of the Gospels regarding Jesus: "Is this the Christ?" (cf. Matt. 2:4; 11:3; Mark 14:61; John 7:26–44). Mark, however, has no doubts about Jesus' messianic credentials; he is the Christ, God's Anointed One (Mark 1:1), the "Lord" whom Isaiah predicted (Mark

---

4. See, for example, James R. Edwards, *The Gospel according to Mark*, Pillar New Testament Commentary (Grand Rapids: Eerdmans, 2002), 249.

1:3), the divine "Son of God," a title with messianic overtones (cf. Mark 14:61; John 20:31) and royal connotations (cf. 2 Sam. 7:12–15; John 1:49). In short, Mark portrays Jesus as a divine messianic King, a motif that is reflected in his subsequent ministry (e.g., Mark 1:15–45).

The reader should not miss the significance of this particular "ful-fillment" motif. All the many messianic Old Testament promises are now being fulfilled in the person of Jesus! Given Jesus' true identity, it is hardly surprising that he does not appear on the scene unheralded. As is commonplace with any prominent visiting dignitary, he has a forerunner or "messenger," John the Baptist (Mark 1:4), to prepare his way (vv. 2–3). Like all the prophets of old, John points to Jesus, and in so doing he lays the groundwork for Jesus' divine ministry of deliverance by sketching for the reader Jesus' credentials. In the circumstances, it is totally fit-ting that no less than John the Baptist should say of this Jesus, "I am not worthy to stoop down and untie [the thongs of his sandals]" (v. 7)!

As we turn our attention to the Old Testament quotation in our text (Mark 1:2–3), it is important to heed our exhortation to identify the source of the quotation and then reflect on its Old Testament context. Mark attributes the quotation to the prophet Isaiah (v. 2a). The quota-tion is, in fact, a conflation of parts of Exodus 23:20, Malachi 3:1, and Isaiah 40:3. This observation, in and of itself, is significant. To credit a conflated quotation to a single source suggests a harmony of purpose between these diverse parts of the Scriptures, while at the same time indicating that the truths revealed are not limited to any one part of the Old Testament canon. But why does Mark single out Isaiah as the lens through which to read this Old Testament material? The Old Tes-tament context of Isaiah's prophecy gives us a clue. Isaiah commenced his prophetic ministry in about A.D. 740, during the reigns of Uzziah, Jotham, Ahaz, and Hezekiah, all kings of Judah (Isa. 1:1). This was a time of political and religious turmoil in Israel's history. The northern kingdom of Israel would fall to Assyrian invaders about twenty years later, in 722 B.C. Although the southern kingdom of Judah was spared this same fate, it would end up in exile a little more than a century later at the hands of the Babylonians in 586 B.C. It is this sixth-century historical scenario that Isaiah addresses in the second part of his proph-ecy, beginning at chapter 40, and culminating in Isaiah's vision of a new heaven and new earth (Isa. 65:17–25). The tone of this part of the prophecy is one of good news as Isaiah addresses the Babylonian exiles: "Comfort, comfort my people, says your God. Speak tenderly to Jerusalem, and proclaim to her . . . that her sin has been paid for" (Isa. 40:1–2). Significantly, Mark quotes from this very section of Isaiah's prophecy, setting a "gospel" or "good news" tone for Jesus' earthly ministry (cf. Isa. 40:3)! Moreover, Mark's subsequent description of John the Baptist's ministry that includes references to "the forgiveness of sins" and the "Judean countryside" and "Jerusalem" provide further points of contact with Isaiah's prophecy and indicate that, with John's ministry, Isaiah's prophecy is in the process of being fulfilled (Mark 1:4–5; cf. Isa. 40:2, 9). Isaiah's "good news" tone is therefore the dominant note that we are to hear as we reflect on these Old Testament words. Mark hereby affirms the good news about Jesus Christ, the Son of God (Mark 1:1).

Although Mark singles out Isaiah for special mention, we should still pause to reflect on the Old Testament contexts of the other components of this quotation. In Malachi 3:1 it is the Lord Almighty speaking: "See, I will send my messenger, who will prepare the way before me. Then suddenly the Lord you are seeking will come to his temple." As Malachi records this prophecy, in the context a clear note of judgment is associated with this coming: "But who can endure the day of his coming? Who can stand when he appears? For he will be like a refiner's fire or a launderer's soap" (Mal. 3:2; cf. 3:5a). How do we reconcile Malachi's "judgment" motif with Isaiah's "good news" motif? It is in this context that the ministry of John the Baptist, Malachi's messenger, is to be understood. On the one hand, John's call to repent is a wake-up call to God's people that the judgment of a holy God looms. On the other hand, his baptism of repentance for the forgiveness of sins is good news to all who confess their sins that this judgment can be averted (Mark 1:4–5). It is in this sense that John prepares the way for the Lord's coming, the coming of God's Messiah, the Lord Jesus Christ!

It is against this background of Malachi's prophecy that Mark's description of John's otherwise strange dress and diet makes sense (Mark 1:6). It bears a striking resemblance to the dress code of the Old Testament prophet Elijah, recasting God's messenger John as an Elijah figure (cf. 2 Kings 1:8). According to Malachi 4:5, God will send to Israel "the prophet Elijah before that great and dreadful day of the LORD comes," a day that will bring judgment on the arrogant and wicked, but blessing to those who revere God's name (Mal. 4:1–3). Mark identifies John the Baptist as the one who fulfills this prophecy (Mark 9:11–13); he comes in the "spirit and power of Elijah" (Luke 1:17), but before the "dreadful day" of judgment (Mal. 4:5), to prepare God's people for the Lord's coming. In keeping with this, Jesus describes John's ministry as a ministry of restoration (Mark 9:12; cf. Mal. 4:6). From this perspective, there really is no tension between Malachi and Isaiah; John's ministry, like that of Jesus, is "good news"! The Old Testament prophets agree, although Malachi adds a note of urgency to the ministry of both John, God's messenger, and Jesus, God's Messiah.

How does the book of Exodus fit into this introduction to the narrative that Mark is crafting? In the Old Testament quotation, both Exodus 23:20 and Malachi 3:1 speak of the divine initiative in the sending of a messenger to prepare the way, and in both prophecies the role of the messenger is good news. But Malachi's messenger prepares the way for the *Lord God's* arrival (Mal. 3:1), whereas, according to the context of the Exodus prophecy, this messenger or "angel" goes ahead of *Israel* in the wilderness (Ex. 23:23). Rather than brush this distinction aside, or view the point as too subtle, we see that it makes good sense of the wilderness setting of our text and explains the need for Jesus' subsequent baptism and temptation whereby he identifies himself with Israel, God's son (cf. Mark 1:4–13; Hos. 11:1). Jesus is thereby also portrayed as a substitute for Israel, once again in the wilderness, but now effecting deliverance for God's people. The picture is that of another exodus, what some commentators call a "new exodus"—yet the deliverance is not from political oppression, but from the bondage of sin, a motif prominent in both the Isaiah and Markan contexts (cf. Isa. 40:1–2; Mark 1:4, 8).[5] This is part of the "good news" that Mark wants his readers to grasp.

The fulfillment of these various strands of prophecy in these opening verses of Mark's Gospel creates the impression that with the coming of Jesus, we have reached a new and defining moment in redemptive history. Mark uses the Old Testament Scriptures to alert the reader to the significance of this event: God's Messiah is here! John the Baptist is appointed to ensure that God's people in the historical context do not

5. See, for example, Rikk E. Watts, *Mark*, Commentary on the New Testament Use of the Old Testament (Grand Rapids: Baker Academic, 2007), 119.

miss its significance either. It is a time of decision before an impending day of judgment. Both John's ministry and his message point to Jesus and his ministry and message of forgiveness (cf. Mark 1:4–5, 8, 15).

Unlike John, Jesus has all the credentials to effect the actual forgiveness of sins (e.g., Mark 2:1–12). His Holy Spirit baptism hints at the fulfillment of prophecies by the Old Testament prophets Joel and Ezekiel that predict the life-giving, and life-changing, ministry of God's Spirit "before the coming of the great and dreadful day of the LORD" (Joel 2:31; cf. Joel 2:28; Ezek. 36:25–27). Once again the overarching message is good news, for, according to Joel, "everyone who calls on the name of the LORD will be saved" (Joel 2:32). It is this same Lord who has drawn near in Jesus to bring this salvation. Like pieces of an intricate puzzle assembled in full, all these promises, rightly understood, paint a brilliant portrait of Jesus Christ and his saving work on the cross. Jesus fulfills these Old Testament promises—or, if you prefer, the Old Testament, rightly understood, is full of Jesus!

A FORWARD READING

The goal of a forward reading is to trace through the rest of the New Testament the development of motifs in our text with a view to their application in the contemporary context. We will select just one prominent motif from our text, "the gospel," to illustrate the value of this step in the exegetical process because it encompasses so many of the other elements present in the text.

Mark initially defines "the gospel" in a personal, Christ-centered way: it is good news, with Old Testament roots, about the presence of Jesus, God's long-awaited Messiah, the divine Son of God, who will deliver his people from their sins (Mark 1:1–8). Thereafter in his narrative, Mark shifts the focus to the gospel message preached: Jesus preaches "the gospel of God" (1:14 ESV), that is, from God, about the presence of God's kingdom, a message demanding repentance and faith (e.g., 1:14–15). According to Jesus, allegiance to this gospel message can be costly for the Christian (e.g., 8:35; 10:29), but it is a message that must be proclaimed to all the world (13:10; 14:9; 16:15). Jesus commences his public ministry in the Gospels by proclaiming this gospel (cf. Matt. 4:17; Mark 1:14–15), alerting the reader to the priority of this gospel in his ministry, a truth affirmed in the subsequent narrative (e.g., Mark 1:35–39).

The noun form of the word *gospel* occurs in Luke's writings in only two places as he records his history of the early church in Acts (Acts 15:7; 20:24). But the verbal form, "to preach the gospel," is far more prevalent. The priority of the preaching of the gospel and the truth that the message is for all people is stressed in this context (Luke 2:10; 4:43; 9:6; Acts 5:42; 8:4, 25, 40; 11:20; 14:7; 16:10).[6] The gospel is central to the apostle Paul's ministry that he receives from the Lord (Acts 20:24); he describes himself as "a servant" of this gospel (e.g., Col. 1:23). Consequently, Paul constantly preaches it (Rom. 1:9, 15; 15:20; 1 Cor. 1:17; 15:1; 2 Cor. 2:12; 10:16; Gal. 1:11; 1 Thess. 2:9), defends it (Rom. 1:16; 1 Cor. 15:1–2; Gal. 1:6–9; Phil. 1:7), and is willing to suffer for it (1 Thess. 2:2; 2 Tim. 1:8, 10–12; 2:9). In his letter to the church at Rome, Paul writes an extended defense of this gospel and, in the process, articulates its tenets and implications. Paul's introduction to Romans echoes Mark's introduction to his Gospel: "Paul, a servant of Christ Jesus, called to be an apostle and set apart for the gospel of God—the gospel he promised beforehand through his prophets in the Holy Scriptures regarding his Son" (Rom. 1:1–3a; cf. Rom. 15:19). The same gospel ingredients are present in both instances. The gospel is from God, its roots are in the Old Testament prophets, and Jesus Christ is at the center (cf. 1 Cor. 15:1–4; Gal. 1:16; 2 Tim. 2:8). For our purposes, this is an important observation. In the transition from the time of Jesus' earthly ministry to the church age in which we live, the gospel remains unchanged, in terms of both its focus on Christ and its priority status (e.g., Rom. 1:15; 1 Cor. 1:17; 9:16). We see these same sentiments in Paul's animated defense of the gospel message in his letter to the Galatians (Gal. 1:6–9) and in John's reference to "the eternal gospel" in Revelation 14:6.

As we reflect on the message of the gospel, we can discover an interesting blending in the New Testament of the various motifs reflected in our Markan text. In the book of Acts, the apostles "day after day, in the temple courts and from house to house, . . . never stopped teaching and proclaiming the good news that Jesus is the Christ" (Acts 5:42). This particular messianic focus makes sense in a Jewish context such

---

6. Interestingly, the apostle John does not use the noun or verbal form of *gospel* in his Gospel or letters. Yet the concept is certainly present in the "believe in Jesus" motif that is stressed in these writings (e.g., John 1:12; 3:16; 3:36; 6:29, 47; 20:31; 1 John 5:13).

as Jerusalem, or in synagogues further afield (cf. 9:22; 17:2; 18:5, 28). In Samaria, Philip preaches "the good news of the kingdom of God and the name of Jesus Christ." Those who believed "were baptized, both men and women" (8:12). In Acts 8:35, Philip, beginning with a passage in Isaiah, tells an Ethiopian eunuch "the good news about Jesus." The eunuch is subsequently baptized (8:38). The obvious parallels here between the gospel, the Old Testament prophets, Jesus, and baptism are also evident in Mark's Gospel.

Significantly, as the mission field expands to include Gentiles, such as Cornelius, the message also expands to include "the good news of peace through Jesus Christ, who is Lord of all" (Acts 10:36; cf. 11:20). The declaration of Jesus' lordship over all not only challenges the apparent supremacy of Caesar in the first-century context, but also alludes to the rule of God inherent in the more Jewish "kingdom of God" concept associated with the gospel (e.g., Mark 1:14–15; Acts 19:8; 28:23, 31), recasting it in terms more familiar to the average Gentile in the Roman Empire (e.g., Acts 11:17; 16:31; 18:8; 20:21; 28:31; Rom. 10:9).[7] The gospel, then, according to Peter, is not only about peace and reconciliation (e.g., Eph. 2:17; 6:15), but also about the rule of God and his Son. It is in this sense that we commonly assert that Jesus is both "Lord and Savior," a designation that Peter is particularly fond of (e.g., 2 Peter 1:11; 2:20; 3:2, 18). Peter's gospel message to Cornelius and his household includes comprehensive "judgment" and "forgiveness" motifs: Jesus will judge all the living and the dead, while, according to the Prophets, all who believe in him will receive forgiveness of sins (Acts 10:42–43; cf. Isa. 33:24). Repentance and faith are requirements for both Jew and Gentile, although on occasion only one requirement is mentioned (Acts 2:38; 14:15; 16:31; 20:21; cf. Mark 1:4, 15). Those who believe the gospel message receive the Holy Spirit, an experience that both John and Jesus designate as the "bapti[sm] . . . with the Holy Spirit" (Mark 1:8b; cf. Acts 1:5; 11:15–17).

Our forward reading underscores the "good news" character of the gospel as it showcases the various facets of the saving work of Jesus: forgiveness of sins and peace with God and man. It is a message of salvation based on faith, not works; grace, not merit. As such, it is good news

---

7. "Kingdom" terminology, however, continues to be part of the church's vocabulary, although it is not as prevalent as in the Synoptic Gospels (e.g., Rom. 14:17; 1 Cor. 4:20; 6:9–10; Col. 1:12–13; 4:11; 2 Thess. 1:5; Heb. 12:28; James 2:5; 2 Peter 1:11; Rev. 11:15; 12:10).

for all who believe, whether Jew or Gentile, slave or free, male or female (Acts 16:31; 1 Cor. 15:2; cf. Gal. 3:28; Eph. 3:6). The New Testament, however, doesn't separate faith in the Lord Jesus Christ from obedience to his rule; those who believe must obey their Lord (cf. Rom. 1:5; Col. 2:6; James 2:24). After all, Jesus is both Lord and Savior!

The apostle Paul is particularly helpful regarding the practical implications of the gospel for the Christian. Paul's rhetoric in Romans reveals that the gospel not only justifies, but also sanctifies; it not only saves, but also makes holy (Rom. 6:1ff.). This same motif is present in Colossians, where Paul exhorts the saints there to continue to live in the Lord Jesus Christ, the One they have received (Col. 2:6). Accordingly, the gospel is not only for the unbeliever, but also for the believer. Christians, according to the apostle, are to conduct themselves "in a manner worthy of the gospel of Christ" and "[contend] as one man for the faith of the gospel" (Phil. 1:27); they are to stand firm on the gospel they have received, "not moved from the hope held out in the gospel," if they are to enjoy its saving benefits of reconciliation, holiness, and freedom from blemish and accusation (Col. 1:22–23; cf. 1 Cor. 15:2). What a glorious hope for those who endure! It brings "life and immortality to light" (2 Tim. 1:10). No wonder Paul refers to this gospel as the "glorious gospel of the blessed God" (1 Tim. 1:11) and is careful to pass on to his Christian readers the same gospel message he received (1 Cor. 15:3).

SUMMARY

A downward reading of our text places the reader's focus squarely on Jesus. Like John the Baptist, the reader is called to publicly venerate this Jesus (e.g., Mark 1:7). A sideways reading highlights the "good news" aspect of Jesus' earthly ministry by omitting the "judgment" motif present in the parallel accounts. A backward perspective on the text enhances our grasp of Jesus' true identity, and the significance of his work, by clearly identifying Jesus as the long-awaited Messiah, bringing deliverance from sin. Finally, a forward reading, focused on the "gospel" motif present in the text, reinforces the priority of this gospel in the life of the church, the "good news" character of its message for all who believe, and consequently the need for the church to receive it, preach it, contend for it, and hold firmly to it.

This "gospel" motif is not detached from the text's focus on Christ; after all, the gospel is about Jesus Christ (Mark 1:1). This Christ-centered perspective on the gospel is important because it functions as a reminder that the gospel's saving work is not based on the faith of the recipient, but rather on the object of that faith, the person and saving work of the Lord Jesus Christ. It is this Jesus whom Mark introduces to the reader at the outset of his Gospel. With the deft use of multiple witnesses, Mark sketches the excellencies of his person to encourage faith and confidence that Jesus will not fail those who entrust their eternal destinies to him by believing his gospel.

3

JESUS HEALS A PARALYTIC

Mark 2:1–12: A few days later, when Jesus again entered Capernaum, the people heard that he had come home. So many gathered that there was no room left, not even outside the door, and he preached the word to them. Some men came, bringing to him a paralytic, carried by four of them. Since they could not get him to Jesus because of the crowd, they made an opening in the roof above Jesus and, after digging through it, lowered the mat the paralyzed man was lying on. When Jesus saw their faith, he said to the paralytic, "Son, your sins are forgiven."

Now some teachers of the law were sitting there, thinking to themselves, "Why does this fellow talk like that? He's blaspheming! Who can forgive sins but God alone?"

Immediately Jesus knew in his spirit that this was what they were thinking in their hearts, and he said to them, "Why are you thinking these things? Which is easier: to say to the paralytic, 'Your sins are forgiven,' or to say, 'Get up, take your mat and walk'? But that you may know that the Son of Man has authority on earth to forgive sins . . . ." He said to the paralytic, "I tell you, get up, take your mat and go home." He got up, took his mat and walked out in full view of them all. This amazed everyone and they praised God, saying, "We have never seen anything like this!"

A DOWNWARD READING

Jesus announces the presence of the kingdom of God, and with the display of a number of key acts of authority, Jesus demonstrates its presence (Mark 1:15ff.):

- Simon, Andrew, and the sons of Zebedee respond to Jesus' call "without delay" (1:16–20).
- Jesus teaches with an amazing authority, "not as the teachers of the law" (1:22b).
- Jesus casts out an evil spirit: "What is this? A new teaching—and with authority! He even gives orders to evil spirits and they obey him" (1:27).
- Jesus banishes disease by healing many who had various diseases (1:34).

Truly, the kingdom of God is present! It is hardly surprising that Jesus becomes popular: "Everyone is looking for you!" (Mark 1:37). No doubt everyone is wanting Jesus to heal the sick. Jesus, however, uses this opportunity to underscore the priority of his preaching ministry: "Let us go somewhere else—to the nearby villages—so I can preach there also. That is why I have come" (v. 38). It is therefore significant that two detailed healing stories immediately follow. The pace of the narrative, so to speak, slows down, to make a particular point. Both of these stories, as we will see, relate back to the issue of Jesus' priorities.

In the first healing story, a leper comes to Jesus, desperate for cleansing: "If you are willing, you can make me clean" (Mark 1:40). The question is not whether Jesus is able to heal; that is beyond dispute in the context. Rather, the question is, given Jesus' priorities—to preach rather than to heal—is he willing to heal? In other words, does Jesus have compassion? Mark leaves the reader in no doubt on this question: "Filled with compassion, Jesus reached out his hand and touched the man. 'I am willing,' he said. 'Be clean!' Immediately the leprosy left him and he was cured" (vv. 41–42). Jesus clearly demonstrates both the power and the willingness to purify those who are ceremonially unclean. Yet this encounter does not end there. Jesus gives the man a directive: "See that you don't tell this to anyone. But go, show yourself to the priest and offer the sacrifices that Moses commanded for your cleansing, as a testimony to them" (v. 44).[1] Remarkably, Jesus is not defiled by his contact with this leper; rather, he is the One who makes clean those who are ceremonially unclean (cf. Lev. 14:2–32; 13:45–46). This story functions to picture and

---

1. This directive portrays Jesus as One who "honored the Mosaic law." James R. Edwards, *The Gospel according to Mark*, Pillar New Testament Commentary (Grand Rapids: Eerdmans, 2002), 71.

anticipate the forgiveness from the defilement of sin that Jesus provides in the encounter that follows (cf. Mark 2:1–12).

Jesus returns home to Capernaum. His presence immediately attracts a crowd. This brings us to the second healing story and our text, the well-known account of the healing of a paralytic who is brought to Jesus by his friends (Mark 2:1–12). The friends obviously intend Jesus to heal their paralytic friend; that is their unspoken intent. The physical need is so obvious, no words are necessary. The physical need is so desperate, the friends are prepared to take the rather extreme measure of digging through the roof above Jesus' head, to bypass the crowds that surround him (vv. 3–4). It is therefore surprising that Jesus' immediate response to this need is a declaration of forgiveness of sins: "When Jesus saw their faith, he said to the paralytic, 'Son, your sins are forgiven'" (v. 5). It is not clear whether "their faith" includes the faith of the paralytic. Either way, Jesus is motivated by their faith in him.

The teachers of the law who are present are not impressed with Jesus: "Why does this fellow talk like that? He's blaspheming! Who can forgive sins but God alone?" (Mark 2:7). Jesus, aware of what they are thinking in their hearts, is not impressed with them either, and challenges their mind-set: "Why are you thinking these things? Which is easier: to say to the paralytic, 'Your sins are forgiven,' or to say, 'Get up, take your mat and walk'?" (vv. 8–9). The answer is obvious. The issue revolves around authority: "But that you may know that the Son of Man has *authority* on earth to forgive sins . . ." (cf. v. 10a). Jesus, as the Son of Man, demonstrates his authority to forgive sins by healing the paralytic: "He said to the paralytic, 'I tell you, get up, take your mat and go home.' He got up, took his mat and walked out in full view of them all" (vv. 10b–12a). This healing provides a visible, public testimony of Jesus' authority to forgive sins. Everyone is amazed, and says, "We have never seen anything like this!" (v. 12b). Jesus does what no one else can do!

The link to the question of Jesus' priorities in the context is not difficult to see (Mark 1:38–39). Jesus does heal this paralytic, but not before he has forgiven his sins. The implication is plain for all to see: more important than any physical healing is the need for the forgiveness of sins! Put differently, our greatest need is hidden from the human eye; it cannot be seen, except by God! This is why Jesus prioritizes his preaching above his healing ministry (vv. 35–39).

23

A SIDEWAYS READING

Matthew, Mark, and Luke all record this incident (cf. Matt. 9:1 8; Luke 5:17–26). Mark highlights the presence of the crowds surrounding Jesus in his house (Mark 2:2). Matthew makes no mention of these bystanders, while Luke is more interested in drawing attention to the presence of religious leaders (Luke 5:17). Mark alone describes Jesus as "preach[ing] the word" to the crowds gathered around him (Mark 2:2b). This is significant in light of Jesus' earlier-stated priority to preach to sinners, rather than to heal the sick (Mark 1:38). This may also explain Jesus' surprising tactic in the context—to declare the forgiveness of his sins, rather than heal the paralytic, as a first step. In any event, Jesus uses the paralytic's intrusion to reveal his authority to forgive sins and to underscore its importance; it is a priority, more important than even the most dire need for physical healing!

Mark alone mentions the number of men carrying the paralytic: "Some men came, bringing to him a paralytic, carried by four of them" (Mark 2:3). The implication seems to be that there were more in the procession, adding to the overcrowding problem around Jesus and necessitating an alternative plan of action. Mark portrays their determination to see Jesus with his reference to their digging through the roof above Jesus (Mark 2:4). This is implied in Luke's account (Luke 5:19).

Jesus declares the paralytic forgiven. The religious leaders are offended. According to Mark, Jesus immediately "knew in his spirit [what the teachers of the law] were thinking in their hearts" (Mark 2:8). This "immediacy" motif is a well-known distinctive of Mark's Gospel, and its presence here enhances Jesus' stature in the context; nothing is hidden from him, ever! This same motif recurs in Mark 2:12, although it is obscured by the NIV translation. The more literal ESV translation makes the point: "And he rose and immediately picked up his bed and went out before them all" (Mark 2:12; cf. Luke 5:25a). Not only is the paralytic able to rise to his feet, but Mark makes the point that his full strength is "immediately" restored by Jesus. Carried in on a mat by four men, he is now able, without any help and without any delay, to take up his mat and walk out in full view of them all. The bystanders are all amazed and praise God, saying, "We have never seen anything like this!" (Mark 2:12b; cf. Luke 5:26). They testify that Jesus' display of authority is unique! Matthew's mention of the response of "the crowd" at this point (Matt. 9:8)—a group distinguished in his Gospel from the teachers of the law (cf. Matt. 7:28–29; 8:18–19)—suggests that Mark's reference to the amazement of "everyone" who witnessed these events should not be understood to include the teachers of the law who were present (Mark 2:6, 12b).

That which is hidden from the eyes of men—the authority of Jesus to forgive sins—he reveals with the visible healing of a paralytic. Unlike some of the other healing miracles in Mark's Gospel, which Jesus intends should remain hidden (e.g., Mark 1:44), Jesus clearly desires that all should see this significant display of divine authority.

A BACKWARD READING

The Old Testament Scriptures were the Bible of Jesus' day. As far as the teachers of the law were concerned, these Scriptures taught that God alone could forgive sins. From their perspective, Jesus' declaration of forgiveness of sins violates this truth (Mark 2:7). Jesus challenges their thinking regarding himself, but not their theology regarding forgiveness. The Old Testament Scriptures do indeed teach unequivocally that God forgives sins. According to the psalmist David, God "forgives all [your] sins and heals all [your] diseases" (Ps. 103:3). Remarkably, this is exactly what Jesus does in his dealings with the paralytic; he both forgives and heals him (Mark 2:1–12). The implication for the reader should be obvious: Jesus is the divine Son of God who forgives all your sins and heals all your diseases! The psalmist lists the forgiveness of sins before the healing of diseases, the same sequence reflected in Jesus' actions. This parallel can hardly be a coincidence.

The Old Testament prophet Isaiah not only affirms the divine origin of forgiveness, but also defines its nature and identifies its gracious foundation: "I [the Lord God], even I, am he who blots out your transgressions, for my own sake, and remembers your sins no more" (Isa. 43:25). Transgressions are blotted out, and sins are remembered no more! And all this is for God's own sake and glory. This striking prophetic portrayal of divine forgiveness is complemented by other vivid word pictures from the Old Testament Scriptures that reflect this "forgiveness" motif:

- Psalm 103:12: "As far as the east is from the west, so far has [God] removed our transgressions from us."

25

- Isaiah 38:17b: "You [God] have put all my sins behind your back."
- Micah 7:19: "You will again have compassion on us; you will tread our sins underfoot and hurl all our iniquities into the depths of the sea."

The paralytic experiences this amazing forgiveness, by faith, as a gift from God in the flesh, Jesus Christ.

There is, however, one other detail in this text, a reference to Jesus as the "Son of Man," that points the reader back to the Old Testament Scriptures: "But that you may know that the Son of Man has authority on earth to forgive sins . . ." (Mark 2:10a). According to many commentators, this reference is a clear allusion to the mysterious "son of man" figure in Daniel 7:13–14:[2] "In my vision at night I looked, and there before me was one like a son of man, coming with the clouds of heaven. He approached the Ancient of Days and was led into his presence. He was given authority, glory and sovereign power; all peoples, nations and men of every language worshiped him. His dominion is an everlasting dominion that will not pass away, and his kingdom is one that will never be destroyed." It is not only the "son of man" terminology that links Jesus to Daniel's prophecy, but also the prominent "authority" motif present in both contexts. Contrary to the Old Testament context, however, Jesus, as "the Son of Man," does not receive authority, but unilaterally exercises the divine authority to forgive sins! The implications regarding the true identity of Daniel's "one like a son of man" should be obvious.

This backward reading of the text places the focus on the question of Jesus' identity. It functions to affirm his true identity as the divine Son of Man with authority on earth to forgive sins (Mark 2:10–12).

A FORWARD READING

This encounter between Jesus and a paralytic is about the forgiveness of sins, its importance, and its source. Our forward reading

---

2. Some commentators assert that *son of man* is rather a designation for "human being" (cf. Ps. 8:4; Ezek. 2:1). Stein, however, contends that it cannot mean "man" in this context; Jesus was not saying that every person had the power to forgive sins. Robert H. Stein, *Mark*, Baker Exegetical Commentary on the New Testament (Grand Rapids: Baker Academic, 2008), 121. This is the first time in Mark's Gospel that this "Son of Man" designation occurs. All in all, it occurs fourteen times in this Gospel, with most references linked to a "suffering" motif (Mark 2:10, 28; 8:31, 38; 9:9, 12, 31; 10:33, 45; 13:26; 14:21 (twice), 41, 62).

will examine this motif. John the Baptist, Jesus' forerunner, preached a baptism of repentance for the forgiveness of sins. But John could baptize only with water (Mark 1:4, 8a); he did not have the authority to actually forgive sins. At best, his baptism symbolized this reality. Jesus, on the other hand, demonstrates in both word and deed that he, as the Danielic "Son of Man" figure, has the power and authority on earth to forgive sins. All those who confess their sins are baptized by John; no merit is involved (Mark 1:5). Water baptism, normally reserved in the historical context for the Gentile, is now also required of the Jew. Deliverance from sin is the same for both Jew and Gentile; it is by faith (e.g., Acts 15:11). Jesus' ministry is also characterized by this same faith principle. It is evident in the message he preaches (cf. Mark 1:15: "Repent and believe the good news!"). It is also evident in the faith principle that motivates Jesus to forgive sins (Mark 2:5).

This faith principle is not vitiated when Jesus subsequently informs his disciples that God, their "Father in heaven," will not forgive their sins if they do not forgive others (Mark 11:25). In the context, Jesus is teaching his disciples about prayer. He points out that faith and a forgiving spirit are essential prerequisites for answered prayer (Mark 11:24–25; cf. Matt. 6:14–15). According to one commentator, "a spirit of forgiveness—accepted, and extended to others—assures us of our welcome before God's throne."[3] But whoever blasphemes against the Holy Spirit will never be forgiven. Jesus describes this as "an eternal sin" (Mark 3:29).

If we trace this "forgiveness" motif through the remainder of the New Testament, we see that it occurs in the canonical writings of Luke, Paul, John, and James and in the book of Hebrews. It is prominent in the conclusion to Peter's all-important Pentecost sermon: "Repent and be baptized, every one of you, in the name of Jesus Christ so that your sins may be forgiven. And you will receive the gift of the Holy Spirit. The promise is . . . for all whom the Lord our God will call" (Acts 2:38–39). Significantly, Peter's concluding exhortation echoes the message of John the Baptist and Jesus, in Mark's Gospel (cf. Mark 1:4–5, 15). The subsequent apostolic preaching recorded in Acts links the forgiveness of sins to the person of Jesus, underscoring its faith,

---

3. Lawrence O. Richards, *The Bible Reader's Companion*, electronic ed. (Wheaton, IL: Victor Books, 1991), 643.

not works, character, its universal scope—for Jew and Gentile—and its Old Testament roots (see Acts 5:31; 10:43; 13:38; 26:18). This is the gospel message that the apostles preached.

The apostle Paul reflects the teaching of Jesus' encounter with the paralytic by ascribing the forgiveness of sins to both God the Father and Jesus the Son (see Eph. 1:7; 4:32; Col. 1:13; 2:13). The prominent doctrine of justification by faith in Paul's letters includes forgiveness of sins. Significantly, Paul quotes from the Old Testament to make the point: "However, to the man who does not work but trusts God who justifies the wicked, his faith is credited as righteousness. David says the same thing when he speaks of the blessedness of the man to whom God credits righteousness apart from works: 'Blessed are they whose transgressions are forgiven, whose sins are covered. Blessed is the man whose sin the Lord will never count against him'" (Rom. 4:5–8, quoting Ps. 32:1–2). This doctrinal link with justification reinforces the faith foundation of forgiveness, while this particular text provides a helpful description of the fruits of forgiveness in the lives of those who believe: their sins are "covered"; the Lord will never "count" their sin against them (cf. Heb. 8:12). This imagery complements the other Old Testament pictures of forgiveness revealed by our backward reading of this motif. Truly, those who are forgiven are blessed!

The apostle John reflects the "forgiveness" motif in his first letter, using the language of ritual purity: "But if we walk in the light, as he is in the light, we have fellowship with one another, and the blood of Jesus, his Son, purifies us from all sin" (1 John 1:7). This reference is worth taking note of for a number of reasons. First, it links forgiveness to the blood of Jesus, shed on the cross (cf. Heb. 9:22). Second, it alludes to the sufficiency of this act to purify "from all sin," or "from every sin," an acceptable translation of this phrase that makes the point (cf. Heb. 9:26; Eph. 1:7). Third, the present tense of the verb *purifies* suggests that forgiveness is an ongoing process, a point made explicit in the verses that follow: "If we claim to be without sin, we deceive ourselves and the truth is not in us. If we confess our sins, he is faithful and just and will forgive us our sins and purify us from all unrighteousness" (1 John 1:8–9). Clearly, forgiveness exonerates the believer from the penalty of all sin, but the presence of sin is not eradicated in the life of the one who is forgiven. Accordingly, Christians are to confess these sins to obtain forgiveness from a "faithful and just" God (cf. James 5:16).

The Christian believer stands completely forgiven before God! This is an amazing truth. The Christian therefore has an obligation to forgive "whatever grievances [he] may have against . . . another"; he is to forgive as the Lord forgave him (Col. 3:13; cf. Matt. 18:21–35; 2 Cor. 2:7–10). A spirit of forgiveness is to be one of the hallmarks of the Christian's walk (e.g., Matt. 6:14–15).

SUMMARY

A downward reading of the text reveals not only Jesus' authority, as the Son of Man, to forgive sins, but also the priority of that forgiveness. Our sideways, comparative reading of the parallel accounts in the Synoptic Gospels draws attention to the priority of Jesus' preaching ministry in the context (Mark 2:2b). It is his message, rather than his miracles, that are most important—spiritual forgiveness, rather than physical healing, that is the priority. The Christian reader needs to heed this important lesson.

A backward reading of the text enhances the stature of Jesus by introducing the reader to the authoritative "son of man" figure in Daniel 7:13–14, now with authority on earth to forgive sins. The various Old Testament descriptions of forgiveness increase our sense of appreciation not only for the divine origin of forgiveness, but also for its comprehensive, "once-for-all," gracious character, truths affirmed by our forward reading of the text (e.g., Mic. 7:19).

As a first step in applying any Gospel account, the reader should always ask: What does this encounter teach me about Jesus? The primary lesson of our text is rather obvious: Jesus has authority on earth to forgive sins! Accordingly, as an initial response, this encounter should encourage the reader to seek forgiveness of sins from Jesus and to rest assured by his healing of the paralytic that he has the authority to grant this forgiveness. As a next step, the portrayal of the priority of forgiveness in this encounter should also motivate Christians to prioritize this forgiveness in their various relationships, both divine and human. This should be done completely to the honor and glory of God and his Son, the One who first forgives us, so that we may forgive others in the same way (see Matt. 6:14–15; 18:21–35).

4

JESUS PRONOUNCES ON THE SABBATH

Mark 2:23–3:6: One Sabbath Jesus was going through the grainfields, and as his disciples walked along, they began to pick some heads of grain. The Pharisees said to him, "Look, why are they doing what is unlawful on the Sabbath?"

He answered, "Have you never read what David did when he and his companions were hungry and in need? In the days of Abiathar the high priest, he entered the house of God and ate the consecrated bread, which is lawful only for priests to eat. And he also gave some to his companions."

Then he said to them, "The Sabbath was made for man, not man for the Sabbath. So the Son of Man is Lord even of the Sabbath."

Another time he went into the synagogue, and a man with a shriveled hand was there. Some of them were looking for a reason to accuse Jesus, so they watched him closely to see if he would heal him on the Sabbath. Jesus said to the man with the shriveled hand, "Stand up in front of everyone."

Then Jesus asked them, "Which is lawful on the Sabbath: to do good or to do evil, to save life or to kill?" But they remained silent.

He looked around at them in anger and, deeply distressed at their stubborn hearts, said to the man, "Stretch out your hand." He stretched it out, and his hand was completely restored. Then the Pharisees went out and began to plot with the Herodians how they might kill Jesus.

A DOWNWARD READING

This text records a double controversy regarding the Old Testament Sabbath command. Jesus' opponents are the Pharisees, self-appointed "religious police," as one commentator describes them.[1] They valued the Torah, or law of Moses, and developed an oral tradition designed to provide detailed guidance for the application of this law in daily life (cf. Mark 7:1–13). Many of the teachers of the law belonged to the sect of the Pharisees (2:16). In the context, the Pharisees do not understand the significance of Jesus' presence. They should be feasting in celebration; instead, they are fasting (2:18–20). Their escalating animosity toward Jesus and his disciples is expressed in a number of searching questions, culminating in a plot to kill him (cf. 2:16, 24; 3:6). Jesus tells a short parable, contrasting the "new" and the "old," to make the point that these Pharisees are out of step with God's redemptive purposes (2:21–22). Their adversarial stance toward Jesus regarding the Sabbath command reflects this disjunction.

The Pharisees were "strict Sabbatarians."[2] A confrontation is triggered by Jesus' disciples as they walk through some grainfields on one Sabbath, picking "heads of grain," an action that the Pharisees consider "unlawful" (Mark 2:23–24). In response, Jesus cites an Old Testament incident that occurred "in the days of Abiathar" when David and his hungry companions ate consecrated bread from the house of God, "which is lawful only for priests to eat" (vv. 25–26). Jesus concludes with a rather cryptic pronouncement: "The Sabbath was made for man, not man for the Sabbath. So the Son of Man is Lord even of the Sabbath" (vv. 27–28).

Commentators debate the exact point of Jesus' response to the Pharisees, due in part to the compressed nature of the reported dialogue.[3] What is clear is that Jesus believes that the Old Testament incident cited exonerates his disciples; that is the implication of his words, "Have you never read . . . ?" (Mark 2:25a). There is no mention in the text that this incident occurred on the Sabbath; the lesson appears to revolve around "what David did" (v. 25), rather than when he did it. David eats "the con-

1. David E. Garland, *Mark*, NIV Application Commentary (Grand Rapids: Zondervan, 1996), 106.
2. Robert H. Stein, *Mark*, Baker Exegetical Commentary on the New Testament (Grand Rapids: Baker Academic, 2008), 145.
3. See for example, ibid., 147.

secrated bread, which is lawful only for priests to eat," and gives some to his companions (v. 26). What is significant, some commentators point out, is that David is not censured for his unlawful actions, apparently because he and his companions "were hungry and in need" (v. 25b).[4] According to one commentator, "[Jesus] cites the incident . . . to establish the principle that the satisfaction of normal human need must take priority over the rulings of various rabbinical schools."[5] This humanitarian principle is then applied to the Sabbath: "The Sabbath was made for man, not man for the Sabbath" (v. 27). Simply put, the Sabbath was intended to be a blessing, not a burden. Jesus' disciples are exonerated on this view of the Sabbath. Jesus thereby overthrows the narrow interpretation of the Pharisees that makes the Sabbath command burdensome. As "Lord" of the Sabbath, Jesus has the authority to do so (v. 28).

This understanding of the text, however, has been challenged by commentators who latch on to the fact that Jesus' disciples are not described as "hungry and in need" in Mark's Gospel, suggesting that human need is not the crux of Jesus' defense in the context (see Mark 2:25b).[6] Rather, Jesus cites this Old Testament incident because it involves David. What is important, from Jesus' perspective, is not what David did, but the fact that it was David, Israel's anointed king, who did it. It must be admitted that the text does place an emphasis on David: "When [David] was in need and was hungry" (ESV), he entered the house of God, ate the consecrated bread, and also gave some to his companions (vv. 25–26). According to this view, Jesus intends to draw a comparison between himself and David, and build an argument from the lesser to the greater: if David and his companions could be exonerated for doing something that was in fact unlawful, how much more so the disciples of Jesus, who is "Lord even of the Sabbath" (v. 28). The issue then revolves around the authority of Jesus.

The Pharisees condemn Jesus' disciples because they fail to recognize Jesus' true authority, as in the case of the paralytic whose sins are forgiven (Mark 2:6–7). Jesus asserts his authority over the Sabbath by making a pronouncement regarding its purpose (2:27); he then demonstrates

---

4. See, for example, R. A. Cole, *Mark*, New Bible Commentary: 21st Century Edition (Downers Grove, IL: IVP Academic, 1994), 955.

5. Brian Wintle, "The New Testament as Tradition," *Evangelical Review of Theology* 19 (1995): 116.

6. See, for example, Robert H. Gundry, *Mark: A Commentary on His Apology for the Cross* (Grand Rapids: Eerdmans, 1993), 142.

this authority by his subsequent healing on the Sabbath of the man with the shriveled hand (3:1 5). The point of Jesus' defense, therefore, is to show his opponents that he "is Lord even of the Sabbath" (2:28). This perspective on the text reflects the broader motif in the Markan context of the presence of God's kingdom, evident in Jesus' authority over evil spirits, all manner of diseases (1:21–45), sins (2:10), and, in this instance, the Sabbath. Jesus' point is therefore primarily Christological. This view is supported by the fact that the text does not end on the humanitarian note struck by Mark 2:27, but rather on a note of personal authority reflected in Mark 2:28. One or two commentators aver that the concluding pronouncement in Mark 2:28 is best understood as a parenthetical remark by Mark.[7] Yet the preceding "Then he said to them" (2:27a) suggests that both verses 27 and 28 should rightly be attributed to Jesus, a conclusion reinforced by the "So" that links them (2:28a).

In a second, related incident, the setting changes from the grainfields to a synagogue that Jesus enters on the Sabbath. There he encounters a man with a shriveled hand (Mark 3:1). "Some of [the Pharisees]" are present; they are "looking for a reason to accuse Jesus," so they watch closely to see whether he will heal the man on the Sabbath (v. 2). The issue is not whether Jesus can heal, but whether he will heal on the Sabbath! The man with the shriveled hand does not come to Jesus looking for healing, but Jesus singles him out and raises his profile by directing him to "stand up in front of everyone" (v. 3). Jesus intends to make his actions public; he wants to make a point. Then Jesus asks them, "Which is lawful on the Sabbath: to do good or to do evil, to save life or to kill?" The answer is self-evident; there is no need for Jesus to argue the point. But the Pharisees remain silent. In effect, Jesus silences his opponents, and in the process exposes their true heart condition. Jesus is angry and "deeply distressed at their stubborn hearts" (vv. 4–5). They are indifferent to the plight of this man; they have made up their minds about Jesus; they are not willing to concede the point to him. Jesus is not deterred or intimidated by their attitude toward him. With a simple command to the man to "stretch out your hand"—hardly a violation of the "no work" Sabbath principle—his hand is "completely restored" (v. 5), demonstrating Jesus' authority as Lord of the Sabbath (cf. 2:28). The religious leaders are unmoved by this miraculous healing. They "immediately"

7. See discussion in Stein, *Mark*, 149.

(ESV) begin to plot with the Herodians, the political leaders, how they might kill Jesus (3:6).

It is worth noting that the reaction of the others who witness this miracle is not recorded (cf. Mark 1:27). The point of the story is not to reveal to them Jesus' miraculous power to heal—that is assumed in the context, even by his enemies (3:2)—or to highlight the faith of the man healed. Rather, the intent is to showcase the response of the leaders of Israel to Jesus—first looking to accuse him, then remaining silent, then plotting to destroy him (3:2, 4, 6). Their hearts are hard; they witness a miracle—Jesus' act of doing good that is lawful on the Sabbath (3:4)—but are unwilling to reconsider their hostile stance toward Jesus. The "old wineskins" of the Pharisees cannot contain the "new wine" of Jesus' ministry (2:22a). Through this incident, Jesus exposes their true heart condition.

A SIDEWAYS READING

All three Synoptic Gospels record these Sabbath controversies (cf. Matt. 12:1–14; Luke 6:1–11). There are a number of differences between these parallel traditions. In the first incident, Mark records details not reflected in Matthew's and Luke's accounts. The most significant are the following: they make no reference to "the days of Abiathar the high priest" (Mark 2:26a) or to the pronouncement in Mark 2:27: "The Sabbath was made for man, not man for the Sabbath." But a number of details in the parallel accounts that are not recorded in Mark's narrative help to shed light on Mark's account:

- Matthew, unlike Mark, explicitly mentions that Jesus' disciples "were hungry" (Matt. 12:1). Although it is possible that this point is implied in Mark's account (see Mark 2:25b), we argue that Mark makes no mention of this detail because it is not part of his argument in the context.
- Mark's reference to "Abiathar the high priest" (Mark 2:26a) has raised questions about the historical accuracy of his account because Ahimelech, not Abiathar, his son, was high priest at the time of this incident (cf. 1 Sam. 21:1–6). The NIV rendering of this phrase, "in the days of Abiathar the high priest," provides

a historically plausible solution to this difficulty. The absence of this historical marker in the parallel accounts may be due to the difficulties raised by this reference.

- Matthew adds an example from "the Law" of the priests in the temple who desecrate the Sabbath and yet are innocent (Matt. 12:5). According to one commentator, "Jesus' argument . . . provides an instance from the law itself in which the Sabbath restrictions were superseded by the priests because their cultic responsibilities took precedence: the temple, as it were, was greater than the Sabbath."[8] These comments make sense of Jesus' subsequent pronouncement in Matthew's account: "One [or "something," ESV] greater than the temple is here" (Matt. 12:6). By implication, service for Jesus and the kingdom, like that of the priests in the temple, supersedes the normal Sabbath restrictions. Although Mark does not include this example, it sheds light on the logic of his argument regarding David (see Mark 2:25–26). Mark is drawing a comparison between David and Jesus to make the point that One greater than David is here! If David had the authority to act as he did, how much more so Jesus, for he is "Lord even of the Sabbath" (Mark 2:28).

- Matthew quotes the words of the prophet Hosea: "If you had known what these words mean, 'I desire mercy, not sacrifice,' you would not have condemned the innocent" (Matt. 12:7, quoting Hos. 6:6). Jesus here identifies the problem with the Pharisees' legal hermeneutic: it is too rigid, it contemplates no exceptions to the Sabbath law, and it is devoid of mercy. The Pharisees have missed the true significance of the law. As one commentator states, "The priority of rules had replaced the priority of relationships."[9] Consequently, they condemn those whom the law does not condemn. Significantly, Mark does not include this Old Testament quotation, enhancing the view that his argument revolves around a comparison between David and Jesus, rather than the humanitarian purpose of the Sabbath.

8. D. A. Carson, "Matthew," in *Matthew, Mark, Luke*, vol. 8 of The Expositor's Bible Commentary (Grand Rapids: Zondervan, 1984), 282.

9. R. J. D. Utley, *The Gospel according to Peter: Mark and I & II Peter*, vol. 2 of Study Guide Commentary Series (Marshall, TX: Bible Lessons International, 2001), 36.

Matthew's more detailed record of Jesus' response to the accusation of the Pharisees enables the reader to better connect the dots, so to speak, of Jesus' more cryptic argument in Mark's Gospel. Jesus' two Old Testament examples in Matthew's account demonstrate that his disciples are exempted from the Sabbath "no work" principle, not on the humanitarian grounds of hunger, but on the grounds that One "greater than the temple" is present (Matt. 12:6). It is for this reason that Mark makes no mention of the hunger or need of the disciples and does not place David's actions on the Sabbath; neither is necessary for his purposes. One commentator provides a helpful analysis of this evidence:

> Strikingly, Mark resists what must have been an almost overpowering urge to mention need, hunger, and eating on the part of the disciples to correspond with the mentioned need, hunger, and eating on the part of David and his companions (so Matthew and Luke). Mark never states that the disciples plucked ears of grain because they were hungry or that they ate what they plucked. Only their breaking the Sabbath by plucking ears of grain comes into the picture. Thus no emphasis falls on the humanitarian purpose of the Sabbath. Instead the emphasis builds up Jesus' authority as Lord of the Sabbath to pronounce on its humanitarian purpose.[10]

Mark's intention, then, is to use this Sabbath controversy to make a telling point about Jesus, the Son of Man—he is "Lord even of the Sabbath" (Mark 2:28). It is worth noting that only Mark's rendition includes the word *even*, an indication that this pronouncement is part of a larger argument that Mark is building in the context concerning "the Son of Man"—not only does Jesus, "the Son of Man," have authority on earth to forgive sins (cf. v. 10), he "is Lord *even* of the Sabbath" (v. 28)! According to one commentator, this "implies that the Sabbath offers the supreme test of Jesus' lordship over religious practice—and he passes."[11]

This particular perspective on the text is not inconsequential. It reinforces the point we made at the outset of our study of Mark's Gospel: the Gospels are primarily biographies of Jesus. The purpose of this incident, then, is to reveal Jesus' true identity—he is "Lord" of the Sabbath;

10. Gundry, *Mark*, 142.
11. Ibid., 143.

it is not a ploy by the early church to justify a more lenient view of the Sabbath command in the church, as some argue.

In Matthew's account of the second Sabbath incident (cf. Matt. 12:9–14; Mark 3:1–6; Luke 6:6–11), the religious leaders, motivated by malice, ask a question that Jesus answers (Matt. 12:10b–12). In the process, Jesus makes a point about the Sabbath: it is lawful to do good on the Sabbath! In Mark's account, by way of contrast, it is Jesus who asks a question, triggering a confrontation, but the religious leaders respond with silence (Mark 3:3–4; cf. Luke 6:9; 14:6). In the process, Jesus makes a point about the religious leaders: their hearts are hard!

The question that the religious leaders pose to Jesus in Matthew's account is narrowly construed: "Is it lawful to heal on the Sabbath?" (Matt. 12:10b; cf. Luke 14:3). Jesus' question in the parallel accounts is couched more broadly and antithetically: "Which is lawful on the Sabbath: to do good or to do evil, to save life or to kill?" (Mark 3:4; cf. Luke 6:9). In a context where the Jewish tradition allowed healing on the Sabbath only if life was threatened (see Luke 13:14), Jesus' question seems to imply that to do good or evil can be equated with saving life or killing (see Mark 3:4). Jesus' answer in Matthew's Gospel argues more generally for doing good on the Sabbath: "He said to them, 'If any of you has a sheep and it falls into a pit on the Sabbath, will you not take hold of it and lift it out? How much more valuable is a man than a sheep! Therefore it is lawful to do good on the Sabbath'" (Matt. 12:11–12; cf. Luke 14:5). Jesus' subsequent act of healing the man in Mark's Gospel demonstrates this truth, answers Jesus' question, and functions as a rebuke to the religious leaders (Mark 3:5). The Sabbath is for doing good, not just for rest from work. It is not Jesus but his opponents who are out of step with God's law.

In Mark's Gospel, Jesus responds to the hard-heartedness of the religious leaders with anger and deep distress (Mark 3:5). The Pharisees respond to Jesus' subsequent public act of healing by initiating a plot to kill Jesus, ironically on the Sabbath, a day intended to save life! They enlist the help of the "Herodians" (Mark 3:6; cf. Luke 6:11). As part of the political establishment, the Herodians are unlikely allies of the Pharisees and, as such, are an indication of the lengths to which the Pharisees would go to destroy Jesus, such is their animosity toward him. Mark alone makes reference to the "Herodians," signaling a more widespread opposition to Jesus (cf. Matt. 12:14; Luke 6:11).

A sideways reading of the parallel traditions in this second incident draws attention to the fact that, in Mark's account, Jesus confronts his opponents by asking them a leading question and then deliberately healing the man in a public place, in a public manner, and on the Sabbath. He could have delayed the healing until after the Sabbath; the man's ailment was not life-threatening. As Lord of the Sabbath (Mark 2:28), Jesus demonstrates his authority by establishing and doing what is "lawful" on the Sabbath. His purpose is to expose the true heart condition of the Pharisees as they plot to kill him (3:4–6). One commentator concludes that "this first mention of a plot to kill Jesus springs not from disputes over the legality of various Sabbath activities but over Jesus' authority. The Sabbath conflicts are not the cause of the plotting but its occasion. Therefore Sabbath disputes were not mentioned at Jesus' trials; in themselves they were never as much an issue as Jesus' claim to be the Sabbath's Lord."[12] The fact that the Pharisees are willing and able to plot against Jesus with the help of the Herodians, a political party, indicates that their opposition to him is not based purely on disputes relating to the Sabbath (see 3:6); Jesus' authority threatens the entire status quo, and hence their standing among the people (see 11:18).

A BACKWARD READING

The fingerprints of the Old Testament are all over this text. It is striking how Jesus points back to these Scriptures to defend his disciples. "Have you never read" is a clear allusion to the authority of the Old Testament in that context. Jesus' purpose is not to abrogate the Sabbath command through some new revelation, but to admonish his critics for overlooking a piece of biblical evidence that exonerates his disciples. The accusation of the Pharisees relates to the actions of Jesus' disciples on the Sabbath.

The Sabbath was instituted by God as "a day of rest, a holy Sabbath to the LORD" (Ex. 16:23), during Israel's wanderings in the wilderness before the giving of the law at Sinai. Significantly, the Sabbath command is listed as one of the Ten Commandments, where its rationale is linked to God's pattern of rest at the end of the creation week (Ex. 20:8–11; cf. Gen. 2:2–3). The Sabbath is subsequently designated

---

12. Carson, "Matthew," 285.

as "a sign" between God and his people for the generations to come so that they may know that it is God who makes them holy (Ex. 31:13; cf. Ezek. 20:12). Anyone who does any work on the Sabbath must be put to death (Ex. 31:15; 35:2). When Moses recounts the giving of the law in Deuteronomy, the rationale for the Sabbath is declared to be Israel's divine rescue from Egypt (Deut. 5:15; cf. Ex. 20:1–2). The Sabbath was intended to be a "delight" to God's people (Isa. 58:13), but instead, Israel had a history of "desecrating" the day (see Neh. 13:17; Ezek. 20:13, 16, 24).

The Pharisees' charge of "unlawful" behavior relates to the issue of reaping on the Sabbath (Mark 2:23–24). The disciples' action of picking heads of grain in the fields of another was lawful (cf. Deut. 23:25), but the Pharisees viewed this as reaping, an activity prohibited on the Sabbath (Ex. 34:21). In response, Jesus cites the Old Testament account, recorded in 1 Samuel 21:1–6, of David, who, when "hungry and in need," enters the house of God, eats "the consecrated bread, which is lawful only for priests to eat," and gives some to his companions (Mark 2:25–26). The relevant Old Testament verses are worth quoting in full:

> David went to Nob, to Ahimelech the priest. Ahimelech trembled when he met him, and asked, "Why are you alone? Why is no one with you?"
>
> David answered Ahimelech the priest, "The king charged me with a certain matter and said to me, 'No one is to know anything about your mission and your instructions.' As for my men, I have told them to meet me at a certain place. Now then, what do you have on hand? Give me five loaves of bread, or whatever you can find."
>
> But the priest answered David, "I don't have any ordinary bread on hand; however, there is some consecrated bread here—provided the men have kept themselves from women."
>
> David replied, "Indeed women have been kept from us, as usual whenever I set out. The men's things are holy even on missions that are not holy. How much more so today!" So the priest gave him the consecrated bread, since there was no bread there except the bread of the Presence that had been removed from before the LORD and replaced by hot bread on the day it was taken away. (1 Sam. 21:1–6)

In the context, David is fleeing from King Saul with the help of his son Jonathan (see 1 Sam. 20). Like Jesus, David is an anointed king-in-waiting (see 1 Sam. 16:11–13) with enemies that threaten his life (1 Sam. 20:31; cf.

Mark 3:6). The Old Testament account makes no mention of Jesus' reference to the hunger and need of David and his companions (Mark 2:25), and the text does not state that this incident occurred on the Sabbath, although this fact may be inferred from the removal and replacement of the "bread of the Presence," which occurred on the Sabbath (1 Sam. 21:6; cf. Lev. 24:8). Jesus' account does not refer to David's apparent deception in the context or to his detailed interaction with Ahimelech, the priest, regarding the consecrated bread. But we may conclude from Jesus' question to the Pharisees, "Have you never read what David did" (Mark 2:25a), that his hearers had some knowledge of these omitted details. In any event, Jesus' citation focuses on "what David did" (Mark 2:25) by entering the house of God, eating the "consecrated bread" reserved for the priests to eat (Mark 2:26; cf. Lev. 24:9), and giving some to his companions, none of which is explicitly mentioned in the Old Testament text, but is clearly implied (see 1 Sam. 21:4b–5). Significantly, David's unlawful act is not censured; that appears to be Jesus' point. Nothing in this Old Testament context derails our earlier conclusion regarding the logic of Jesus' argument. His intent is to claim an authority for himself as the Son of Man that not only parallels but exceeds that of David (Mark 2:28; cf. Matt. 12:6), thereby exonerating his disciples.

Critics point out that Jesus erred by identifying Abiathar, and not Ahimelech, his father, as the "high priest" when this incident occurred (cf. Mark 2:26; 1 Sam. 21:1). Evangelical commentators have countered with various plausible proposals to reconcile the historical data. Some commentators suggest that Ahimelech and Abiathar each had both names (cf. 1 Sam. 22:20; 2 Sam. 8:17; 1 Chron. 18:16; 24:6).[13] Others cite Mark 12:26 as evidence that, in the absence of chapters and verses in the Old Testament, New Testament authors would identify a passage by means of an important character in that section of the canon.[14] In this case, Abiathar was considered more important than Ahimelech (cf. 1 Sam. 22:20). One commentator makes the suggestion, a compelling fit in the Markan context, that Jesus' reference to Abiathar is intended as an allusion to his later role in the Old Testament narrative where he sides with David,

13. See discussion in James R. Edwards, *The Gospel according to Mark*, Pillar New Testament Commentary (Grand Rapids: Eerdmans, 2002), 95n42.

14. William Lane, *The Gospel of Mark*, New International Commentary on the New Testament (Grand Rapids: Eerdmans, 1974), 116.

becoming his chief priest, which in effect affirms God's presence with David and furnishes additional evidence that God did not sanction him for eating the consecrated bread (1 Sam. 22:20–23; cf. 22:9–15).[15] Whatever the solution to this historical tension, rather than being evidence of historical error in the Bible, ironically, it is possible to cite this reference as evidence that Mark carefully preserved Jesus' historical sayings, even if difficult, just as he received them.

Jesus' concluding pronouncements in Mark 2:27–28 also echo the Old Testament Scriptures at a number of points. Jesus' declaration in Mark 2:27 regarding the humanitarian purpose of the Sabbath reflects the all-encompassing "no work" motif so prominent in the Sabbath command (see Deut. 5:14–15) and the prophetic language of "delight" experienced by those who honor the command (Isa. 58:13). Jesus' pronouncement in Mark 2:28 regarding his authority over the Sabbath incorporates the "Son of Man" motif introduced in Mark 2:10. Some commentators argue that this "Son of Man" terminology should be understood as a reference to mankind in general. Jesus' argument would then read as follows: "The Sabbath was made for man . . . . So man is lord even of the Sabbath" (Mark 2:27–28).[16] If this were the case, however, it would be highly unlikely that Jesus would use the terminology of "lordship," with its connotations of divinity (Mark 1:3), to make the point. There are good reasons in the context for rather connecting the "Son of Man" language to Daniel's authoritative "son of man" figure (Dan. 7:13). First, the force of Jesus' argument from the Old Testament places the focus on his authority, not mankind's, over the Sabbath. Second, the broader Markan context has a discernible emphasis on the authority of Jesus (cf. Mark 1:22, 27; 2:10). Third, to quote one commentator, "Here, as always when 'Son of Man' appears on the lips of Jesus, it carries the definite article, '*the* Son of Man,' referring to Jesus' unique vocation as the Son of Man with divine authority and power from Daniel 7:14."[17] In the Markan context, this divine authority and power is revealed in Jesus' authority, as the Son of Man, to forgive sins (Mark 2:10) and to "even" regulate the use of the Sabbath (Mark

---

15. Rikk E. Watts, *Mark*, Commentary on the New Testament Use of the Old Testament (Grand Rapids: Baker Academic, 2007), 141.

16. See discussion in Edwards, *The Gospel according to Mark*, 96–97.

17. Ibid., 97.

2:28). The Old Testament points forward to Jesus, the One greater than David and the temple, the Lord of the Sabbath!

In the second Sabbath incident, Jesus seeks to establish what is "lawful" on the Sabbath, but his opponents remain silent, refusing to discuss this question (Mark 3:4). The antithetical structure of Jesus' question could be an echo of the choices depicted in Deuteronomy 30:15: "See, I set before you today life and prosperity, death and destruction." Jesus responds by demonstrating that healing a non-life-threatening ailment is a lawful activity. It is possible that an Old Testament passage such as Micah 6:8 is hovering in the background of Jesus' thinking in this incident: "He has showed you, O man, what is good. And what does the LORD require of you? To act justly and to love mercy and to walk humbly with your God."

A FORWARD READING

These incidents reveal and establish Jesus' authority over the Sabbath. As Lord of the Sabbath, Jesus uses this authority to define the proper purpose of the Sabbath (Mark 2:27) and to establish what is "lawful" activity on this day (3:4). Jesus, in the process, does not abrogate the Sabbath command. The obvious question that arises, then, is how the Christian should relate to the Sabbath. Simply put, is the Christian still required to obey the Sabbath command today? Anyone familiar with the literature on this topic will know that this is a contentious issue that continues to generate disagreement in the contemporary church. One writer calls it "a perennial debate" in the church.[18]

Some Christians insist on the need to keep the Sabbath today because it is a "creation ordinance," that is, based on the pattern of the creation week, and because it is part of the Decalogue (or Ten Commandments). Yet most of these same Christians "hallow" not the seventh day, as required by the Sabbath command, but the Sunday, or first day of the week (cf. Ex. 20:11). Is this legitimate obedience to the Sabbath command? Or perhaps more to the point, would the Lord of the Sabbath consider this "lawful" obedience to the Sabbath command? A forward reading of this motif in the New Testament will help the reader to identify the

---

18. Richard B. Gaffin Jr., "Sabbath," in *New Dictionary of Theology*, electronic ed. (Downers Grove, IL: IVP Academic, 2000), 606.

relevant biblical data. Our interpretation of this biblical data may differ, but this, in and of itself, does not invalidate a forward reading of the text.

In the Acts of the Apostles, the Sabbath does not appear to be an issue in the life of the early church. When "the Sabbath" is mentioned, it is usually in connection with gospel outreach in the synagogues where the people of God gathered on the Sabbath. We are told that in Thessalonica, Paul, "as his custom was, . . . went into the synagogue, and on three Sabbath days he reasoned with them from the Scriptures" (Acts 17:2; cf. 13:14, 42, 44; 16:13; 18:4). There is no indication that this same pattern was adopted when the church met together (cf. 20:7).

What is surprising is that, outside of the Gospels and Acts, there are only two references to "Sabbath" in the New Testament writings: Colossians 2:16 and Hebrews 4:9. The former reference is often used to argue for the abrogation of the Sabbath command, while the latter is sometimes used to argue for the contrary. According to Paul, "Do not let anyone judge you by what you eat or drink, or with regard to a religious festival, a New Moon celebration or a Sabbath day. These are a shadow of the things that were to come; the reality, however, is found in Christ" (Col. 2:16–17; cf. Gal. 4:9–11). The writer to the Hebrews, for his part, refers to a still-future "Sabbath-rest" for the people of God (Heb. 4:9). The former view tends to highlight the notion of typological fulfillment in the ministry of Christ, while the latter places greater emphasis on the still-future eschatological dimension of the rest he offers (cf. Matt. 11:28–30).

A variant approach to this question identifies the "faith" motif as a key component of the Sabbath command. In the context of God's providing manna for his people in the wilderness, the Israelites were commanded to refrain from work on the Sabbath and to trust God's provision for their needs on that day; to work signified a lack of trust in God, who had covenanted to provide for them (see Ex. 16:23–30). According to this view, keeping the Sabbath under the old covenant was a symbolic reminder of these truths that are now fulfilled under the new covenant in a life of faith centered on the Lord Jesus Christ (Heb. 3:16–4:13). So the Christian keeps the Sabbath today by trusting God to meet his or her every need every day. Thus, "in Christ, every day is the Sabbath!"[19]

---

19. Scott J. Hafemann, *The God of Promise and the Life of Faith* (Wheaton, IL: Crossway, 2001), 224n4; see also 84–87.

How does the Christian respond to this unsettled landscape of views regarding the validity of the Sabbath command today? In our opinion, the reader should factor in the following observations when formulating a response to this issue: First, although Jesus does not abrogate the Sabbath in the Gospels, and there is no reference to the early Christians' doing so either, the biblical evidence suggests that these Christians early on began to gather together "on the first day of the week," the Sunday, apparently in recognition of Christ's resurrection on this day. There are indications that this day was used for communal worship, mutual encouragement, and the celebration of the Lord's Supper (Acts 20:7–12; 1 Cor. 16:2; Heb. 10:25; cf. Rev. 1:10). This pattern of meeting together provides a biblical precedent for the general practice of the church today to gather on a Sunday for communal worship. Second, when Christians today speak of keeping the Sabbath day holy, it is typically a reference to setting aside the Sunday for this purpose. It needs to be recognized, however, that no biblical text explicitly mentions that this "first day" of worship was viewed as a replacement for the Sabbath day of rest. Third, the Bible recognizes that certain matters of practice generate disagreements among Christian believers on occasion. Paul designates these as "disputable matters" (Rom. 14:1). It appears as though the Sabbath command may be included on a list of such matters. According to the apostle, "One man considers one day more sacred than another; another man considers every day alike" (v. 5). This is an apt description of the current status of the Sabbath debate. Paul's advice? "Each one should be fully convinced in his own mind. He who regards one day as special, does so to the Lord" (vv. 5b–6a). So, to quote one writer, "whether under the new covenant we honor one day of the week above another . . . is a matter of personal preference and conscience before the Lord."[20] And in a context in which such disagreements persist, Christians should avoid judging or despising one another because the Lord alone is the Judge of us all (v. 10). Instead, the Christian's energies should be directed toward actions that lead "to peace and to mutual edification" within the body of Christ (v. 19).

SUMMARY

Mark has designed these Sabbath conflict stories to reveal Jesus' authority over the Sabbath. As one writer puts it rather aptly, "The

---

20. Ibid., 224n4.

clash . . . is not over the rules but over *who* rules."[21] Thus, our text is concerned with the true identity of Jesus. This view of the text is evident from our downward reading of the narrative, and is reinforced by both a sideways and a backward reading of the text. This perspective raises a more pressing matter for the reader to confront than the question of the validity of the Sabbath command today, the focus of our forward reading—the reader's attitude toward Jesus! In our text, the religious leaders do not recognize the authority of Jesus; the conflict over the Sabbath is a symptom of this failure on their part. Jesus responds to their "stubborn hearts" with anger and deep distress (Mark 3:5). This combination of emotions is attributed to Jesus only this once in the Gospels, and therefore it is a striking indictment of this mentality. Consequently, while it may be important to have clear biblical convictions about the validity of the Sabbath command today, it is far more important to have first bowed the knee to the Lord of the Sabbath!

A similar perspective is reflected by the writer to the Hebrews when he adopts the "Sabbath-rest" motif to exhort his readers to avoid the grave consequences of hardening one's heart against Christ (Heb. 3:11–4:11). He reminds his readers of the wilderness generation that Moses led out of Egypt, who heard God's "voice" but rebelled against him because of unbelief. God was angry with them. Consequently, they did not enter his rest; their "bodies fell in the desert" (3:15–19). The good news is that there remains a "Sabbath-rest for the people of God" (4:9). Those who believe the gospel message enter that rest (4:2–3). The writer concludes with an exhortation: "Let us, therefore, make every effort to enter that rest, so that no one will fall by following their example of disobedience" (4:11). It is striking how the writer includes himself in this exhortation, indicating the need for self-examination among the people of God. Any application of these Sabbath conflict stories today should reflect this perspective.

---

21. William Willimon, quoted in Garland, *Mark*, 117 (emphasis in original).

5

JESUS TEACHES IN PARABLES

Mark 4:1–20: On another occasion Jesus began to teach by the lake. The crowd that gathered around him was so large that he got into a boat and sat in it out on the lake, while all the people were along the shore at the water's edge. He taught them many things by parables, and in his teaching said: "Listen! A farmer went out to sow his seed. As he was scattering the seed, some fell along the path, and the birds came and ate it up. Some fell on rocky places, where it did not have much soil. It sprang up quickly, because the soil was shallow. But when the sun came up, the plants were scorched, and they withered because they had no root. Other seed fell among thorns, which grew up and choked the plants, so that they did not bear grain. Still other seed fell on good soil. It came up, grew and produced a crop, multiplying thirty, sixty, or even a hundred times."

Then Jesus said, "He who has ears to hear, let him hear."

When he was alone, the Twelve and the others around him asked him about the parables. He told them, "The secret of the kingdom of God has been given to you. But to those on the outside everything is said in parables so that,

"'they may be ever seeing but never perceiving,
     and ever hearing but never understanding;
otherwise they might turn and be forgiven!'"

Then Jesus said to them, "Don't you understand this parable? How then will you understand any parable? The farmer sows the word.

Some people are like seed along the path, where the word is sown. As soon as they hear it, Satan comes and takes away the word that was sown in them. Others, like seed sown on rocky places, hear the word and at once receive it with joy. But since they have no root, they last only a short time. When trouble or persecution comes because of the word, they quickly fall away. Still others, like seed sown among thorns, hear the word; but the worries of this life, the deceitfulness of wealth and the desires for other things come in and choke the word, making it unfruitful. Others, like seed sown on good soil, hear the word, accept it, and produce a crop—thirty, sixty or even a hundred times what was sown."

A DOWNWARD READING

In our text, Jesus teaches a large crowd "many things by parables" (Mark 4:1–2). This is not the first time that Jesus teaches in parables (see 2:19–22; 3:23), but our text represents the first substantial block of Jesus' teaching material in Mark's Gospel, and so merits our close attention. The context is one of opposition and conflict. Jesus' own family criticizes him (3:20–21), and the teachers of the law accuse him of casting out demons by "the prince of demons" (3:22). By attributing an "evil spirit" to Jesus, they are "guilty of an eternal sin"; they will never be forgiven (3:29–30)! When Jesus' family subsequently seeks him out, he uses the opportunity to redefine the family of God; it is not dependent on biology, but on doing "God's will." So we find Jesus' family standing "outside," while Jesus identifies those "seated in a circle around him" as "my mother and my brothers" (3:31–35)! Jesus' words would have been startling to his hearers, and no doubt shocking to his family. According to this scenario, Mark divides Jesus' hearers into "insiders" and "outsiders," a distinction evident in the parabolic teaching that follows (4:10–12). Jesus' audience is now so large that he takes to a boat on the lake, where he sits down to teach by parables as they gather along the water's edge to listen to him (4:1).

These verses have a clear structure: The parable (Mark 4:1–9) and its interpretation (vv. 14–20) sandwich Jesus' teaching about parables in Mark 4:10–13, suggesting that Mark intended these verses to be understood as a unit. The details of this oft-quoted parable are well known.

A farmer sows his seed, scattering it widely.[1] Some falls on the path and is eaten up; some falls on "rocky places"; it springs up quickly, but withers when the sun comes up because the seed has no root; other seed falls among thorns, which grow up and choke the plants, so they do not bear grain. Still other seed falls on good soil, and it grows and produces a crop, "multiplying thirty, sixty, or even a hundred times" (vv. 3–9), a good harvest in that context (cf. Gen. 26:12).

In Jesus' subsequent explanation of the parable, he identifies the "seed" as "the word" (Mark 4:14). The sower, or "farmer," is a reference to Jesus in the context, while the various soils—"the path," "rocky places," "thorns," and "good soil"—represent different "people" or hearers who respond differently to the word that is sown (vv. 14, 15a, 16, 18, 20). One commentator summarizes Jesus' explanation as follows: "Even in the case of those ready to listen, shallow response is a danger. Careless or superficial listeners, who have no root, or those whose lives are too full of worries or pleasures (sometimes equal dangers) will bear no fruit. Only those who listen, accept and act will be fruitful."[2] The parable and its interpretation end on a positive note. According to one commentator, "In summary, the good hearers welcome the word immediately, so that Satan cannot snatch it away. They welcome it deeply, so that persecution because of it cannot induce them to apostatize. They welcome it exclusively, so that other concerns do not stifle it."[3]

This parable is commonly referred to as the "parable of the sower" (Matt. 13:18), although the emphasis falls on the seed and type of soil it encounters, particularly in Jesus' interpretation of the parable (Mark 4:14–20). Interpreters understand this parable differently. Some argue that Jesus intends to convey the point that the kingdom of God is present even though some reject it. Others suggest that Mark's intention is to encourage his audience to continue to share the gospel in spite of the opposition and rejection of the message; it will bear some fruit. According to to this view, the nonreception of the message of the kingdom is not due to any deficiencies with the messenger or his message, but is due to the

---

1. Mark does not actually use the word *seed* in his account; he uses pronouns instead to refer to the seed.

2. R. A. Cole, *Mark*, New Bible Commentary: 21st Century Edition (Downers Grove, IL: IVP Academic, 1994), 958.

3. Robert H. Gundry, *Mark: A Commentary on His Apology for the Cross* (Grand Rapids: Eerdmans, 1993), 206.

type of hearer the message encounters. But these perspectives don't do justice to the "hearing" motif, so prominent in this parable, which places the focus on what one commentator calls "the exhortation to hear/heed the word of God" (Mark 4:3a, 9; cf. 4:15, 16, 18, 20, 24a).[4] In our opinion, Jesus' commands to "listen" are prescriptive, not descriptive.

At the heart of this text is Jesus' response to a question by "the Twelve and the others around him" who ask about the parables (Mark 4:10). Jesus draws a distinction between insiders and outsiders. The insiders are those to whom "the secret of the kingdom of God has been given" (v. 11), a reference to "the Twelve and the others around him" (v. 10). Jesus does not elaborate on "the secret," but the context suggests, according to one commentator, that "the secret has to do with the kingdom of God coming in a veiled way in the person, words, and works of Jesus."[5] Jesus does not identify the giver of this "secret," but his hearers would know that he is referring to God, the gracious Giver. But "those on the outside" have turned away from God. For them "everything is said in parables" (v. 11) so that they hear Jesus' teaching, but do not perceive or understand it, "lest they should turn and be forgiven" (v. 12 ESV). This is a clear allusion to Jesus' opponents and their mounting animosity toward him and his ministry.

A parable has been likened to a modern political cartoon—some viewers, like Jesus' outsiders, see only a picture and look no further, but others, who have insider knowledge, grasp that an analogy is intended, and respond in a more reflective way. Parables, then, are designed to provoke reflection. The outsiders in Jesus' context witness Jesus' ministry and hear his teaching, but do not understand its meaning. Jesus' parables function to confirm them in their unbelief and hard-heartedness. In keeping with this, Jesus does not explain the meaning of the parable to these outsiders, but to the insiders, those who have been given "the secret of the kingdom of God" (Mark 4:10–20). Accordingly, Jesus challenges his hearers to listen carefully to his message, lest they find themselves to be among the outsiders (4:3a, 9; cf. 4:24a; 3:29). The encouragement to listen is reinforced by the conclusion of the parable that pictures a

4. Robert H. Stein, *Mark*, Baker Exegetical Commentary on the New Testament (Grand Rapids: Baker Academic, 2008), 221.

5. David E. Garland, *Mark*, NIV Application Commentary (Grand Rapids: Zondervan, 1996), 158.

productive hearing of Jesus' message (4:20). Producing "a crop" is evidence that one has heard the message and understood it.

Jesus' subsequent question to these insiders, however, reveals that insider status does not guarantee immediate or complete understanding of his teaching: "Don't you understand this parable? How then will you understand any parable?" (Mark 4:13). The reader can detect a note of exasperation in this rhetorical question. Jesus clearly expects some level of comprehension from them, although the disciples in Mark's Gospel are characteristically portrayed as dull regarding spiritual matters (cf. 8:17, 21; 9:32). Nevertheless, the question provides Jesus with an opportunity to give these insiders an interpretation of this parable as a model for understanding "any parable" (4:13). Jesus' point seems to be that a proper listening to his teaching in the context is the key to understanding parables.

It is apparent that the difference between insiders and outsiders lies in this: not that the one understands parables and the other doesn't, but that the insider wants to know and understand, while the outsider does not. This much is evident from the insiders' question to Jesus about the parables (Mark 4:10). Unlike the outsiders, they gather around Jesus, seeking an explanation from him. The outsiders, on the other hand, remain indifferent to Jesus' teaching; they do not pursue him for an explanation, and so the message is lost.

A SIDEWAYS READING

All three Synoptic Gospels record Jesus' parabolic teaching about the sower and the seed (cf. Matt. 13:1–23; Luke 8:4–15). There is considerable overlap between these parallel accounts, particularly in the case of Mark and Matthew, but also several significant differences that should be noted:

- Mark alone begins his parabolic discourse with a command to "listen" (Mark 4:3a). This addition alerts the reader to Mark's purpose in this text: to promote a careful hearing of Jesus' message (cf. 4:9, 24a).
- Mark alone mentions that the seed that falls among the thorns "yield[s] no fruit" (Mark 4:7b KJV; cf. Matt. 13:7; Luke 8:7). The

reference to "no fruit" here functions as a contrast to the fruitfulness of the "good soil" that is subsequently described (Mark 4:8).

- According to Mark's account, the seed that falls on "good soil" produces a crop, multiplying "thirty, sixty or even a hundred times" (Mark 4:8, 20), while in Matthew's account the order is reversed to read: "a hundred, sixty or thirty times what was sown" (Matt. 13:8). Luke, for his part, mentions only "a hundred times more than was sown" (Luke 8:8). Mark's sequence appears to reflect a call for increasing fruitfulness in the lives of those who hear.

- Mark alone mentions that others are present who, together with his disciples, ask Jesus about "the parables" (Mark 4:10; cf. Matt. 13:10; Luke 8:9). This is a significant addition, indicating that the insiders cannot be limited to the Twelve.

- Mark speaks of the singular "secret of the kingdom of God" (Mark 4:11), while both Matthew and Luke mention the plural "knowledge of the secrets of the kingdom" (Matt. 13:11; Luke 8:10). One commentator ascribes the difference to Matthew's "preference for the plural" (cf. Matt. 4:3; Luke 4:3, "stone[s]"), but the presence of the plural in both Matthew and Luke suggests that they have in view not only Mark's allusion to the veiled presence of the kingdom of God, but other matters in Jesus' teaching as well.[6]

- Mark alone mentions "those on the outside" for whom "everything is said in parables" (Mark 4:11; cf. Luke 8:10). Mark is simply reinforcing the distinction between insiders and outsiders, and the consequences of outsider status. For them everything literally "happens" in parables (Mark 4:11b; cf. KJV). In Mark's account, unlike Matthew's or Luke's, "everything" about Jesus and his ministry, not just his teaching, is obscure to the outsider—Jesus' identity, the significance of his miracles, the meaning of his teaching, and so on (see Mark 4:11b; cf. Matt. 13:13; Luke 8:10).[7] Consequently, there is no forgiveness for them (Mark 3:29–30).

6. D. A. Carson, "Matthew," in *Matthew, Mark, Luke*, vol. 8 of The Expositor's Bible Commentary (Grand Rapids: Zondervan, 1984), 308.

7. George R. Beasley-Murray, *Preaching the Gospel from the Gospels* (Peabody, MA: Hendrickson, 1996), 174–75.

- In Mark 4:12, Mark alone makes reference to forgiveness (cf. Matt. 13:15; Luke 8:10), thereby forging a link between this saying and the unforgivable sin of the teachers of the law (Mark 3:28–29). They are among the outsiders that Jesus is referring to in the context.
- Mark 4:13 has no parallels in the other accounts: "Then Jesus said to [the Twelve and the others around him], 'Don't you understand this parable? How then will you understand any parable?'" There is an implied rebuke in Jesus' questions. It could be for this reason that the parallel accounts omit it. Jesus' questions, however, alert the reader to the fact that the "secret of the kingdom of God" given to his disciples, the insiders, does not confer automatic understanding of Jesus' parables, even of this most basic parable!
- Mark alone identifies "the birds" (Mark 4:4) as "Satan" (Mark 4:15), his preferred designation for the devil (cf. Mark 1:13; 3:22, 26; cf. Matt. 13:19: "the evil one"; Luke 8:12: "the devil").
- The mention of "the desires for other things" is unique to Mark's account (Mark 4:19; cf. Matt. 13:22; Luke 8:14), and expands the description of metaphorical "thorns" that grow up and "choke" the Word of God, making it "unfruitful."
- Mark's account of the "good soil" describes those who not only hear the Word but also "accept it" (Mark 4:20), while Matthew's account speaks of those who understand it (Matt. 13:23), a prominent motif in both accounts (Matt. 13:13–15, 19, 23, 51; cf. Mark 4:12–13, 33). Mark's choice of terminology at this point could be designed to show the reader that more than a mere intellectual assent to the Word of God is in view; the Word is actually accepted or embraced by the hearer.

Of all these Markan distinctives, most noteworthy are Jesus' command to "listen" at the outset of his teaching (Mark 4:3a), the definition of an insider that includes "the others around him" (v. 10), and the consequences of insider and outsider status in Jesus' ministry—the insider has been given "the secret of the kingdom of God," but does not necessarily understand Jesus' parabolic teaching (vv. 11, 13), while the outsider hears Jesus' parabolic teaching, but does not turn and receive forgiveness from sin (v. 12).

A BACKWARD READING

A backward reading of the text sheds light on Jesus' reference to the "secret" or "mystery of the kingdom of God" (Mark 4:11 KJV). This term occurs only here and, in plural form, in the Gospel parallels (cf. Matt. 13:11; Luke 8:10). The fact that this term occurs in Jesus' teaching, without explanation and without query, suggests that his Jewish hearers had some inkling of its intended meaning. Their Old Testament Scriptures provide us with a clue. Daniel's prophetic writings have a cluster of eight references to the word *mystery* that provide a window into Jesus' use of the term (cf. Dan. 2:18–19, 27–30, 47).[8] In that seventh-century B.C. context, Nebuchadnezzar, king of Babylon, has a dream about the destiny of the kingdoms of this world. Daniel, with the help of God, provides the king with an interpretation of his dream (v. 28). In his vision, Nebuchadnezzar sees a statue representing successive kingdoms on the earth. It is completely "swept . . . away without leaving a trace" (v. 35), destroyed and replaced by a rock "not [cut] by human hands" (v. 34), which becomes a "huge mountain" and fills "the whole earth" (v. 35). This, in the opinion of commentators, is an obvious reference to the future coming and consummation of the kingdom of God that triggers the obliteration of the kingdoms of this world at the end of the age.[9] But wherein lies the "mystery"? In the Old Testament, the establishment of God's kingdom was expected to coincide with the final day of judgment, when God's people would be saved and all his enemies destroyed (cf. Isa. 35:4). According to Daniel, however, God will set up his kingdom "*in the time of those kings*" (Dan. 2:44a). Daniel's prophecy envisages the presence of God's kingdom "in the time of those kings." In view is a time of coexistence, and conflict, between the kingdom of God and the "kings" of this world. Only at some future date will God's kingdom "crush all those kingdoms and bring them to an end, but it will itself endure forever" (Dan. 2:44b).

Contrary to the popular Old Testament belief in Jesus' day, this prophecy reveals a two-stage deployment of God's kingdom: an initial presence that encounters opposition from the kings and kingdoms of this world, and a second-stage presence that will obliterate all this opposition. This is evidently the "mystery" to which Daniel refers. According to one

8. Ibid., 174.

9. See, for example, Ronald S. Wallace, *The Message of Daniel*, The Bible Speaks Today (Downers Grove, IL: InterVarsity Press, 1979), 58–59.

commentator, "It is not a mystery in the sense that it is incomprehensible, but it is a 'secret' in that not everyone yet knows it."[10] This prophetic depiction of God's kingdom has led to the formulation of such slogans as the "already–not yet" presence of God's kingdom, or the "fulfillment without consummation" nature of the kingdom promises. Applied to Jesus' ministry, it refers to the truth that the kingdom of God is present in Jesus' earthly ministry, but not in its consummate fullness; that awaits his second coming! Thus, Jesus proclaims that the kingdom of God "is at hand" (Mark 1:15 ESV), but he continues to experience opposition from Israel's religious and political elite because the consummation of the kingdom, and the destruction of God's enemies, is still future (see 3:6). The reader detects this same scenario in Jesus' parable of the sower. Jesus sows "the word," but it encounters opposition from the world, the flesh, and the devil (4:14–20)! Notwithstanding this opposition, the insiders recognize that in the person of Jesus, and his words and works, the kingdom of God is present. This veiled presence of the kingdom is "the secret of the kingdom of God" that has been given to them (4:11). Consequently, they "hear" and "accept" Jesus' parabolic teaching and, in due course, "produce a crop" (4:20).

At the heart of our text is Jesus' teaching regarding the purpose of parables (Mark 4:12). The indented format of Jesus' words at this point in our Bibles alerts the reader to the presence of an Old Testament quotation, which can be traced to Isaiah 6:9–10 (cf. Matt. 13:14): "Go and tell this people: 'Be ever hearing, but never understanding; be ever seeing, but never perceiving.' Make the heart of this people calloused; make their ears dull and close their eyes. Otherwise they might see with their eyes, hear with their ears, understand with their hearts, and turn and be healed."

This particular quotation in Mark's Gospel has troubled some readers because the "so that" conjunction that introduces the quotation suggests that Jesus utilizes parables to deliberately exclude outsiders from the kingdom (Mark 4:12a; cf. Matt. 13:13; Luke 8:10). The reality, however, is that these outsiders have already rebelled and hardened their hearts against Jesus (Mark 3:5). To use the language of Isaiah, they have already "turned" from God (see Isa. 6:10b). The parables are simply designed to expose their true heart condition. Consequently, they hear

10. Garland, *Mark*, 157.

the message of the kingdom, but do not turn to Christ to receive his forgiveness (Mark 4:12b). It is on these grounds that parables are typically described as a "two-edged sword," both revealing truth to insiders and at the same time concealing truth from outsiders. According to one commentator, parables are

> like the cloud which separated the fleeing Israelites from the pursuing Egyptians. It brought "darkness to the one side and light to the other" (Exod. 14:20). That which was blindness to Egypt was revelation to Israel. The same event was either a vehicle of light or of darkness, depending on one's stance with God.[11]

Mark paraphrases Isaiah 6:9–10 in Mark 4:12. He reverses the "hearing" and "seeing" sequence of ideas in Isaiah 6:9, possibly to emphasize the fact that not only Jesus' teaching that they hear but also his actions that these outsiders see remain obscure to their hard hearts. After all, according to Mark's account, "everything," including both Jesus' teaching and his actions, literally "happens in parables" (Mark 4:11b). Mark also omits the first part of Isaiah 6:10, probably because, in Jesus' ministry, the hearts of his opponents are already "calloused," their "ears dull," and "their eyes [closed]." Most notably, Mark substitutes "be forgiven" for Isaiah's "be healed," creating an explicit link with the actions of the teachers of the law that disqualify them from forgiveness in the context (Mark 3:29).

The Old Testament context of Isaiah 6:9–10 is instructive. God's people have rebelled against him (Isa. 1:4–5; 3:14). He is not impressed with their veneer of piety and hypocritical displays of devotion to him (1:11–15). According to Isaiah, the leaders of Judah "have rejected the law of the LORD Almighty and spurned the word of the Holy One of Israel. Therefore the LORD's anger burns against his people; his hand is raised and he strikes them down" (5:24–25; cf. 1:23). Against this background God commissions the prophet Isaiah to preach to a people that will not heed his message (cf. 6:9–10). Jesus quotes Isaiah at this point because he is encountering an analogous situation in his own ministry; what was true in Isaiah's day is true in Jesus' day—God's Word is rejected. In both

11. James R. Edwards, *The Gospel according to Mark*, Pillar New Testament Commentary (Grand Rapids: Eerdmans, 2002), 138.

contexts, God's rule is met with "rebellion cloaked in piety, especially on the part of the nation's . . . leaders."[12] Consequently, Jesus responds in parables, which expose the rebellion of the outsiders. Judgment is inevitable for them (Mark 3:23; 4:12; 12:8–12).

But in Jesus' ministry there is an important difference: unlike Judah and Jerusalem in Isaiah's day, there is still the opportunity for Jesus' listeners to "listen" and to "hear" (Mark 4:3a, 9). This is hardly surprising in view of Mark's presentation of Jesus as "good news" to those who will repent and believe his message (e.g., Mark 1:15). Thus, this prophetic word from Isaiah acts as a warning for Jesus' hearers who will not listen to him. If they turn from Jesus, they will remain on the outside, without hope and consigned to judgment. It may be for this reason that Jesus converts the second-person orientation of Isaiah 6:9–10 into the third-person form, to create a distinction between Isaiah's hearers, who will not respond to his message, and Jesus' hearers, who, like the insiders, are responding to his message. Clearly, then, in God's purposes, judgment is not the final word, a truth also hinted at by Isaiah in his subsequent reference to "the holy seed . . . in the land" that introduces what one commentator calls "a faint, but sure, ray of hope" to this prophecy, a hope that is developed elsewhere in Isaiah (Isa. 6:13b; cf. 4:3; 10:20; 65:8–9).[13] Given this emphasis on hearing the Word of God, one commentator detects "a deliberate echo" of Israel's *Shema* at this point (cf. Deut. 6:4–5).[14]

A FORWARD READING

A number of important motifs could legitimately be the focus of the forward reading of this text. For example, the interpretation of the parable of the sower contains eight references to "the word" sown, indicative of the centrality of God's Word to God's kingdom (see Mark 4:14–20). But we will focus our attention on the thrust of this text, Jesus' exhortation to "hear" the word he preaches: "He who has ears to hear, let him hear" (v. 9; cf. v. 3a). Exactly the same note is struck in Jesus' subsequent parable of a lamp on a stand: "If anyone has ears to hear,

12. Rikk E. Watts, *Mark*, Commentary on the New Testament Use of the Old Testament (Grand Rapids: Baker Academic, 2007), 154.

13. John N. Oswalt, *The Book of Isaiah: Chapters 1–39*, New International Commentary on the Old Testament (Grand Rapids: Eerdmans, 1986), 190.

14. Watts, *Mark*, 154.

let him hear" (v. 23). There is a gracious, "good news" quality about this exhortation: it applies to "anyone" and everyone who has ears to hear! Jesus provides the necessary motivation, both positive and negative, to heed his exhortation: "Consider carefully what you hear . . . . With the measure you use, it will be measured to you—and even more. Whoever has will be given more; whoever does not have, even what he has will be taken from him" (vv. 23–25). It is striking that this command is directed at the insiders of Jesus' ministry.

The command to "hear" or "listen"—the same word in the original Greek—occurs at a number of strategic places in the subsequent New Testament story:

- When Jesus identifies what defiles a man, he prefaces his comments with an exhortation to the gathered crowd to "listen": "Listen to me, everyone, and understand this" (Mark 7:14). Although Jesus addresses the crowd at this point, only his disciples inquire about the meaning of the parable that follows (vv. 17–19).
- On the Mount of Transfiguration, God exhorts Peter, James, and John, in the presence of Elijah and Moses, to "listen" to Jesus (Mark 9:7; cf. Acts 3:22–23)!
- At Pentecost, Peter exhorts the "men of Israel" to "listen" to his words regarding "Jesus of Nazareth" (Acts 2:22). The response is positive: "Those who accepted his message were baptized, and about three thousand were added to their number that day" (v. 41).
- At his trial before the Sanhedrin, Stephen challenges his Jewish "brothers and fathers" to "listen" to him as he recounts God's dealings with Israel throughout redemptive history (Acts 7:2). Their violent response to his message is a reflection of their disobedience to God's law (vv. 51–59).
- In a synagogue in Pisidian Antioch during his first missionary journey, Paul commences his "message of salvation" to the assembled worshipers with the following injunction: "Men of Israel and you Gentiles who worship God, listen to me!" (Acts 13:16; cf. 13:26). He concludes with a sobering reference to the Old Testament prophet Habakkuk: "Take care that what the prophets have said does not happen to you: 'Look, you scoffers, wonder and perish, for I am

going to do something in your days that you would never believe, even if someone told you'" (Acts 13:40–41, quoting Hab. 1:5).

- After Paul's first missionary journey, at the so-called Jerusalem Council, James, tasked with adjudicating the contentious issue of the place of the Mosaic law in the church (Acts 15:1–2), delivers the concluding address, beginning with an exhortation directed at all the delegates: "Brothers, listen to me" (v. 13). The outcome is a letter sent to "the Gentile believers in Antioch, Syria and Cilicia," to convey the Council's decree (vv. 22–29).
- When Paul is arrested in Jerusalem after his third missionary journey, he exhorts the gathered crowd to "listen": "Brothers and fathers, listen now to my defense" (Acts 22:1). The crowd listens to Paul until he speaks of his divine calling to the Gentiles, at which point they turn violent (vv. 21–22).
- James challenges his Christian readers not to engage in discrimination—along economic lines—in the early church: "Listen, my dear brothers" (James 2:5).
- The letters to the seven churches in the book of Revelation (Rev. 2–3) are of special interest to us at this point because they echo the language of Jesus in Mark 4:9, suggesting a parabolic quality to the visions that John sees: "He who has an ear, let him hear what the Spirit says to the churches" (Rev. 2:7, 11, 17, 29; 3:6, 13, 22). In the context, it is the resurrected Jesus who speaks to the churches (see 1:10–20; 2:1, 8, 12, 18; 3:1, 7, 14). These churches are called to "overcome" a variety of challenges, which one writer describes as the dangers of compromise, persecution, and complacency.[15] Encouragement to heed this call is provided in each of the letters, with a promise of blessing and reward to those who "overcome" (cf. 2:7b, 11b, 17b, 26–28; 3:5, 12, 21). It is worth noting that the sequence of parallel exhortations to "hear" in Revelation 2–3 includes the singular, "ear," and plural, "churches," the point being that every ear must listen to every message to every one of the seven churches!
- Tucked away in the middle of John's subsequent description in Revelation of the so-called unholy trinity, comprising the dragon or Satan, the beast "coming out of the sea," and the beast

---

15. Craig R. Koester, *Revelation and the End of All Things* (Grand Rapids: Eerdmans, 2001), 56.

"coming out of the earth" (Rev. 13:1, 11), is a similar injunction: "He who has an ear, let him hear" (v. 9). Linked to what follows, it "stresses the inevitability of persecution and death for the faithful," according to one commentator, and calls for "patient endurance and faithfulness on the part of the saints" (v. 10).[16] Like seed sown "along the path" and seed sown on "rocky places" in Jesus' parable (Mark 4:15–17), the opposition of Satan and the threat of persecution remain realities in the life of the church this side of eternity (cf. Rev. 20:10).

Implicit in all these injunctions to "listen" is the authority of God's Word and the significance of the truth it proclaims, whether it be about things that defile, Jesus of Nazareth, the message of salvation, the relevance of the Mosaic law today, discrimination in the church, or the perseverance of the saints in the midst of many trials and dangers. What is striking about all these commands to "listen" profiled above is the fact that they are all, without exception, addressed to religious audiences, whether they be insiders, Israelites, Gentile God-fearers, Christian brothers, or the Christian church. This suggests that there may be a tendency among the religious at times, perhaps based on a presumption of insider status, to listen superficially to God's Word and therefore miss its message (see Heb. 2:1). This, of course, is the point of the parable of the sower!

This same scenario is in view in the conclusion to the Sermon on the Mount (Matt. 7:24–27). Jesus there distinguishes between the "wise" and "foolish" builders, a metaphor for those who hear Jesus' words and put them into practice and those who hear him but fail to obey his words. The consequences for the foolish builder are disastrous; his "house" falls "with a great crash" (Matt. 7:27). James, the brother of Jesus, writes to "the twelve tribes scattered among the nations," a designation for the Jewish Christian recipients of his letter (cf. James 1:1; 2:1), warning them about the danger of a superficial response to God's Word: "Do not merely listen to the word, and so deceive yourselves. Do what it says" (James 1:22). In the broader context, James deals with the negative impact of material wealth on the Christian community that he is addressing (cf.

16. Robert H. Mounce, *The Book of Revelation*, New International Commentary on the New Testament (Grand Rapids: Eerdmans, 1998), 253.

James 1:10–11; 2:1–7; 5:1–6). It may well be that, like seed sown among the thorns in Jesus' parable, this wealth has in some instances "choke[d] the word," making these hearers "unfruitful" (Mark 4:18–19). In any event, the New Testament continues to issue warnings to the Christian about the dangers of material wealth (cf. 1 Tim. 6:6–10, 17–19).

The writer to the Hebrews gives the ominous example of the Israelites who heard "the gospel" in the wilderness, but perished because they did not combine the message with faith (Heb. 4:2; cf. Eph. 1:13; Col. 1:6); they did not experience God's "rest" because of their "disobedience" (Heb. 4:6). Consequently, he exhorts the "holy brothers, who share in the heavenly calling" (3:1), to "pay more careful attention" to the message of salvation they have heard. Notice how he includes himself in this exhortation: "We must pay more careful attention, therefore, to what we have heard, so that we do not drift away. For if the message spoken by angels was binding, and every violation and disobedience received its just punishment, how shall we escape if we ignore such a great salvation?" (2:1–3a). His subsequent exhortation to these readers is an exhortation to every hearer of God's Word: "Today, if you hear his voice, do not harden your hearts" (4:7, quoting Ps. 95:7–8; cf. Heb. 3:7–8), like the wilderness generation and the outsiders of Jesus' ministry, both of whom perished because of "their stubborn hearts" (Mark 3:5).

The parable of the sower in Mark's Gospel emphasizes the hearer's responsibility to "listen" to God's Word. There is, of course, the divine side to this equation. Jesus hints at it in his discussion about parables: "The secret of the kingdom of God has been given to [the insiders]" (Mark 4:11a). This so-called divine passive construction was the accepted way in Jesus' context of identifying God as the Giver, without mentioning his name. At times the Word of God emphasizes the human side of the "hearing" equation and at other times the divine side: "God gave them a spirit of stupor, eyes so that they could not see and ears so that they could not hear, to this very day" (Rom. 11:8, quoting Deut. 29:4). If we couch this verse in positive terms, we have a clear definition of the divine role in the process of hearing: "God gave them . . . eyes so that they could see and ears so that they could hear, to this very day." Simply put, spiritual insight comes from God! On occasion, both the human and divine roles are mentioned side by side: "When the Gentiles heard this, they were glad and honored the word of the Lord; and all who were appointed for eternal life believed" (Acts 13:48). And again: "The Lord opened [Lydia's] heart to respond to Paul's message" (Acts 16:14b).

A divine perspective on the process of hearing has the advantage of generating a sense of peace and expectation in the one proclaiming the Word of God. This is Paul's perspective in Rome where he is under house arrest at the end of Acts (Acts 28:16–31). Paul has the freedom to declare the truth about God's kingdom and God's Messiah, Jesus. When his Jewish audience rejects his message, it is nothing more, according to Paul, than another fulfillment of Isaiah's prophecy concerning his hearers (Acts 28:25–27, quoting Isa. 6:9–10)—the same prophecy, coincidentally, referred to by Jesus in his discussion about parables (see Mark 4:12). God's prophet anticipated this rejection. Consequently, Paul is not discouraged. The Gentiles will listen (Acts 28:28)! And so "boldly and without hindrance he preached the kingdom of God and taught about the Lord Jesus Christ" (Acts 28:31).

SUMMARY

A downward reading of this text reveals a focus in Jesus' teaching on his hearers' responsibility to listen carefully to his words (Mark 4:3a, 9). In the process, Jesus alerts them to the ever-present danger of a superficial and inadequate response, because the Word that is "sown" is "susceptible to being devoured, withered, and choked."[17] A sideways perspective on the text reinforces this call to "listen."

A backward reading of the text uncovers the meaning of the "secret of the kingdom of God" (Mark 4:11a; cf. Dan. 2:44); it refers to the veiled presence of the kingdom in the ministry of Jesus, a presence hidden from these outsiders. An Old Testament perspective on the text also reveals a parallel between the hard hearts of Isaiah's hearers and some of Jesus' hearers: they see but never perceive; they hear but never understand (Mark 4:12, quoting Isa. 6:9–10). Unlike those under Isaiah's ministry, however, Jesus' hearers still have the opportunity to listen and to turn from their sin. A forward reading of the text reveals a possible tendency among those who hear the Word of God to listen to it superficially.

17. Garland, *Mark*, 157.

This, of course, is the point of the parable of the sower, and it is from this perspective that this text should be applied to today's hearers. The good news is that whoever "has ears to hear" can respond, by God's grace; it is "good news" for all who will "listen"! A valid hearing produces "a crop," the fruit of obedience—"thirty, sixty or even a hundred times what was sown" (Mark 4:20b). Clearly, unproductive hearing is deficient hearing. The parable ends not with the threat of judgment, but with the promise of fruitfulness—a feature no doubt designed to encourage the hearer of Christ's words to "listen" to them (cf. Mark 4:3a, 9).

6

JESUS HELPS THE HELPLESS

Mark 5:21-43: When Jesus had again crossed over by boat to the other side of the lake, a large crowd gathered around him while he was by the lake. Then one of the synagogue rulers, named Jairus, came there. Seeing Jesus, he fell at his feet and pleaded earnestly with him, "My little daughter is dying. Please come and put your hands on her so that she will be healed and live." So Jesus went with him.

A large crowd followed and pressed around him. And a woman was there who had been subject to bleeding for twelve years. She had suffered a great deal under the care of many doctors and had spent all she had, yet instead of getting better she grew worse. When she heard about Jesus, she came up behind him in the crowd and touched his cloak, because she thought, "If I just touch his clothes, I will be healed." Immediately her bleeding stopped and she felt in her body that she was freed from her suffering.

At once Jesus realized that power had gone out from him. He turned around in the crowd and asked, "Who touched my clothes?"

"You see the people crowding against you," his disciples answered, "and yet you can ask, 'Who touched me?'"

But Jesus kept looking around to see who had done it. Then the woman, knowing what had happened to her, came and fell at his feet and, trembling with fear, told him the whole truth. He said to her, "Daughter, your faith has healed you. Go in peace and be freed from your suffering."

While Jesus was still speaking, some men came from the house of Jairus, the synagogue ruler. "Your daughter is dead," they said. "Why bother the teacher any more?"

Ignoring what they said, Jesus told the synagogue ruler, "Don't be afraid; just believe."

He did not let anyone follow him except Peter, James and John the brother of James. When they came to the home of the synagogue ruler, Jesus saw a commotion, with people crying and wailing loudly. He went in and said to them, "Why all this commotion and wailing? The child is not dead but asleep." But they laughed at him.

After he put them all out, he took the child's father and mother and the disciples who were with him, and went in where the child was. He took her by the hand and said to her, "*Talitha koum!*" (which means, "Little girl, I say to you, get up!"). Immediately the girl stood up and walked around (she was twelve years old). At this they were completely astonished. He gave strict orders not to let anyone know about this, and told them to give her something to eat.

A DOWNWARD READING

Mark 4 concludes with Jesus and his disciples' encountering "a furious squall" on the Sea of Galilee that threatens to swamp their boat (Mark 4:35–41). With a word, Jesus rebukes the wind and the waves, and there is complete calm (4:39). The response of his disciples is one of fear: "They were terrified and asked each other, 'Who is this? Even the wind and the waves obey him!'" (4:41). They cross over to the other side of the lake. Jesus is confronted by the so-called Gadarene demoniac, a man possessed by an evil spirit named "Legion"—for "we are many"—and confined to living among the tombs in that region (5:1–9). Legion is so powerful that he tears apart the chains that bind him, and breaks the irons on his feet. No one is strong enough to subdue him (5:4). One commentator describes him as "the most intimidating of demonic power."[1] With a simple command, however, Jesus banishes all the evil spirits into "a large herd of pigs" nearby, numbering two thousand, all of which plunge into a lake and are drowned (5:8–13). Jesus is portrayed as being more powerful than literally thousands of demons! The lesson

---

1. R. T. France, *The Gospel of Mark*, New International Greek Testament Commentary (Grand Rapids: Eerdmans, 2002), 234.

of this encounter is obvious: Not only do "the wind and the waves obey" Jesus, but even Legion obeys him! Thus, Mark's primary purpose in this incident, as a number of commentators point out, is Christological, that is, it tells us something about who Jesus really is.[2] It is worth noting, however, that both the location and the presence of the pigs indicate a Gentile context, indicating that Jesus' great power extends over Gentile territory as well. In the set of encounters that follow, Jesus' power is once more on display, but now he is portrayed as being more powerful than disease and death!

Mark sandwiches together into a unit the stories of Jesus' encounters with Jairus, a synagogue ruler, and with a sick woman by inserting the healing of this woman into the middle of the Jairus account (Mark 5:21–43). At first glance, these two encounters may appear to have nothing in common. Yet if we place ourselves, for a moment, in the shoes of Jairus and the woman, we realize that they are both powerless to help themselves, and both have no one but Jesus to turn to for assistance. Jairus's daughter, in due course, dies; he has no other option but to trust Jesus to intervene (vv. 22–23, 35). The woman has a bleeding problem. We are told in no uncertain terms that she is beyond the help of medical science (vv. 25–26). So in desperation she turns to Jesus for assistance. Both Jairus and the woman fall at Jesus' feet (vv. 22b, 33b)—the one to beg for help, the other to bear testimony to her healing, but both in acknowledgment of his great power.

There are also notable differences between Jairus and the woman. Jairus's problem is life-threatening, while the woman's problem is chronic. He is a man of standing in the community, a synagogue ruler. It is no coincidence that Mark identifies Jairus by name (Mark 5:22). The woman, however, is nameless. There is no mention of her station in life, only her condition. Like the Gadarene demoniac, she has been marginalized on the periphery of Jewish society as unclean because of her physical ailment. Unlike Jairus, who pleads publicly with Jesus for his help, this woman approaches Jesus from behind, and seeks a mere touch of his garment (cf. vv. 22–23, 27–28). Significantly, however, Jesus helps both of them—the marginalized woman and the privileged Jairus—"both those at the

2. Robert H. Stein, *Mark*, Baker Exegetical Commentary on the New Testament (Grand Rapids: Baker Academic, 2008), 257.

bottom of the social scale . . . and those at the top."[3] If one also factors in the plight of the Gentile Gadarene demoniac and Jesus' subsequent intervention, it is apparent that the crises of life know no ethnic, gender, or social boundaries, nor does Jesus' help!

Against this background we can now turn our attention to the details of the text. Jesus' encounter with Jairus takes place on "the other side of the lake" (Mark 5:21); the exact location is not important for Mark's purposes. The focus shifts from a Gentile Gadarene to "one of the [Jewish] synagogue rulers" (v. 22). When Jairus sees Jesus, he falls at his feet and pleads "earnestly" with him to heal his daughter: "My little daughter is dying. Please come and put your hands on her so that she will be healed and live" (v. 23). The reader can discern the desperation in Jairus's demeanor, but can also detect a note of confidence in Jesus' ability to heal his daughter. A "large crowd [is] gathered around [Jesus]," indicating a public setting for this encounter (v. 21; cf. v. 24b). But such is Jairus's desperation that he is not deterred by the possible stigma attached to a synagogue ruler's publicly requesting help from Jesus. Without comment, Jesus goes with him (v. 24a).

The focus in the narrative changes abruptly to a woman "who had been subject to bleeding for twelve years" (Mark 5:25). Her chronic condition has caused her a great deal of suffering and drained her financial resources, spent on doctors who have failed to help her; indeed, her condition has deteriorated (v. 26). No doubt these Markan comments are intended to underscore just how persistent her medical condition is. After twelve years of this suffering, she too is desperate for healing. When she hears about Jesus, she comes up behind him in the crowd and touches his cloak, "because she thought, 'If I just touch his clothes, I will be healed'" (vv. 27–28). Her approach to Jesus may be motivated in part by her reluctance to publicize her unclean condition. But such is her confidence in Jesus' power to heal that she believes a mere touch of his clothes will suffice. In an instant, she is completely healed: "Immediately" her bleeding stops and she is freed from her suffering (v. 29)! According to one commentator, "Twelve years of shame and frustration are resolved in a momentary touch of Jesus."[4]

---

3. Ben Witherington III, *The Gospel of Mark*, A Socio-Rhetorical Commentary (Grand Rapids: Eerdmans, 2001), 186.

4. James R. Edwards, *The Gospel according to Mark*, Pillar New Testament Commentary (Grand Rapids: Eerdmans, 2002), 164.

Jesus "immediately" knows that power has "gone out from him" (Mark 5:30; cf. KJV). The woman's action cannot be hidden from him. But why, then, Jesus' question: "Who touched my clothes?" (v. 30b)? The question, as we will see, is for the benefit of the others who are present. Jesus' disciples are perplexed by Jesus' question: "'You see the people crowding against you,' his disciples answered, 'and yet you can ask, "Who touched me?"'" (v. 31). But Jesus "looked round about to see *her* that had done this thing" (v. 32 KJV). This KJV translation captures the sense of the text, the reference to *her* suggesting that Jesus knows that the person concerned is a woman. Significantly, as is evident in the more literal KJV translation, Jesus uses the feminine gender in this grammatical construction, indicating that he knows the person concerned is a woman. What matters, from Jesus' perspective, is what this woman has done, and not what he has done. Jesus' desire is to expose her identity so that he can showcase her faith to all who are present. Then the woman, "knowing what had happened to her," comes and falls at Jesus' feet, "in fear and trembling," and tells him the whole truth (vv. 32–33 ESV). This same "fear" motif is reflected in the two prior incidents recorded in Mark's Gospel, where Jesus calms a storm and heals the Gadarene demoniac (cf. 4:41; 5:15). As on this occasion, the fear is a human response to the miracle-working power of Jesus and, as such, demonstrates that Jesus' power in the context is so awesome, it is fear-inducing!

Jesus commends the woman for her faith: "Daughter, your faith has healed [literally, "saved"] you. Go in peace and be freed from your suffering" (Mark 5:34). Her faith is worthy of commendation—a mere report about Jesus draws her, and a simple touch of his clothes heals her (cf. vv. 27–28). Moreover, according to one commentator, "Despite her embarrassing circumstances, she pushes through both crowd and disciples to reach Jesus. Her gender, namelessness, uncleanness, and shame—none of these will stop her from reaching Jesus."[5]

The focus then shifts back to Jairus and his daughter. In the interim, she has died: "While Jesus was still speaking, some men came from the house of Jairus, the synagogue ruler. 'Your daughter is dead,' they said. 'Why bother the teacher any more?'" (v. 35). They believe that it is too late for Jesus to do anything. The sentiments expressed by these messengers are clear: Jesus can heal the sick, but he cannot raise the dead! One commentator, however, observes that "the readers of Mark . . . unlike the messengers from the house

5. Ibid., 168.

of Jairus, have learned in the preceding chapters of the Gospel that no situation is hopeless for Jesus, the Son of God, for he, like God, possesses mastery over nature, demons, and illness. In anticipation they await to learn what this mighty Son of God will do."[6]

The double reference to "daughter" in Mark 5:34–35—referring first to the healed woman, and then to Jairus's dead daughter—not only reinforces the link between these two stories, but also introduces an element of hope into an otherwise bleak report: if faith can literally "save" one "daughter," it can also save another, Jairus's daughter! Significantly, then, in response to the news about Jairus's daughter, Jesus tells him: "Don't be afraid; just believe" (v. 36). Jairus has just heard the woman's testimony and Jesus' commendation of her faith. In effect, Jesus commends the faith of the healed woman to Jairus. According to one commentator, "This woman exemplifies and defines faith for Jairus, which means to trust Jesus despite everything to the contrary. That faith knows no limits—not even the raising of a dead child!"[7] It now becomes apparent why Jesus, en route to heal Jairus's desperately ill daughter, delays his journey in order to heal the woman and commend her faith; she functions as a beacon of hope for Jairus and his daughter. Yet the challenge for Jairus is far greater; he must now believe, in the face of death, that Jesus has the power to raise his daughter!

Jesus appears unhurried and in control in the midst of all this frenetic activity, with people coming and going and the crowds swirling around him. One commentator says, "The interruption, so profitable to the woman, has cost the life of Jairus's daughter."[8] Yet the text does not indicate that Jesus' delaying encounter with the sick woman is a deliberate ploy on his part to allow for the onset of Jairus's daughter's death (cf. John 11:4–6). Rather, Jesus uses the healing of the woman to identify, for the benefit of Jairus, the role of faith—"just believe"—in experiencing his miracle-working power, even in the face of death (Mark 5:36b; cf. John 11:14–15). Moreover, by pausing to help this woman in the face of Jairus's need, Jesus demonstrates a concern for "the vulnerable and marginalized."[9]

---

6. Stein, *Mark*, 271–72.
7. Edwards, *The Gospel according to Mark*, 168.
8. Ibid., 166.
9. Witherington, *The Gospel of Mark*, 185.

Jesus allows only Peter, James, and John to follow him (Mark 5:37). Jesus' actions at this point may be motivated by a desire for privacy—"the supreme miracle of raising the dead is . . . for their eyes only" (cf. vv. 40, 43), a return to the insider-outsider theme, according to one commentator.[10] No doubt Jesus also intends for them to act as apostolic eyewitnesses of the miracle about to be performed. When they arrive at Jairus's home, Jesus sees "a commotion, with people crying and wailing loudly" (v. 38). These people are generally identified as professional mourners. If nothing else, their presence functions to confirm the death of Jairus's daughter, and the general anguish of soul and sense of helplessness that accompanies death. Yet Jesus challenges them: "Why all this commotion and wailing? The child is not dead but asleep." But they all laugh at him (vv. 39–40). Jesus' declaration should not be misinterpreted to mean that Jairus's daughter is not dead (cf. Mark 5:35; Luke 8:53). Rather, Jesus uses the term *sleep* to indicate that she will "wake up" from death, and that with his presence, death is temporary; it will not have the final word. Death is no match for Jesus' power; she is "asleep"!

Jesus "put[s] them all out" of the home and takes a select few with him—the child's father and mother and the disciples with him—to where the child is (Mark 5:40). Jesus takes her by the hand and addresses her with the words, "'*Talitha koum!*' (which means, 'Little girl, I say to you, get up!')." The italicized words reveal that Jesus' mother tongue is Aramaic. The translation that follows indicates that for at least some of Mark's readers it is not. She "immediately" stands up and walks around (vv. 41–42). There is no delay; Jesus' power over death is immediate. The reference to her twelve years of age provides another link to the woman "who had been subject to bleeding for twelve years" (v. 25), a gentle reminder that the faith principle is once again at work in this miracle. In this case, however, Jairus's faith, not that of the little girl, is in view. With a mere two words, Jesus raises the dead. His power is amazing. Not surprisingly, those who witness this miracle are "completely astonished" (v. 42b; cf. 1:27; 2:12).

Jesus gives them "strict orders not to let anyone know about this [miracle]" (Mark 5:43a). This is rather surprising in view of the fact that it would be difficult to conceal this miracle once people see the little girl alive. The command, however, is not without precedent in Mark's Gospel, where is it designed to protect Jesus' messianic identity from

---

10. Edwards, *The Gospel according to Mark*, 166.

what one commentator terms "premature and false understandings" (cf. 1:25, 34, 44; 3:12; 7:36; 8:26).[11] Another commentator suggests that this injunction is temporary so that Jesus can make good his "getaway."[12] Jesus, however, may simply be requesting of the eyewitnesses that the details of his involvement in the miracle be kept hidden. Jesus instructs them to give the girl something to eat, perhaps to affirm, for the benefit of those present, that her physical restoration is real and complete.

Still another commentator summarizes the thrust of these various encounters as follows: "Jesus has just exorcised a demon from a man that no one could control; now he heals a woman that no physician can cure and restores to life a girl when all hope is gone."[13] This last incident functions as a climax of the various demonstrations of Jesus' power: Jesus even has power over death!

A SIDEWAYS READING

Mark devotes twenty-three verses to this story, more than either Matthew (nine verses) or Luke (seventeen verses). This is significant in view of the fact that Mark is the shortest of the Synoptic Gospels. The most noteworthy differences in these parallel accounts may be summarized as follows:

- Mark, in sketching the geographical setting of our text, alone makes reference to "the other side of the lake" (Mark 5:21; cf. Matt. 9:18; Luke 8:40). This reference echoes the geographical setting of the two previous incidents, in which Jesus calms the storm and heals the Gadarene demoniac (cf. Mark 4:35b; 5:1). Thus, it functions to connect and unite these three accounts in Mark's Gospel around the common theme of Jesus' awesome displays of power.
- Mark alone describes the size of the crowd that gathers around Jesus at the lake as "large" (Mark 5:21; cf. Luke 8:40). This testifies to Jesus' continued popularity despite the high-profile

11. Ibid., 65.
12. Robert H. Gundry, *Mark: A Commentary on His Apology for the Cross* (Grand Rapids: Eerdmans, 1993), 276.
13. Garland, *Mark*, 220.

opposition he experiences. A short while later, Mark reiterates this description regarding the size of the crowd. Significantly, he tells the reader that this "large crowd followed and pressed around [Jesus]" when he encounters the woman "who had been subject to bleeding" (Mark 5:24–25; cf. Luke 8:42). No doubt "a large crowd" pressing around Jesus would be a deterrent for anyone, especially an "unclean" woman, seeking to approach him to touch his clothes. Yet she is not deterred in her approach to Jesus—a testimony to her faith that Jesus, in due course, commends (Mark 5:34).

- Mark alone describes Jairus as pleading "earnestly" with Jesus to come and heal his dying "little daughter" (Mark 5:23; cf. Matt. 9:18; Luke 8:41–42). This earnestness reveals the extent of Jairus's desperation and his sense of helplessness as his little daughter faces death, contributing to the marvel of the subsequent miracle-working power of Jesus.

- In Matthew's account, Jairus asks Jesus to "put [his] hand on [his daughter], and she will live" (Matt. 9:18b). According to Mark, Jairus requests that "she will be healed and live" or, more literally, "be saved and live" (Mark 5:23b). If Mark intends an allusion to the more literal rendering, "be saved and live," it would carry "overtones of salvation" from eternal destruction, according to one commentator (cf. Mark 8:35; 10:26; 13:13, 20).[14] This would suggest that Jairus's daughter's death, and subsequent raising, has spiritual connotations.

- The details of Mark 5:26 pertaining to the woman with the bleeding problem are unique to Mark: "She had suffered a great deal under the care of many doctors and had spent all she had, yet instead of getting better she grew worse." Luke merely records that "no one could heal her" (Luke 8:43). Several commentators suggest that Luke, a medical doctor, omits the parallel Markan details out of deference to his profession.[15] Be that as it may, the Markan account highlights the woman's great suffering, her deteriorating condition, and the inability of anyone else to heal

14. Stein, *Mark*, 266–67.
15. See, for example, Walter L. Leifeld, "Luke," in *Matthew, Mark, Luke*, vol. 8 of The Expositor's Bible Commentary (Grand Rapids: Zondervan, 1984), 916.

her. Jesus' great power alone can reverse her condition and bring relief from her suffering.

- Mark 5:29b is unique to Mark: "and she felt in her body that she was freed from her suffering." One commentator states, "Mark's unflattering account of the medical profession provides a sharp . . . contrast with the completeness and immediacy of the cure she receives through touching Jesus."[16]

- According to Mark 5:30, Jesus asks the large crowd, "Who touched my clothes?" This could simply be another way of asking, "Who touched me?" (Luke 8:45a).

- After the woman is healed by Jesus and asked to identify herself, according to Mark, "Then the woman, knowing what had happened to her, . . . told him the whole truth" (Mark 5:33). Luke unpacks "the whole truth" for the benefit of his readers: "In the presence of all the people, she told why she had touched him and how she had been instantly healed" (Luke 8:47b).

- After Jesus commends the woman for her faith, Mark alone informs us that Jesus also tells her to "be freed from your suffering" (Mark 5:34b). At least one commentator suggests that Jesus may hereby be restoring her to society by publicly removing the "unclean" stigma that had attached to her physical condition, and had caused her not only physical but also psychological suffering.[17]

- We have argued that when Jesus informs the professional mourners that Jairus's daughter "is not dead but asleep" (Mark 5:39b), Jesus' words should not be interpreted literally—Jairus's daughter was in fact dead; neither the messengers nor the mourners were mistaken (see Mark 5:35–38). We find corroborating evidence for this conclusion in Matthew's condensed account, where Jairus, and not the messengers from his home, informs Jesus that his "daughter has just died" (see Matt. 9:18). Matthew's condensed version of events at this point also casts further doubt on the notion that Jesus intends the healing of the woman to provide what one commentator calls "time for [the girl] to die."[18] In Mat-

16. France, *The Gospel of Mark*, 236–37.
17. Ibid., 238.
18. Stein, *Mark*, 271.

thew's account, she is already dead before Jesus encounters the woman. Rather, the purpose of the incident appears to be to highlight the role of faith in relation to Jesus' miracle-working power (Matt. 9:22).

- Only Mark records that Jesus "took the child's father and mother and the disciples who were with him, and went in where the child was" (Mark 5:40). In the context, the reader is told that Jesus "put . . . all [the mourners] out [of Jairus's home]" before performing the miraculous raising of his daughter (v. 40). The implication appears to be that the miracle was not intended for these scoffers to witness. According to one commentator, "those who offer nothing but disdain and ridicule are excluded."[19] The few that do attend will act as eyewitnesses to the miracle-working power of Jesus over death.

- Jesus' words, "*Talitha koum!*," the actual Aramaic words he addresses to Jairus's dead daughter, are unique to Mark's account. One commentator views them as "typical of [Mark's] interest in vivid recreation of a scene."[20] There is no hint of a magical formula in these words, translated for the benefit of Mark's Greek readers as: "Little girl, I say to you, get up!" (Mark 5:41).

- "At this [miracle] they were completely astonished" (Mark 5:42b), according to Mark. Luke, for his part, records that "her parents were astonished" (Luke 8:56a). Commenting on Mark's account, one writer observes that "the reaction of the five witnesses, while powerfully expressed, is no more extravagant than after previous lesser miracles (cf. Mark 1:27; 2:12; 4:41; 5:15–17)."[21] This may be Mark's way of linking these various displays of power together to make the point that all these miracles are equally impressive, and that none is more difficult for Jesus than another!

- Unlike Luke, who records that Jairus's daughter was "a girl of about twelve" at the outset of this incident (Luke 8:42), Mark makes reference to her age only at the conclusion of the incident, after she has been raised from the dead (Mark 5:42). The age reference, as we have pointed out above, reinforces the link

19. Ibid., 274.
20. France, *The Gospel of Mark*, 240.
21. Ibid.

between this miracle and the healing of the woman who had "been subject to bleeding for twelve years" (Mark 5:25b). By implication, the same faith in Jesus that heals this woman is at work raising Jairus's daughter. In the case of Jairus, however, this faith is implied, not stated.

A BACKWARD READING

This text contains no explicit Old Testament quotations. Yet a number of Old Testament motifs are hovering in the background and may help to explain some of the details of the text.

First is the matter of ritual or ceremonial impurity in the redemptive-historical context. In our text, Jesus would be considered unclean because of his contact with the woman and with Jairus's dead daughter. According to Leviticus 15, anyone who touches a woman during her monthly period becomes ritually unclean (Lev. 15:19). And "when a woman has a discharge of blood for many days at a time other than her monthly period or has a discharge that continues beyond her period, she will be unclean as long as she has the discharge, just as in the days of her period" (Lev. 15:25). This uncleanness extends to the clothes that come into contact with her person (Lev. 15:27). After she is "cleansed from her discharge," the law stipulates the requirements for making priestly "atonement for her before the LORD" for her unclean discharge (Lev. 15:28–30). The same scenario applies with regard to contact with dead bodies (cf. Num. 5:2; 19:11–13).

The concept of "clean" and "unclean" occurs earlier in Mark's Gospel (see Mark 1:40–44), but this language is not reflected in our text. It is possible, however, that Jesus' attitude toward the laws of purity, as depicted in this sequence of encounters in our text, is designed to prepare the way for Jesus' subsequent declaration in Mark's Gospel that the Old Testament distinction between "clean" and "unclean" is no longer valid (7:19b; cf. 7:1–23). Moreover, this "unclean" motif, although not explicit in our text, may explain the reluctance of the woman to approach Jesus more directly to request healing from her bleeding (cf. 5:27–28). In any event, "her long and fruitless search for a cure [would have been] motivated not only by physical distress but by her social and religious isolation," according to one commentator, and "the effect of her cure" would be "to remove her impurity and restore her to a normal place in society."[22]

Second, Jesus' raising of the dead is not without precedent in the Bible. In the Old Testament, both Elijah and Elisha raise the dead (1 Kings 17:17–24; 2 Kings 4:18–37). There is no indication in our text that Mark's account is consciously borrowing from either of these two earlier incidents. Yet it is noteworthy that, in contrast to these two Old Testament miracles, Jesus raises Jairus's daughter "with a minimum of fuss."[23] Unlike Elijah, there is no need for Jesus to stretch "himself out on the [child] three times" and cry out to the Lord for help (1 Kings 17:21); and unlike Elisha, there is no need for Jesus to pray to the Lord and stretch himself out on the child, "mouth to mouth, eyes to eyes, hands to hands" (2 Kings 4:34). Jesus takes Jairus's dead daughter by the hand, and with a simple "*Talitha koum!*" she comes to life—such is his divine power!

Third is the matter of faith. Jesus commends the woman "subject to bleeding" for her faith (Mark 5:25, 34). Some readers believe that the Old Testament is all about the law and is devoid of faith. This point of view is sometimes formulated as follows: In the Old Testament, salvation was by the works of the law, while in the New Testament, salvation is by faith in Christ Jesus. Yet while it is true that the word *faith* does not frequently occur in the Old Testament, this view is refuted by the Old Testament prophet Habakkuk, who commends faith: "But the righteous will live by his faith" (Hab. 2:4b; cf. Rom. 1:17b; Gal. 3:11b). Moreover, the concept of faith is also expressed in such a well-known word as *believe*. We see this conceptual link in our text where Jesus first commends the woman for her faith (Mark 5:34a) and then encourages Jairus to "just believe" (Mark 5:36b). A key Old Testament reference to *believe* occurs in Genesis 15:6: "Abram believed the LORD, and he credited it to him as righteousness." The apostle Paul selects this verse to prove to his Christian readers in Rome that salvation has always been by faith, whether for the Jew or for the Gentile (cf. Rom. 4:1–12). The point of all this discussion is to show that the concept of faith stretches back to the earliest pages of redemptive history; it is nothing new. It is probably for this reason that none of Jesus' hearers query the concept of faith when he speaks of it in the context.

22. Ibid., 236, 238.
23. Ibid., 240.

Finally, there is Jesus' concluding command to the woman to "go in peace" (Mark 5:34). Why this specific wording? Jesus is here drawing on the Old Testament concept of *shalom*, or "peace." As a greeting, it indicates the Lord's approval or favor (cf. Judg. 18:6; 1 Sam. 1:17; 2 Kings 5:19), suggesting that the woman, because of her faith in Jesus, has found divine approval. Her faith has literally "saved" her (Mark 5:34a). Her restoration with God and men is complete!

A FORWARD READING

We can pursue a number of motifs with benefit in this forward reading of the text. For example, the words *faith* and *believe* are prominent motifs in our text (e.g., Mark 5:34–36) and in the remainder of the New Testament, each occurring about 250 times. Well-known verses such as John 3:16 ("Whoever believes in [God's Son] shall not perish but have eternal life") and Romans 3:22 ("This righteousness from God comes through faith in Jesus Christ to all who believe") illustrate the importance of these concepts in the New Testament. It is evident that Jesus' command to Jairus to "only believe" (Mark 5:36b ESV) continues to echo through the pages of the New Testament as the governing paradigm for relating to God (e.g., Eph. 2:8–10). But we will instead focus our attention on the dominant motif of divine power, at work in and through Jesus, that undergirds these two encounters described in our text (e.g., Mark 5:30).

In our text, Jesus' power brings healing to a woman and life to Jairus's daughter. It is worth pointing out in this context that the combination of words Mark uses to refer to the raising of Jairus's daughter—"get up" and "stood up" (Mark 5:41-42)—reoccurs in Mark's Gospel when referring to Jesus' resurrection, suggesting that the same divine power that raises the young girl also raises Jesus from the dead (cf. Mark 8:31; 9:31; 10:34; 14:28; 16:6–7). This power will also, in due course, raise the Christian from the dead (1 Cor. 6:14; cf. Phil. 3:10)!

This power that raises the dead is at work in the believer in a number of different ways (see Eph. 1:19; 3:20). According to Acts 1:8, Jesus informs his disciples, after his resurrection from the dead and just before his heavenly ascension, that they will "receive power when the Holy Spirit comes on [them], and [they] will be my witnesses . . . to the ends of the earth." Here is power to witness, and testify, about Jesus (cf. Matt. 28:1;

Acts 4:33). And where the gospel is preached, God's power is at work to effect conversions (Rom. 1:16; 1 Cor. 1:18; 1 Thess. 1:5). Jesus' power is also at work through his apostles, and those associated with them, to perform miraculous signs, wonders, and healings of various kinds, to establish his church on earth. Invariably the divine source of this power is stressed (cf. Acts 3:12–16; 4:7–10; 6:8; 8:13–20; 19:11; Rom. 15:19; 1 Cor. 12:10, 28; 2 Cor. 12:12; Gal. 3:5; Heb. 2:4).

The New Testament letters contain a number of references to God's power, strengthening and sustaining his people in the midst of their sufferings, struggles, and spiritual warfare on earth (see 2 Cor. 13:4; Eph. 3:16; 6:10–11; Col. 1:11). A few examples make the point: Paul exhorts Timothy to "join with me in suffering for the gospel, by the power of God" (2 Tim. 1:8b). And Peter encourages his Christian readers by reminding them that "through faith [they] are shielded by God's power until the coming of [their] salvation . . . , though now for a little while [they] may have had to suffer grief in all kinds of trials" (1 Peter 1:5–6). In a similar vein, Paul, alluding to our human frailty, points out that as believers "we have this [gospel] treasure in jars of clay to show that this all-surpassing power is from God" (2 Cor. 4:7). This same perspective is reflected in Paul's discussion of his "thorn in [the] flesh": "[God's] power is made perfect in weakness" (2 Cor. 12:9). Yet God's power not only sustains his people, but also equips and enables them to honor and serve him (see Eph. 3:7; 2 Thess. 1:11; 2 Tim. 1:7). A particularly encouraging verse is 2 Peter 1:3: "[God's] divine power has given us everything we need for life and godliness." This divine enabling, however, does not mean struggle-free service for God (cf. Col. 1:29).

This snapshot of the biblical data provides a sobering corrective to those readers who insist on the more spectacular displays of God's power as the only valid evidence of this power in the life of the believer today. The biblical data suggest otherwise (e.g., Matt. 7:21–23). We have seen in Mark's Gospel that the reaction of complete astonishment to Jesus' miracle-working power in the case of Jairus's daughter is no different from the response to so-called lesser miracles (Mark 5:42b; cf. 1:27; 2:12; 4:41; 5:15–17). Accordingly, we argue that the miracle of conversion is no less spectacular than the miracle of being raised from the dead. For that matter, a life of godly obedience and perseverance in the midst of the most challenging of circumstances is no less a reflection of God's power than Jesus' healing a chronic disease. The so-called *Wow!* factor in each case should be the same. Both are a reflection of God's power at work; both are equally impressive.

This survey of the biblical data also provides enormous encouragement for the Christian reader, however, no matter what his or her circumstances or calling; God's power is at work in the lives of his children to effect his purposes, whether they are witnessing, suffering, serving, struggling, or striving for godliness! It is with this truth in mind that the Christian should seek to honor and serve God (see 2 Peter 1:3–10). The believer must learn to trust in this power on a daily basis, that God's name may be glorified in all that the person does!

Paul's doxology in his letter to the Ephesians provides a fitting climax to our forward reading of this "power" motif in our text: "Now to him who is able to do immeasurably more than all we ask or imagine, according to his power that is at work within us, to him be glory in the church and in Christ Jesus throughout all generations, forever and ever! Amen" (Eph. 3:20–21).

SUMMARY

Mark combines three stories in Mark 5 around the common theme of divine power displayed by Jesus. Our downward reading of the text reveals the display of this power in a context where all other powers have failed. This perspective is reinforced by a sideways reading of the text, which highlights the fact that Jesus is able to heal a woman whom medical science has dismally failed to help (Mark 5:25–26). In effect, Jesus is able to do what no one else can do! A backward reading, among other things, contrasts the miracle-working power of Jesus with the acts of Elijah and Elisha, raising the dead. In comparison, Jesus raises Jairus's daughter from the dead with a minimum of fuss.

Finally, our forward reading of the text focuses on the motif of divine power and makes the point that Jesus' same miracle-working power is at work today in the Christian, albeit in less spectacular ways— sustaining, equipping, and enabling God's people to serve and honor him, no matter how difficult their circumstances. Moreover, this power is at work in the lives of all of God's people, whether it is the Jairuses of this world or the "unclean" women of this world. Accordingly, the Christian should be encouraged to persevere and serve Christ in the knowledge of this truth, and in dependence on this power!

7

JESUS FEEDS THE
FIVE THOUSAND

Mark 6:34–44: When Jesus landed and saw a large crowd, he had compassion on them, because they were like sheep without a shepherd. So he began teaching them many things.

By this time it was late in the day, so his disciples came to him. "This is a remote place," they said, "and it's already very late. Send the people away so they can go to the surrounding countryside and villages and buy themselves something to eat."

But he answered, "You give them something to eat."

They said to him, "That would take eight months of a man's wages! Are we to go and spend that much on bread and give it to them to eat?"

"How many loaves do you have?" he asked. "Go and see."

When they found out, they said, "Five—and two fish."

Then Jesus directed them to have all the people sit down in groups on the green grass. So they sat down in groups of hundreds and fifties. Taking the five loaves and the two fish and looking up to heaven, he gave thanks and broke the loaves. Then he gave them to his disciples to set before the people. He also divided the two fish among them all. They all ate and were satisfied, and the disciples picked up twelve basketfuls of broken pieces of bread and fish. The number of the men who had eaten was five thousand.

A DOWNWARD READING

The so-called feeding of the five thousand is the only miracle recorded in all four Gospels (Matt. 14:15–21; Mark 6:34–44; Luke 9:12–17;

John 6:1–15). Its significance in Mark's Gospel is signaled by two subsequent references to this miracle in Mark 6:52 and 8:17–21. In the context, a striking contrast is drawn between the self-serving, self-indulgent King Herod, who orders the death of John the Baptist, and a compassionate Jesus, Israel's true Shepherd-King, who feeds the flock by "teaching them many things" and satisfying their physical needs (6:14–44).

Mark sets the scene for the miraculous feeding of the five thousand: A large crowd is present with Jesus and his disciples. It is "late in the day," and they are in a "remote place" (Mark 6:35). Mark does not consider it necessary to be more specific. The disciples exhort Jesus to "send the people away so they can go to the surrounding countryside and villages and buy themselves something to eat" (v. 36). "You give them something to eat," says Jesus. Jesus' command puts his disciples on the spot: "That would take eight months of a man's wages [literally, "two hundred denarii," ESV]! Are we to go and spend that much on bread and give it to them to eat?" (v. 37). It would prove extremely costly to feed the crowds in the context. But Jesus is in control of the situation. This is evident from his instructions that follow.

Jesus commands his disciples to "go and see" how many loaves they have (Mark 6:38). The disciples find five loaves and two fish (v. 38b). Given the magnitude of the need, these resources are "ludicrously inadequate."[1] The scene is now set for Jesus to display his power. He directs his disciples to have "all the people sit down in groups on the green grass." So they sit down "in groups of hundreds and fifties" (vv. 39–40). He then takes the five loaves, and looking up to heaven, probably as an act of praise, and to signify his dependence on God, he gives thanks, breaks the loaves, and gives them to his disciples to "set before the people." Jesus also divides the two fish "among them all" (v. 41). Commenting on this sequence of events, one writer points out that

> the blessing and the breaking are simply recorded as facts without reference to duration or repetition, but the handing out of the bread is described by an imperfect as a continuous process, so that we conclude that having [once for all] blessed and broken the bread,

1. R. T. France, *The Gospel of Mark*, New International Greek Testament Commentary (Grand Rapids: Eerdmans, 2002), 267.

[Jesus] multiplied it by continuing to hand it out without exhausting the scanty stock: the multiplication thus took place in the hands of [Jesus] Himself.[2]

Mark records that everyone eats and is "satisfied," and the disciples pick up "twelve basketfuls of broken pieces of bread and fish" (Mark 6:42–43). The account closes with a reference to the number of men, "five thousand" in all, who had eaten (v. 44). It is evident that Jesus meets the physical needs of the crowd through his disciples, who distribute the multiplied loaves and fishes to all who are present (v. 41). One commentator draws attention to the magnitude of Jesus' miraculous act:

> The conclusion of this miracle story involves three statements that serve to heighten the miraculous nature of the incident. The first is that they "all ate and were satisfied" (Mark 6:42). . . . The second . . . is that after eating, the disciples took up "twelve basketfuls" full of fragments. . . . The third . . . is that those who ate the loaves numbered . . . "five thousand men" . . . [emphasizing] the exceptional nature of the miracle.[3]

A SIDEWAYS READING

Even though Mark's Gospel is the shortest overall, his version of this incident is the longest of the synoptic accounts, indicating its relative importance in his Gospel narrative. Mark's account reveals a number of interesting distinctives:

- According to Mark 6:34, "When Jesus landed and saw a large crowd, he had compassion on them, because they were like sheep without a shepherd. So he began teaching them many things." Matthew, in his parallel account, makes no mention of the "sheep" and "a shepherd," and instead of teaching them, Jesus heals their sick (cf. Matt. 14:14; Luke 9:11). These differences highlight the potential significance of the "shepherd" motif for

2. Maximilian Zerwick, *Biblical Greek Illustrated by Examples*, English ed., adapted from the 4th Latin ed. (Rome: Editrice Pontificio Instituto Biblico, 1963), 91.
3. Robert H. Stein, *Mark*, Baker Exegetical Commentary on the New Testament (Grand Rapids: Baker Academic, 2008), 317.

Mark, and reflect the priority of Jesus' teaching in his Gospel, a motif stressed earlier in his ministry (see Mark 1:38).

- Mark and John alone refer to the possible cost of feeding such a large crowd: "That would take eight months of a man's wages! Are we to go and spend that much on bread and give it to them to eat?" (Mark 6:37; see John 6:7; cf. Matt. 14:17; Luke 9:13). In John's account, Jesus' disciple Philip remarks that this amount of money "would not buy enough bread for each one to have a bite!" (John 6:7). The effect of this response by the disciples is to provide the reader with an indication of the enormity of the need and, consequently, the magnitude of Jesus' subsequent miracle that not only will satisfy the hunger of the large crowd, but also will produce an abundance of leftovers!

- Mark alone records Jesus' question and directive to his disciples: "'How many loaves do you have?' he asked. 'Go and see'" (Mark 6:38; cf. Matt. 14:17; Luke 9:13). Clearly, Jesus' instruction to his disciples is intended to expose the fact that they do not have the necessary resources to feed the crowds. Jesus' directive to "go and see" hints at the fact that Jesus intends for his disciples to take a supply inventory among the crowds as well. All they find is the five loaves and two fish (Mark 6:38b; cf. Matt. 14:17; Luke 9:13)—resources that are hopelessly inadequate to meet the physical needs of the large crowd.

- Mark's description of the seating arrangements for the crowd includes some distinctives: he alone mentions that the grass on which the crowds sit is "green," an indication of eyewitness testimony (Mark 6:39; cf. Matt. 14:19). Mark records that "they sat down in groups of hundreds and fifties" (Mark 6:40), while in Luke's Gospel, Jesus directs his disciples to seat the crowds "in groups of about fifty each" (Luke 9:14). The size of these groupings, particularly in the case of Mark's Gospel, gives the reader an indication of the large numbers present (cf. Mark 6:37), while the arrangement of the groupings suggests that Jesus has a particular plan and purpose in mind when he multiplies the loaves and fishes (see John 6:6).

- Mark, unlike Luke, concludes his account of the miracle with a reference to the number of men who eat the loaves and fishes

(Mark 6:44; cf. Luke 9:14). Matthew, unlike Mark and Luke, adds "besides women and children," indicating the presence of a much larger crowd, with the implication that they also ate from Jesus' provision (Matt. 14:21).

- The record of this miracle in John's Gospel has some notable differences with the synoptic parallels. First, there is a reference in the context to the nearness of the Passover Feast, a possible allusion to the symbolic significance of the miracle in John's Gospel (see John 6:4, 35). Second, it is Jesus, not his disciples, who raises the issue of buying bread for the approaching crowds. Jesus' question is intended to "test" his disciple Philip (vv. 5–6). Third, John is explicit about Jesus' already having a plan at the outset of this incident to feed the crowds (v. 6). Fourth, Jesus' disciples source the small loaves and fishes from "a boy" in the crowd: "Another of his disciples, Andrew, Simon Peter's brother, spoke up, 'Here is a boy with five small barley loaves and two small fish, but how far will they go among so many?'" (vv. 8–9). The point is explicitly made that these "small" resources are totally inadequate to meet the enormous physical needs of those present. The implication appears to be that these are the only resources available among all those present on the occasion. Fifth, it is Jesus, and not his disciples as in the synoptic accounts, who distributes the loaves and fishes to "those who were seated as much as they wanted" (v. 11; cf. Mark 6:41). Sixth, significantly, the crowd's response to the miracle is recorded: "After the people saw the miraculous sign that Jesus did, they began to say, 'Surely this is the Prophet who is to come into the world.' Jesus, knowing that they intended to come and make him king by force, withdrew again to a mountain by himself" (John 6:14–15). It is interesting to note that Jesus' miraculous actions carry both prophetic and royal connotations for his Jewish audience (see Deut. 18:15–19).

By way of contrast, the synoptic accounts do not mention the response of the crowd to Jesus' miracle (see Mark 1:27–28; 2:12). Obviously, the significance of this incident lies elsewhere for Mark. Mark's account concludes with a reference to "twelve basketfuls of broken pieces" picked up by the disciples and the five thousand men who ate (6:43–44). It is the number of basketfuls picked up by the disciples that Jesus highlights when he subsequently refers to this miracle in Mark's Gospel (8:19), suggesting that the point of the miracle is located in this detail of the story. This is hardly surprising, since the thrust of a biblical narrative is invariably found in the conclusion of the story. What, then, do we make of this detail? The point, of course, is that five thousand men eat and are satisfied, but such is Jesus' provision that there is still enough left over to fill twelve basketfuls!

A BACKWARD READING

A backward reading of the text uncovers a rich Old Testament background to this miracle. It includes allusions to such biblical characters as Moses, Joshua, David, Elijah, and Elisha, and to motifs such as the exodus, manna in the wilderness, and shepherding. Our backward reading of this text will seek to develop some of these connections for the reader.

According to Mark 6:34, Jesus has compassion on the large crowd "because they [are] like sheep without a shepherd." A number of commentators latch on to this "shepherd" reference, but develop it along different lines. Some point out that the language of Mark 6:34 echoes Numbers 27:17. In that context, Moses, disqualified from leading the people of God into the Promised Land because of his disobedience, asks God to appoint a successor to him "so the LORD's people will not be like sheep without a shepherd." God appoints Joshua, "a man . . . to go out and come in before them, . . . a man in whom is the spirit" (Num. 27:16b–18). According to this scenario, Jesus—the Greek version of *Joshua*—is a type of Joshua, God's anointed servant who will lead his people to their appointed destination.[4]

Others draw a connection with the Davidic shepherd of Ezekiel 34:23. In that Old Testament context, the Lord prophesies against "the shepherds of Israel": "Woe to the shepherds of Israel who only take care of themselves! Should not shepherds take care of the flock?" (Ezek. 34:2). This indictment fits neatly with Mark's description of the self-serving King Herod in the context (see Mark 6:14–29). So the Lord God himself intervenes: "I will place over them one shepherd, my servant David, and

4. Ibid., 313.

he will tend them; he will tend them and be their shepherd" (Ezek. 34:23). Jesus is then presented as the divine Shepherd-King, who takes care of the sheep by teaching and guiding them, by feeding them, and by giving them rest on the "green grass" (Mark 6:34b, 39; cf. Ps. 23:1–3; Ezek. 34:14).

Others identify numerous allusions to the "exodus" motif in the Old Testament, and contend that Mark pictures Jesus as leading a new Israel in a new exodus. According to one commentator:

> The repeated references to the wilderness (Mark 6:31,32,35) recall Israel's sojourn in the wilderness following the Exodus from Egypt; the multiplication of the loaves (Mark 6:41) recalls the gift of manna (Ex. 16:14–15); and Jesus' leading the people as a shepherd (Mark 6:34) recalls Moses leading a fledging nation. Like Moses (Ex. 18:21,25), Jesus divides the crowd into groups (Mark 6:39–40).[5]

We might add that Jesus' teaching agenda in this "remote place" mirrors Moses' instruction in the law of God (cf. Mark 6:34b–35; Deut. 5:1–21). These parallels are very striking and point to the greater deliverance— from the bondage to sin—that Jesus will accomplish, in due course, on a cross in Jerusalem (see Luke 9:31 NLT).

The reader should not feel compelled to choose between these various scenarios. All these Old Testament characters just listed point to Jesus in some way, and he in some way perfects or supersedes their ministries. This truth is particularly evident in Jesus' miraculous provision of enough loaves and fishes to feed this large crowd, and then some! Jesus' abundant provision at this point is anticipated by one or two Old Testament feeding miracles in which God provides more than enough for the needs at hand. Both Elijah (1 Kings 17:8–16) and Elisha (2 Kings 4:42–44) perform feeding miracles, but these instances pale into insignificance when compared to Jesus' miracle. The Elisha miracle, in particular, shows remarkable parallels with the feeding of the five thousand, and is worth quoting in full:

> A man came from Baal Shalishah, bringing the man of God twenty loaves of barley bread baked from the first ripe grain, along with some heads of new grain. "Give it to the people to eat," Elisha said.

5. James R. Edwards, *The Gospel according to Mark*, Pillar New Testament Commentary (Grand Rapids: Eerdmans, 2002), 195.

87

"How can I set this before a hundred men?" his servant asked.

But Elisha answered, "Give it to the people to eat. For this is what the LORD says: 'They will eat and have some left over.'" Then he set it before them, and they ate and had some left over, according to the word of the LORD. (2 Kings 4:42–44)

One commentator contrasts this incident with Jesus' miracle as follows: "This mighty work of Jesus . . . makes Elisha's feeding of one hundred people with twenty loaves . . . seem almost trivial. Jesus feeds fifty times more with one-fourth of what Elisha had and has a greater surplus left over!"[6] In all these stories, we have the same spectacle of inadequate human resources followed by abundant divine provision to meet the needs at hand (cf. Num. 11:13, 21–22). In the case of Jesus' miracle, however, these features receive greater emphasis, accentuating the power of Jesus to provide for the overwhelming needs of his people. Jesus is presented as being greater than these Old Testament prophets.

The wilderness setting of Jesus' miracle provides an obvious link to God's provision of manna and quail for the people of God in their wilderness wanderings, and the inevitable comparison between the leadership of Moses and Jesus (cf. Mark 6:35; Ex. 16:14–15). While the sheer scale of God's ongoing provision for his people during their Old Testament wilderness wanderings dwarfs Jesus' miracle (see Num. 11:21–23), there is no mention in that Old Testament context of surplus "leftovers"; the emphasis instead appears to be on the sufficiency of God's provision each day for every Israelite, including on the Sabbath when no manna was provided (Ex. 16:18–30). Against this background, the twelve basketfuls of leftovers after Jesus' miracle may be an allusion to the twelve tribes of Israel and, as such, may signify the sufficiency of Jesus' provision for the needs of the Jews. Certainly the appointment of twelve apostles in Mark's Gospel (see Mark 3:14; 6:7), signifying a so-called new Israel in the context, supports this notion.

In the subsequent Markan account of the miracle of the feeding of the four thousand in Gentile territory (Mark 8:1–10), the seven basketfuls of leftovers—"seven" symbolizing completeness (cf. Gen. 1)—would then signify the sufficiency of Jesus' provision for the Gentiles. These connections, however, are disputed by some commentators. According

6. Stein, *Mark*, 317–18.

to one, "the later reference in the feeding of the four thousand to a 'few small fish' (Mark 8:7) suggests that Mark is not interested in promoting symbolic significance in these numbers, and the difficulty of finding symbolism in the numbers 'two,' 'five thousand,' and 'four thousand' weakens the alleged symbolism of the other numbers."[7] Be that as it may, we should point out that when Jesus subsequently refers to these two feeding miracles, he appears to place the emphasis on the amount of leftovers. The phrasing of Jesus' questions at this point is telling: "'When I broke the five loaves for the five thousand, how many basketfuls of pieces did you pick up?' 'Twelve,' they replied. 'And when I broke the seven loaves for the four thousand, how many basketfuls of pieces did you pick up?' They answered, 'Seven'"—suggesting that there is some significance in these actual numbers (Mark 8:19–20; cf. 6:42–44).

In the context of this discussion, it is worth noting another allusion to these feeding miracles in Mark's Gospel that tends to support a symbolic reading of these figures. Sandwiched between the feeding of the five thousand and the feeding of the four thousand is Jesus' encounter with a Gentile Syrophoenician woman, who begs Jesus to help her demon-possessed daughter (Mark 7:24–30). References to "bread" or "loaves" and "satisfaction" occur in all three accounts, suggesting a link between them (6:41–42; 8:6–8; cf. 7:27). This is evident from a more literal translation of Jesus' response to her request: "First let the children be *satisfied*," he told her, "for it is not right to take the children's bread and toss it to their dogs" (7:27). The woman understands that Jesus is referring to the priority of the Jews in receiving God's provision. Yet she is not deterred: "'Yes, Lord,' she replied, 'but even the dogs under the table eat the children's crumbs'" (7:28). To her credit, she recognizes that even the "crumbs" of God's grace manifested in Jesus Christ are more than sufficient to meet her needs as a Gentile! Jesus commends her reply, and her daughter is healed (7:29–30). God's grace is indeed sufficient to satisfy the needs of both Jew and Gentile, the point of both of Jesus' feeding miracles (cf. 6:42; 8:8)!

A backward reading of this particular text highlights the value of accessing the Old Testament background of the Gospels. If nothing else, it reinforces the truth that with Jesus' earthly ministry, we are living in the age of prophetic fulfillment. In any event, this Old

---

7. Ibid., 314–15.

Testament perspective elevates the dignity of Jesus by portraying him as Israel's compassionate and faithful Shepherd, in the mold of Moses, Joshua, and David, who guides and feeds his flock, satisfying all their needs. The many other Old Testament allusions outlined above, however, suggest that Jesus cannot be reduced to a single type or category; he is a Shepherd, to be sure, but as a Teacher, Prophet, and King, he is far more!

A FORWARD READING

One or two commentators identify parallels between the feeding of the five thousand and the Lord's Supper; in both instances, Jesus gives thanks, breaks the bread, and then gives it to his disciples (cf. Mark 6:41; 14:22).[8] Others see in Jesus' miraculous actions a possible anticipation of the future messianic banquet (see 14:25). While these connections are disputed, they do raise an interesting set of questions for the Christian reader by way of application: Does Jesus provide for the physical needs of his people today, as depicted in this miracle? Or should we, as in the Lord's Supper, spiritualize this provision—or should we, as in the messianic banquet, relegate the physical provision to some future eschatological scenario? This is one important set of questions that flows out of Jesus' feeding miracles.

Right at the outset, it should be recognized that these so-called feeding miracles are few and far between in redemptive history (cf. Ex. 16:14–15; 1 Kings 17:8–16; 2 Kings 4:42–44; Mark 6:34–44 and parallels; Mark 8:1–10 and parallels). Even in the case of God's provision of manna for an extended period of forty years, this too came to an end once God's people reached the border of Canaan (Ex. 16:35). These instances were God's provision for his people in a time of need, but in very specific circumstances. And when Jesus feeds the five thousand (Mark 6:35–44), followed by the feeding of the four thousand (Mark 8:1–10), there is no indication in the records of these events that Jesus is establishing a pattern for providing for God's people. Rather, when Jesus feeds the four thousand, he replicates his earlier feeding miracle, but now in a Gentile context, to make the theological point that his provision is more than sufficient for not only the Jew, but also the Gentile.

8. See, for example, ibid., 316.

Jesus, in his Sermon on the Mount, exhorts his disciples not to be anxious about their basic need for food and clothing; rather, they are to "seek first the kingdom of God and his righteousness" and God will "give" them these things as well (Matt. 6:25–33). When Jesus sends out the Twelve on a mission, however, there is the expectation that those they minister to will provide for their needs because "the worker is worth his keep" (10:10b). Rightly understood, there is no tension between these two perspectives. God supplies the physical needs of his people just as he "feeds" the "birds of the air," yet these birds must still forage for their food (6:26). So God provides for the physical needs of his people, but through their own labors or the kindness of others (10:10b). It is worth noting in passing that even Jesus had a support team in place to minister to his physical needs (Matt. 27:55)! Christians must therefore go about their daily work to provide for their needs, but all the while trusting in God's provision. Jesus' concern in the Sermon on the Mount to trust God for the provision of daily needs is therefore not a call to idleness or irresponsibility; it is a call to recognize that Christians have a Father in heaven who knows their every need and is well able to supply it. And so believers pray, as Jesus commanded, "Our Father in heaven, . . . Give us today our daily bread" (6:9, 11).

We see this same pattern in the life and teaching of the early church. God provides for and sustains his church, but not at the expense of human agency. It is in this context that the verses that advocate sharing with one another should be understood (cf. Rom. 12:13; 15:27; Eph. 4:28; 1 Tim. 6:18; Heb. 13:16). So we read in the book of Acts, where the Spirit of God is mightily at work, that the first Christians "[sold] their possessions and goods, [and] gave to anyone as he had need" (Acts 2:45; cf. 4:34; 11:29). The apostle Paul, for strategic reasons, supports himself and his gospel ministry through his own labors, although he is entitled to receive support from those he ministers to (1 Cor. 9:3–14; 1 Thess. 2:9; cf. Acts 20:34; 2 Cor. 11:9). He holds up this model as an example to challenge those who are idle, ostensibly because they believe that Jesus' second coming is imminent. His teaching at this point is worth quoting in full:

> In the name of the Lord Jesus Christ, we command you, brothers, to keep away from every brother who is idle and does not live according to the teaching you received from us. For you yourselves know how you

ought to follow our example. We were not idle when we were with you, nor did we eat anyone's food without paying for it. On the contrary, we worked night and day, laboring and toiling so that we would not be a burden to any of you. We did this, not because we do not have the right to such help, but in order to make ourselves a model for you to follow. For even when we were with you, we gave you this rule: "If a man will not work, he shall not eat."

We hear that some among you are idle. They are not busy; they are busybodies. Such people we command and urge in the Lord Jesus Christ to settle down and earn the bread they eat. (2 Thess. 3:6–12)

The divine element of God's provision is more evident when Paul writes to thank the Philippians for their financial support (Phil. 4:10–20). While he is grateful for their support gifts, he confesses that "I know what it is to be in need, and I know what it is to have plenty. I have learned the secret of being content in any and every situation, whether well fed or hungry, whether living in plenty or in want. I can do every-thing through him who gives me strength" (vv. 12–13). Paul's experience of God's provision in his life and ministry in this fallen world includes not only times of "plenty," but also times of "want." This pattern hardly constitutes a failure on the part of God to provide for the needs of his servant; after all, Paul lives to tell the tale! In any event, if needs never existed, there would be no opportunity to experience God's provision through the generosity of others. Consequently, Paul strongly endorses the ethic of giving to supply the needs of others—it is "good" and con-stitutes a "[sharing] in [the] troubles [of others]" (v. 14); it is "credited" to the "account" of the giver (v. 17); it is "a fragrant offering, an acceptable sacrifice, pleasing to God" (v. 18)—at the same time, Paul recognizes that it is God who meets all our "needs according to his glorious riches in Christ Jesus" (v. 19). Accordingly, God must get all the glory (v. 20)!

We see similar sentiments reflected in Paul's discussion, in his Corinthian correspondence, regarding the collection among the churches for the saints back in Jerusalem (2 Cor. 8–9). According to Paul, giving to others is a "grace" that God gives to his people, so ultimately, we may conclude, Christians give because God has first given to them (8:1). It follows that God must then get the glory even though he uses the giving of others to meet needs (see 9:12–15). In this context, Paul speaks of the abundance of God's gracious provision to meet the needs of his people:

And God is able to make all grace abound to you, so that in all things at all times, having all that you need, you will abound in every good work. As it is written:

"He has scattered abroad his gifts to the poor;
   his righteousness endures forever."

Now he who supplies seed to the sower and bread for food will also supply and increase your store of seed and will enlarge the harvest of your righteousness. You will be made rich in every way so that you can be generous on every occasion, and through us your generosity will result in thanksgiving to God. (2 Cor. 9:8–11, quoting Ps. 112:9; cf. 1 Tim. 6:17)

God abundantly supplies the needs of his people so that they, in turn, may be generous to others. Paul's reference above to "seed to the sower and bread for food" verifies our contention that the divine provision includes the supply of the believer's physical needs. In these verses, there is a seamless blending of the divine provision through human agency. We see this same principle reflected in Jesus' feeding miracles—he uses his disciples to distribute the loaves and fishes to the crowds. By first exposing their inadequate resources to meet the needs at hand, however, Jesus demonstrates the truth that ultimately he is the One who supplies all our physical needs. This is the consistent pattern of biblical teaching.

By way of conclusion, on the one hand, while it remains true that Jesus is the "bread of life" who satisfies all our spiritual needs (cf. John 6:35, 58), even this brief forward reading shows that there is no need to always spiritualize God's provision of our needs, nor is there any need to relegate it to some future eschatological scenario. On the other hand, God's provision should not be misunderstood to imply manna falling miraculously from heaven. Significantly, when the New Testament does include this Old Testament incident in a discussion about giving, the emphasis is on the human gathering of the manna, and not the divine provision of this sustenance (2 Cor. 8:14–15). God consistently employs the hands of his people to meet their needs. Moreover, God's provision does not mean that God's people will not experience times of hunger and deprivation in his service; Paul's life and teaching provide ample proof of this reality (see 2 Cor. 11:27). And yet it remains true that God's provision in Christ Jesus is sufficient to satisfy all our needs. This is the teaching of Jesus' feeding miracles, and the consistent experience of all of God's people!

SUMMARY

The miracle of the feeding of the five thousand, recounted in all four Gospels, is one of the best-known miracle stories in the Bible. In the Markan account, it follows a series of demonstrations of Jesus' divine power over nature, demonic power, disease, and even death (see Mark 4:35–5:43). Jesus has the power to do what no one else can do! Thus, there is no need to search for a naturalistic explanation, as some moderns have done, to explain Jesus' miraculous multiplication of the loaves and fishes. But our downward reading of the text also reveals a striking contrast between Jesus and King Herod in the context (6:14–29). Herod, the self-serving and self-indulgent leader of Israel, has John the Baptist put to death, in stark contrast to Jesus, who, moved with compassion, satisfies the physical needs of a large crowd. The sufficiency of Jesus' provision is reinforced by the abundance of leftovers collected by his disciples (6:42–44).

Our sideways reading of this account draws attention to the significant "shepherd" motif in the narrative (see Mark 6:34), while at the same time identifying Markan distinctives that accentuate the enormous physical need of the crowd following Jesus (see v. 37). Our backward reading of this miracle story reveals a rich tapestry of Old Testament allusions that portray Jesus, among other things, as a type of Moses and Joshua, leading God's people on a new exodus, and as a Shepherd-King, like David, guiding and feeding God's flock.

In the miracle story, Jesus' disciples have a role to play in the supply chain of his provision, but the emphasis does not fall on their role. Moreover, it is striking that the actual miracle is not described at all, nor is the response of the disciples or the crowds. It is the result of the miracle, the sufficiency of Jesus' provision, that is emphasized (Mark 6:42–44). It is this motif that we explored in our forward reading of the text, concluding that Jesus continues to satisfy the physical needs of his people, but also through the agency of his people. The Christian reader should therefore be challenged by this feeding miracle to bring his or her inadequate resources to Jesus, mindful that in his hands, they are sufficient to achieve his purposes, even in the face of overwhelming need. To him be all the glory and the honor!

8

JESUS HELPS A GENTILE

Mark 7:24-30: Jesus left that place and went to the vicinity of Tyre. He entered a house and did not want anyone to know it; yet he could not keep his presence secret. In fact, as soon as she heard about him, a woman whose little daughter was possessed by an evil spirit came and fell at his feet. The woman was a Greek, born in Syrian Phoenicia. She begged Jesus to drive the demon out of her daughter.

"First let the children eat all they want," he told her, "for it is not right to take the children's bread and toss it to their dogs."

"Yes, Lord," she replied, "but even the dogs under the table eat the children's crumbs."

Then he told her, "For such a reply, you may go; the demon has left your daughter."

She went home and found her child lying on the bed, and the demon gone.

A DOWNWARD READING

In this text, Jesus casts out a demon. We may therefore conclude that the point of this story is to show the reader that Jesus has power over evil—or, put differently, that the coming of God's kingdom eradicates evil (cf. Mark 1:15). Yet this point has already been made in Jesus' ministry; he casts out many demons, too numerous to mention (1:34, 39), and on one occasion, when Jesus casts out "Legion," an extended narrative is devoted to making the point (5:1–20). In that particular account, the demons are driven out into a herd of pigs in the Gentile region of the Gerasenes, indicating that Jesus' power extends into Gentile territory. So the question we have to ask is this: What is different about this occasion?

We are given a clue in the immediate literary context: Jesus has just declared "all foods" ceremonially "clean" (Mark 7:19b). But Jesus then encounters a situation that, from a Jewish perspective, has "unclean" written all over it. He enters an obviously Gentile area, Tyre, and meets an obviously Gentile woman whose daughter, significantly, is possessed by an "unclean" spirit (7:24–26 ESV). But here, unlike Jesus' encounter with Legion (5:1–20), the emphasis is not on the unclean spirit, but rather on the identity of the woman and her interaction with Jesus (7:26–28). How will Jesus respond to this Gentile woman's request to "drive the demon out of her daughter" (7:26b)? Jesus displays an initial reluctance to help, but after the woman's response, Jesus makes clean that which is unclean, banishing the demon from her daughter (7:28–30).

The episode ends on a positive note, with "the demon gone" (Mark 7:30b), and so the reader is left with the distinct impression that Jesus' initial reluctance to help the woman is one of timing, rather than one of principle (v. 27). Mark intends to show his readers that the boundaries of God's people cannot be limited to the Jews. Put differently, Jesus may be a Jewish Messiah, but the "good news" of his kingdom is not only for the Jew, but also for the Gentile. To apply Jesus' teaching from the preceding context, it is not only "all foods" that Jesus declares "clean," but also "unclean" Gentiles (v. 19b)!

This incident occurs in the vicinity of Tyre (Mark 7:24). This is foreign soil; this is enemy territory. According to the first-century Jewish historian Josephus, the people of Tyre were "notoriously our bitterest enemies."[1] Jesus does not want anyone to know about his presence there, possibly because he wants a respite for himself and his disciples from the crowds seeking healing (cf. 6:31). Not surprisingly, Jesus cannot keep his presence hidden; his reputation as a worker of miracles has spread far and wide, among Jews and Gentiles.

---

1. Quoted in Robert H. Stein, *Mark*, Baker Exegetical Commentary on the New Testament (Grand Rapids: Baker Academic, 2008), 350.

As soon as she hears about Jesus—"But immediately" (ESV)—a woman whose "little daughter [is] possessed by an evil spirit" (literally, "an unclean spirit") comes, and like Jairus, desperate for Jesus' help, she falls at his feet (Mark 7:25; cf. 5:22). Before Mark records her plea for help, he emphasizes the woman's identity: she is "a Greek, born in Syrian Phoenicia" (7:26a). According to one commentator, her description "reads like a crescendo of demerit: she is a woman, a Greek Gentile, from the infamous pagans of Syrian Phoenicia."[2] As a Gentile pagan, she would be considered ceremonially unclean from a Jewish perspective (cf. Acts 10:28). Another commentator states that she has "no claim on the God of the covenant."[3]

The woman begs Jesus "to drive the demon out of her daughter" (Mark 7:26b). One commentator observes that "the humble request of this Gentile woman . . . creates dramatic tension. Will Jesus be as gracious to this lady from Tyre as he was to the unclean outcasts within Israel (cf. Mark 5:1ff.)?"[4] Jesus' recorded response to her request has caused consternation among some readers: "'First let the children eat all they want,' he told her, 'for it is not right to take the children's bread and toss it to their dogs'" (7:27). At first glance, Jesus' response seems out of character; after all, he has consistently shown himself to be willing to help all who come to him (e.g., 1:40–42; 3:8–10). It is worth noting, however, that the woman does not take offense at Jesus' response. Instead, she detects in Jesus' words an element of hope for her daughter: "'Yes, Lord,' she replied, 'but even the dogs under the table eat the children's crumbs'" (7:28). When Jesus mentions "the children" and "their dogs," there is broad agreement that he is referring to Jews and Gentiles, respectively, in the context.[5]

The key to unlocking Jesus' response, according to many commentators, is found in the chronological marker "first": "First let the children eat all they want [literally, "be satisfied"]" (Mark 7:27a).[6] According to Jesus, the needs of the Jews must first be "satisfied"; "it is not right" to favor the

2. James R. Edwards, *The Gospel according to Mark*, Pillar New Testament Commentary (Grand Rapids: Eerdmans, 2002), 218.

3. D. A. Carson, "Matthew," in *Matthew, Mark, Luke*, vol. 8 of The Expositor's Bible Commentary (Grand Rapids: Zondervan, 1984), 353.

4. David E. Garland, *Mark*, NIV Application Commentary (Grand Rapids: Zondervan, 1996), 288.

5. Walter W. Wessel, "Mark," in *Matthew, Mark, Luke*, vol. 8 of The Expositor's Bible Commentary (Grand Rapids: Zondervan, 1984), 682.

6. See, for example, Stein, *Mark*, 352.

Gentiles over the Jews (v. 27b). The woman, for her part, does not challenge the priority of the Jews to receive God's blessings. Rather, as a Gentile, she is content with the "crumbs" that fall from their table: "'Yes, Lord,' she replied, 'but even the dogs under the table eat the children's crumbs'" (v. 28). When these dogs eat the "children's crumbs" that fall from the table, according to one commentator, "they do not rob children of their food; they simply eat what is theirs from the surplus of the children."[7]

Some commentators see an allusion at this point to the earlier miraculous feeding of the five thousand in a Jewish setting (see Mark 6:43), and an anticipation of the later feeding of the four thousand in Gentile territory (see 8:8).[8] In that context, all eat "bread" and are "satisfied"— terminology that Jesus uses in our text (7:27)—with an abundant surplus left over afterward (cf. 6:42–43; 8:8). The point is that Jesus' provision is more than enough to satisfy not only "the [Jewish] children," but also the Gentiles! This Gentile woman, remarkably, recognizes this truth.

Jesus commends her for this reply, and grants her request: "For such a reply, you may go; the demon has left your daughter" (Mark 7:29). One commentator points out that "no word of command [is] recorded; the removal of the demon is simply spoken of as already a past event."[9] When she returns home, she finds "her child lying on the bed" and, true to Jesus' word, "the demon gone" (v. 30). Such is Jesus' power that the presence of the child is not required to cast out the demon; a mere declaration, at a distance, will suffice! Such is her trust in Jesus' power that the woman is willing to take him at his word! But it must be admitted that the emphasis in the text is not on the exorcism, which is not even described, but rather on the dialogue between Jesus and the woman. What is significant, then, is not only what Jesus does for this Gentile woman, but why he does it.

A SIDEWAYS READING

Only Matthew and Mark record this incident (Matt. 15:21–28; Mark 7:24–30). It is possible, as some suggest, that Luke does not include this

---

7. Edwards, *The Gospel according to Mark*, 221.

8. See, for example, ibid.

9. R. T. France, *The Gospel of Mark*, New International Greek Testament Commentary (Grand Rapids: Eerdmans, 2002), 299.

incident in his Gospel because Jesus' apparent reluctance to heal a Gentile woman's daughter may be misunderstood by his predominantly Gentile readers (Mark 7:27). The parallel accounts reveal a number of significant differences:

- Mark locates the encounter in the "vicinity of Tyre," whereas Matthew places it in the "region of Tyre and Sidon" (cf. Mark 7:24; Matt. 15:21). Mark alone reports Jesus' entering a house to escape attention, "yet he could not keep his presence secret" (Mark 7:24). Even in this distant Gentile location, Jesus' ministry has attracted attention (cf. Mark 3:8).
- The wording of Mark 7:25 is more or less unique to Mark: "In fact, as soon as she heard about him, a woman whose little daughter was possessed by an evil spirit came and fell at his feet." The reference to the literally "unclean spirit" (ESV) creates a link between this episode and Jesus' teaching on "clean" and "unclean" in the preceding context (cf. Mark 7:1–23).
- Mark, unlike Matthew, does not identify this woman at the outset of his narrative; instead, he mentions her identity alongside her request for help (cf. Mark 7:26; Matt. 15:22, 25), creating literary tension in the context: Will Jesus help this pagan woman? Mark provides a more detailed description of her ethnicity than Matthew—"a Greek, born in Syrian Phoenicia" (Mark 7:26; cf. Matt. 15:22). "This description prepares for the coming dialogue, which depends on her daughter's non-Jewishness: neither culturally nor lineally is she Jewish. Mark may also design the description to capture the interest of his mainly Gentile audience, who will take great encouragement from the outcome of the story."[10]
- Mark does not record all the details of Matthew 15:22–25. Consequently, he makes no reference to Jesus as "Son of David" or to "the lost sheep of Israel" in his account. If Mark had access to these sayings, it is hardly surprising that they are recorded only in Matthew's more Jewish Gospel; they would be of less interest to Mark's Gentile readers. But the fact that in Matthew's account the woman addresses Jesus as "Lord, Son of David," suggests that

10. Robert H. Gundry, *Mark: A Commentary on His Apology for the Cross* (Grand Rapids: Eerdmans, 1993), 372.

when "Lord" occurs elsewhere on the lips of this woman, even in Mark's Gospel, she has in mind a more exalted view of Jesus than merely "Sir" (cf. Matt. 15:25, 27; Mark 7:28).

- The first part of Mark 7:27 is unique to Mark's Gospel: "First let the children eat all they want." This saying, a reference to the Jews in the context, highlights Israel's priority in redemptive history, and the sufficiency of God's provision for their needs, while at the same time leaving the door open for the Gentiles to also experience that provision.

- In Mark's Gospel, the woman responds to Jesus with the words "even the dogs under the table eat the children's crumbs" (Mark 7:28), whereas in Matthew's account, she counters Jesus with the words "but even the dogs eat the crumbs that fall from their masters' table" (Matt. 15:27). It is evident here that Mark's account places a greater emphasis on the "children" motif (Mark 7:27–28). One commentator points out that the woman uses a different, more inclusive term than Jesus in referring to the Jews as "children" (see Mark 7:27–28), implying both children and servants in a household: "The change in terminology suggests that the woman understands the mercies of God to extend beyond ethnic Israel."[11]

- In Mark's Gospel, Jesus commends the woman for her reply (Mark 7:29), whereas in Matthew's account, Jesus commends her for her "great faith" (Matt. 15:28). Mark's Gospel focuses on what the woman says to Jesus, rather than her "faith" motivation.

- Mark alone records that "she went home and found her child lying on the bed, and the demon gone" (Mark 7:30). According to Matthew's account, Jesus grants her request, and the woman's daughter is "healed from that very hour" (Matt. 15:28). It is surely significant that in Mark's Gospel, the woman's daughter is now referred to as her "child" for the first time (cf. Mark 7:25, 26, 29), thereby indicating her membership in the family—not as the family pet dog, but as one of "the children," eating bread at the table mentioned earlier in this incident (Mark 7:27–28).

11. Edwards, *The Gospel according to Mark*, 220.

A BACKWARD READING

No Old Testament quotations appear in our text, but a backward reading reveals a number of allusions to these Scriptures, which help to illuminate a significant element of the text: Jesus' attitude to the Gentiles.

The focus in the preceding incident in Mark's Gospel is on the issue of ceremonial "cleanness" (see Mark 7:14–23). The Old Testament book of Leviticus is full of the distinction between "clean" and "unclean." According to one commentator, "the whole concept of ritual purity . . . [was] of central importance to Jewish culture and identity. Together with the rite of circumcision and their observance of the Sabbath, the literal adherence to these . . . laws served to mark out the Jews as the distinctive people of God, and to separate them socially from other people."[12] Leviticus 11 focuses on the distinction between clean and unclean food, the topic of Mark 7:14–23. In that Old Testament context, the Lord clearly identifies those animals that are considered unclean for God's covenant people, and declares them off-limits for his people: "You must not eat their meat or touch their carcasses; they are unclean for you" (Lev. 11:8; cf. 11:1–7). Those who touch their carcasses must wash their clothes, and they will be considered unclean until evening (Lev. 11:25). Jesus, however, declares all foods "clean"; it is only what "comes out of a man" that makes him unclean (Mark 7:19b–20). Despite Jesus' declaration to this effect, this remains an issue as the church begins to expand among the Gentiles, as recorded in the book of Acts—a reflection of how controversial Jesus' declaration is in the historical context (cf. Acts 10:9–16; 15:1–29).

Both the literary context and Mark's mention of the daughter's "unclean spirit" connect our text to Jesus' declaration in Mark 7:19–23 (cf. Mark 7:25). Jesus' initial reluctance to cast out this "unclean spirit," curious and unexpected at this point in Mark's narrative, alerts the uninformed Gentile reader that something more significant than a simple exorcism is in view here. Moreover, Jesus' reference to Gentiles as "dogs" in the context may be an allusion to their ceremonial uncleanness (Mark 7:27b). A backward reading of this term reveals that, on occasion, human beings are referred to as "dogs" in the Old Testament Scriptures, with connotations of being despised and defiled (1 Sam. 17:43; 24:14; 2 Sam. 9:8; 16:9; 2 Kings 8:13; Ps. 22:16; Eccl. 9:4; cf. Matt. 7:6; Phil. 3:2; Rev. 22:15).

12. France, *The Gospel of Mark*, 277.

One commentator points out that "dogs" were associated with uncleanness "because they ate garbage, carrion, and corpses (Ex. 22:31; 1 Kings 21:23; 22:38; 2 Kings 9:36)."[13]

Some commentators seek to reduce the apparently offensive nature of Jesus' comments by pointing out that Jesus uses the diminutive form of the noun *dogs*, meaning "house pets"—a term not found in the Old Testament—rather than the unclean mongrels that prowl the streets.[14] While this fits with the picture of the dogs "under the table eat[ing] the children's crumbs" (Mark 7:28), it is debatable whether the notion of a pet dog, when compared to children, entirely removes the derogatory nature of the designation. It must be admitted, however, that the woman does not appear to take offense at Jesus' reference to dogs, an obvious allusion to her and her daughter in the context (v. 28). In any event, it is clear from what subsequently transpires that Jesus does not share the prevailing Jewish prejudice against the Gentiles (vv. 29–30).

When Jesus responds to the woman's plea for help, he is quick to point out Israel's "first" place in God's plan of redemption (Mark 7:27). In so doing, Jesus is simply reflecting the priority that Israel enjoyed in God's plan of salvation. After God's judgment on the nations of the world at the tower of Babel (Gen. 11:1–9), God does not turn his back on them; rather, he raises up Abraham, the forefather of Israel, to be his instrument to bless these nations (Gen. 12:1–3). God forms Abraham's descendants into the nation of Israel under Moses, and into a united kingdom under David. He enters into covenants with both these leaders, and Israel experiences God's blessings, in fulfillment of the promises made to Abraham (cf. Gen. 17:6; Ex. 2:24; 19:5; 2 Sam. 7:12–16).

It is through Israel that God raises up a Messiah to fulfill the promises of the Abrahamic covenant; he is the "seed" of Abraham, the One through whom God will bless the nations (Gen. 12:3; Gal. 3:16). In Isaiah's prophecy, God describes this Messiah figure as "my servant" and declares, "It is too small a thing for you to be my servant to restore the tribes of Jacob and bring back those of Israel I have kept. I will also make you a light for the Gentiles, that you may bring my salvation to the ends of the earth" (Isa. 49:6). Although "the tribes of Jacob" enjoy priority status in the servant's work of restoration, God will also make him "a light for the

---

13. Edwards, *The Gospel according to Mark*, 219.
14. Ibid., 220.

Gentiles" to bring God's salvation "to the ends of the earth." We see this same global redemptive perspective taught repeatedly in the prophetic literature of the Old Testament (cf. Isa. 2:2–4; 11:10; 42:1–9; 51:4–5; 55:1–5; 56:6–8; 60:1–3; Mic. 4:1–5; Zech. 8:20–23).

There is evidence of this redemptive pattern in Jesus' earthly ministry. After calling his disciples, Jesus begins his teaching ministry in the local synagogue in Capernaum, and his ministry continues to follow this pattern (see Mark 1:16–21, 39). Clearly, Israel is first in line. At various points in Mark's narrative, however, we glimpse in Jesus' ministry and teaching a future mission to the Gentiles (see 4:30–32; 5:1–20; 12:9; 13:10; 14:9). Clearly, then, Jesus' initial response to this Gentile woman's request for help cannot be understood as a rejection of the Gentiles (7:27). Rather, his response simply reflects the Scripture's redemptive priorities—Israel first, and then the nations—and so, in due course, he grants the Gentile woman's request and banishes the demon from her daughter (7:28–30).

One commentator draws a connection between this incident and the story of Elijah and the widow of Zarephath recorded in 1 Kings 17:7–24.[15] While these stories do share some interesting similarities—the Syrophoenician setting, the references to bread, the women and their children in need of divine help, and the word of the Lord that does not fail—there are also some differences. Accordingly, while it is to go beyond the evidence to suggest that this Elijah incident anticipates Jesus' encounter with this woman, it does give the reader of the Old Testament a glimpse of God's desire to bless the Gentile nations and, as such, anticipates the fulfillment of God's promises to Abraham (cf. Gen. 12:1–3).

A FORWARD READING

At the heart of this incident is the place of the Gentiles in God's plan of salvation. It should be clear from our backward reading of the text that the Gentiles do have a place in God's redemptive purposes. The fulfillment of God's Old Testament promise to bless "all peoples on earth" (cf. Gen. 12:3), glimpsed in the ministry of Christ, comes to full expression in the life of the early church as they, with God's enabling, obey Christ's so-called Great Commission to "make disciples of all nations" (Matt. 28:18–20).

15. Ibid., 218n8.

God's Messiah, Jesus, is sent to redeem "the lost sheep of Israel," in fulfillment of the covenant promises that he has made to them (Matt. 15:24; cf. Gen. 12:1–3; Acts 3:26). It is premature during Jesus' earthly ministry for his disciples to take the gospel to the Gentiles before Israel has an opportunity to respond (Matt. 10:6). All of this changes after Jesus' resurrection. The witness of Jesus' disciples is to extend to "the ends of the earth" (Acts 1:8; cf. Luke 24:47). In due course, "the Lord" raises up the apostle Paul, who has a specific calling to take the gospel to the Gentiles (Acts 9:15; cf. Gal. 1:16; 2:7). Yet Israel still enjoys a redemptive-chronological advantage, even in Paul's mission (cf. Acts 13:46; 18:6; 26:20; 28:25–27). The gospel is, after all, "to the Jew first and also to the Greek" (Rom. 1:16 ESV; cf. Mark 7:27), according to the apostle.

This pattern should not, however, be misinterpreted to mean that Israel is God's "favorite" among the nations. Peter makes this point explicitly in his message to the Gentile Cornelius and his household: "I now realize how true it is that God does not show favoritism but accepts men from every nation who fear him and do what is right" (Acts 10:34–35). The good news of the gospel is that "everyone who believes in [Jesus—Jew or Gentile] receives forgiveness of sins through his name" (10:43). God makes "no distinction" between Jew and Gentile; he purifies the hearts of both by faith; both are saved by grace alone (15:9, 11). There is now, accordingly, no need for the Gentile to be circumcised (15:1–29).

Paul showcases these truths in his letter to the Romans. All have sinned, Jew and Gentile, and fallen short of the glory of God, and are justified freely by his grace, through the redemption that came by Jesus Christ (Rom. 3:23–24). God is not the God of the Jews only; he is also the God of the Gentiles, "since there is only one God, who will justify the circumcised by faith and the uncircumcised through that same faith" (3:30; cf. 4:1–12). A corollary of this truth is that Gentiles are not accorded second-class citizenship in the kingdom of God; they are members of the one people of God, the church. Paul uses the analogy of a single olive tree, representing the people of God, to reflect this point. The natural branches represent Israel, while the "wild olive shoot," grafted into the same olive tree "by faith," represents the Gentiles (11:17–21). Paul uses different imagery to make essentially the same point in his letter to the Ephesians. He is worth quoting in full at this point:

Therefore, remember that formerly you who are Gentiles by birth and called "uncircumcised" by those who call themselves "the circumcision" (that done in the body by the hands of men)—remember that at that time you were separate from Christ, excluded from citizenship in Israel and foreigners to the covenants of the promise, without hope and without God in the world. But now in Christ Jesus you who once were far away have been brought near through the blood of Christ.

For he himself is our peace, who has made the two one and has destroyed the barrier, the dividing wall of hostility, by abolishing in his flesh the law with its commandments and regulations. His purpose was to create in himself one new man out of the two, thus making peace, and in this one body to reconcile both of them to God through the cross, by which he put to death their hostility. He came and preached peace to you who were far away and peace to those who were near. For through him we both have access to the Father by one Spirit.

Consequently, you are no longer foreigners and aliens, but fellow citizens with God's people and members of God's household, built on the foundation of the apostles and prophets, with Christ Jesus himself as the chief cornerstone. In him the whole building is joined together and rises to become a holy temple in the Lord. And in him you too are being built together to become a dwelling in which God lives by his Spirit. (Eph. 2:11–22; cf. Gal. 3:28)

This truth is reinforced by the glorious picture of the church triumphant in the book of Revelation, comprising people "from every nation, tribe, people and language," but depicted in the context as "144,000 from all the tribes of Israel" (Rev. 7:4–9). This vision should encourage the Christian reader today to bear witness to both Jew and Gentile about Christ and his gospel. There is place for both in the redemptive purposes of God. This is the lesson of our text, and the teaching of the entire New Testament (e.g., Rom. 11:25–27).

SUMMARY

Our downward reading of the text shows how Jesus uses the persistence of a Gentile woman to teach the important truth that God's mercy is more than sufficient for all, both Jew and Gentile! Our sideways reading of the text highlights elements in Mark's account that reinforce this truth: First, Mark emphasizes the woman's Gentile identity

(Mark 7:26). Second, he alludes to the priority of Israel in God's plan of redemption (v. 27). Third, by referring to the Gentile woman's daughter as her "child" (v. 30), Mark signals her right to share the "children's bread" (v. 27). Our backward reading reveals that God has always had a place for the Gentiles in his redemptive purposes (cf. Gen. 12:1–3), while our forward reading of the text demonstrates how God faithfully fulfills these redemptive promises through the church's mission to both Jew and Gentile, in recognition that Jesus is the Messiah of all!

Today, in acknowledgment that the mercy of God is more than sufficient to bless both Jew and Gentile, Christian readers should not limit their witness to others in any way, whether because of prejudice or fear. They need to remember that it is not externals, such as ethnicity, that defile, but what comes from within that makes one "unclean" (Mark 7:20–23).

9

JESUS PREDICTS HIS DEATH AND RESURRECTION

Mark 8:27–38: Jesus and his disciples went on to the villages around Caesarea Philippi. On the way he asked them, "Who do people say I am?"

They replied, "Some say John the Baptist; others say Elijah; and still others, one of the prophets."

"But what about you?" he asked. "Who do you say I am?"

Peter answered, "You are the Christ."

Jesus warned them not to tell anyone about him. He then began to teach them that the Son of Man must suffer many things and be rejected by the elders, chief priests and teachers of the law, and that he must be killed and after three days rise again. He spoke plainly about this, and Peter took him aside and began to rebuke him.

But when Jesus turned and looked at his disciples, he rebuked Peter. "Get behind me, Satan!" he said. "You do not have in mind the things of God, but the things of men."

Then he called the crowd to him along with his disciples and said: "If anyone would come after me, he must deny himself and take up his cross and follow me. For whoever wants to save his life will lose it, but whoever loses his life for me and for the gospel will save it. What good is it for a man to gain the whole world, yet forfeit his soul? Or what can a man give in exchange for his soul? If anyone is ashamed of me and my words in this adulterous and sinful generation, the Son of Man will be ashamed of him when he comes in his Father's glory with the holy angels."

A DOWNWARD READING

This passage represents a significant turning point in Mark's Gospel, where the focus of the narrative shifts to Jesus' death and resurrection (Mark 8:31; 9:31; 10:33–34). This particular focus is bound up with Jesus' identity. The reader is alerted to this fact by a series of questions that Jesus asks (literally, "was asking") his disciples: "Who do people say I am? . . . Who do you say I am?" (8:27b, 29b). The imperfect tense of *ask* suggests that some unreported discussion regarding these questions takes place between Jesus and his disciples. The disciples' response indicates that Mark provides the reader with only a brief summary of this interaction (8:28–29). The setting is "on the way" to "the villages around Caesarea Philippi," an area located north of the Sea of Galilee (Mark 7:27a). Jesus' question in this geographical context is hardly accidental. Caesarea Philippi was a city dedicated to false gods. Significantly, in our text Jesus is contrasted with false views of his true identity.

The disciples' response to Jesus' first question—"Who do people say I am?" (Mark 8:27)—reveals a variety of opinions in the historical context regarding his identity: "They replied, 'Some say John the Baptist; others say Elijah; and still others, one of the prophets'" (8:28). These opinions are a repeat of the various views ventured earlier in Mark's narrative regarding Jesus' identity (see 6:14–16). Jesus does not respond to these opinions regarding his identity. The reader of Mark's Gospel, however, knows that all these views are misguided and incorrect; Jesus is, Mark tells us, "the Christ, the Son of God" (1:1b). Jesus then turns the spotlight on his disciples: "But what about you [plural]?" Jesus asks. "Who do you say I am?" Peter answers on behalf of his fellow disciples: "You are the Christ" (8:29). Peter's response is prompt and clear, and at variance with the views of the "people" in the historical context (see 8:27–28). Interestingly, Jesus does not directly comment on Peter's answer. Once again, however, the reader of Mark's Gospel knows that Peter's view is correct, in a formal sense at least (see 1:1b). Surprisingly, Jesus at this point warns his disciples not to tell anyone about him (8:30). The language is forceful (cf. 1:25; 3:12; 4:39). Jesus does not give any reason for this warning, but based on the subsequent interaction between Jesus and Peter, it appears as though it is premature for the disciples to reveal his true identity (cf. 8:31–33).

Jesus then begins to speak about the suffering, rejection, and death of the "Son of Man" at the hands of the religious leaders—"the elders, chief priests and teachers of the law"—and his resurrection three days later (Mark 8:31). Peter obviously understands this "Son of Man" reference as a self-designation for Jesus, because in response to Jesus' "plain" talk about these matters, he takes Jesus "aside" and begins "to rebuke him" (8:32b). Peter clearly is unhappy with Jesus at this point; he finds the concept of a suffering "Christ" unpalatable. He apparently cannot reconcile the miracle-working Jesus he follows with the notion of a suffering "Christ" who is "killed" by his enemies (8:31b; cf. 3:10). Jesus, in turn, rebukes Peter: "Get behind me, Satan!" he says. "You do not have in mind the things of God, but the things of men" (8:33). Jesus detects in Peter's rebuke human, or worldly, thinking. At this point, Peter is Satan's instrument, and a stumbling block to Jesus' ministry.

Some commentators see a connection between Peter's understanding, or rather misunderstanding, of Jesus' identity at this point and the unique two-stage healing of a blind man at Bethsaida in the preceding context (Mark 8:22–26).[1] Peter's understanding of Jesus' identity is "blurred" at Caesarea Philippi, like the blind man after Jesus' first healing touch (8:23–24). Arguably, the second healing touch of the miracle occurs only at the cross, where through a centurion's confession we see clearly for the first time who Jesus is, "the Son of God!" (cf. 15:39).[2] This view dovetails with Mark's introduction to Jesus as both the "Christ" and the "Son of God" (1:1), which Mark progressively defines in his narrative through these two telling confessions, which climax at the cross (8:29; 15:39). Simply put, one cannot understand who Jesus is apart from his work on the cross!

Jesus now turns his attention to his would-be followers. He casts his net wide, so to speak, by calling the crowds to himself along with his disciples (Mark 8:34a). Jesus wants everyone to hear this teaching and understand it (cf. 7:14). His teaching applies to all of them: "If anyone" (8:34); there are no exceptions. Jesus calls his hearers to become his followers, but the standard is demanding: "If anyone would come after me,

---

1. See, for example, James R. Edwards, *The Gospel according to Mark*, Pillar New Testament Commentary (Grand Rapids: Eerdmans, 2002), 245.
   2. Ibid.

he must deny himself and take up his cross and follow me" (Mark 8:34b). In the historical context, the cross signifies the Roman instrument of death. One writer prefers to translate the word for *cross* as "execution stake," to make the point.[3] Jesus' hearers would have understood this. Following Jesus is no easy thing. It requires self-denial and a willingness to lay down one's life! Paradoxically, however, this is the pathway to life. Jesus makes this clear in the saying that follows: "For whoever wants to save his life will lose it, but whoever loses his life for me and for the gospel will save it" (8:35). Jesus and the gospel are more important than preserving any earthly existence!

No doubt mindful of the exacting nature of this call to follow him, Jesus proceeds to furnish his hearers with additional motivation to heed this call. First, Jesus informs them that the "soul" is more precious than anything this world has to offer: "What good is it for a man to gain the whole world, yet forfeit his soul? Or what can a man give in exchange for his soul?" (Mark 8:36–37). Second, Jesus challenges them to have an eternal perspective on this present life, and warns them of the cost of not following him: "If anyone is ashamed of me and my words in this adulterous and sinful generation, the Son of Man will be ashamed of him when he comes in his Father's glory with the holy angels" (v. 38). The call is not to side with "this sinful and adulterous generation" that has displaced God with the idolatry of this present world that is passing away. Glory awaits those who are willing to publicly follow Jesus and identify with him, no matter what the cost.

This text reveals a pattern: suffering, rejection, and death are experienced in this life, followed by resurrection glory in the next. We cannot have the one without the other: "The Son of Man *must*" (Mark 8:31). No suffering, no glory—this is true for both Jesus and his followers! This text is a sobering reminder to Jesus' followers that their allegiance to the miracle-working, all-powerful Jesus and his gospel does not mean deliverance from suffering in the midst of this "adulterous and sinful generation" (v. 38). Indeed, like Jesus, his disciples should expect that this allegiance will provoke opposition from the religious leaders, suffering at their hands, and even death. Yet in the process, they will save their lives (cf. v. 35)!

3. David Stern, quoted in David E. Garland, *Mark*, NIV Application Commentary (Grand Rapids: Zondervan, 1996), 335.

A SIDEWAYS READING

All three Synoptic Gospels record this incident in the life of Jesus (Matt. 16:13–27; Mark 8:27–38; Luke 9:18–26). For the most part, Mark's account is reflected in the parallel accounts at various points. The more significant differences between Mark and these parallel accounts may be summarized as follows:

- Whereas Peter identifies Jesus as "the Christ" in Mark's Gospel (Mark 8:29), in Matthew's account, Jesus is identified as "the Christ, the Son of the living God" (Matt. 16:16). Mark combines these two titles in his introduction (Mark 1:1), but separates them into two distinct confessions in his Gospel, the second at the cross (cf. Mark 8:29; 15:39), probably as a mechanism to emphasize the centrality of the cross in understanding Jesus' true identity.
- Mark's account does not include the teaching of Matthew 16:17–19 that focuses on Peter and the church. Mark's account is more narrowly concerned with the question of Jesus' identity. These particular verses in Matthew's parallel account, however, provide affirmation by Jesus that Peter's confession in Mark's Gospel is correct: "Blessed are you, Simon son of Jonah, for this was not revealed to you by man, but by my Father in heaven" (Matt. 16:17). The "divine revelation" motif present in this saying is arguably reflected in the previous context in Mark's Gospel, in the two-stage healing of the blind man at Bethsaida (Mark 8:22–26). Alluding to the miraculous touch of Jesus in this miracle, one commentator states that the miracle shows how "the disciples who 'have eyes but fail to see' (Mark 8:18), can also be made to see . . . [an] ability . . . [that] is a gift from God."[4]
- Matthew's account, at various points, clarifies some of the otherwise unexplained details in Mark's narrative:
  - According to Mark, Jesus warns his disciples "not to tell anyone about him" (Mark 8:30). Matthew's parallel account makes it clear that Jesus' warning relates to his identity; his disciples are "not to tell anyone that he [is] the Christ" (Matt. 16:20).
  - Peter rebukes Jesus, but Mark does not explain the nature of this rebuke (Mark 8:32). Matthew, however, clarifies its

4. Edwards, *The Gospel according to Mark*, 244–45.

nature: "Never, Lord! . . . This shall never happen to you" (Matt. 16:22). In the context, Peter is adamant that Jesus will not suffer and die at the hands of the religious leaders in Jerusalem (Matt. 16:21; cf. Mark 10:33).

- Mark includes some details not found in the parallel accounts:
  - Mark alone makes reference to all the "disciples" in the context of Jesus' rebuke (cf. Mark 8:33; Matt. 16:23a), possibly indicating that his rebuke is also intended for their ears. In other words, Jesus knows that Peter's misconceptions about "the Christ" are also their misconceptions.
  - Mark includes losing one's life "for the gospel" (Mark 8:35b; cf. Matt. 16:25; Luke 9:24), reflecting the prominent "gospel" motif in this Gospel (cf. Mark 1:1; 10:29; 13:10; 14:9).
  - Mark alone mentions "this adulterous and sinful generation" (Mark 8:38; cf. Matt. 10:33; Luke 9:26; 12:9), not only providing the setting for Christian discipleship, but also alluding to the hostile nature of that environment.
- Whereas Jesus refers to the "soul" in Mark's account (Mark 8:36; cf. Matt. 16:26), Luke's account speaks instead of "self" (Luke 9:25), indicating that Jesus has in mind the entire person, rather than just the inner being.

A BACKWARD READING

Mark mentions a number of key Old Testament characters in this text: "John the Baptist" (Mark 8:28), "Elijah" (v. 28), "the Christ" (v. 29b), and "the Son of Man" (v. 31). Each of these individuals requires some explanation.

- John the Baptist's ministry is recorded in the pages of the New Testament Gospels. In reality, however, he is an Old Testament prophet described in Mark's narrative as God's "messenger" sent to "prepare the way for the Lord" (Mark 1:2–3). Although his ministry more or less overlaps with Jesus, after John the Baptist's death, some people believe Jesus is John "raised from the dead, and that is why miraculous powers are at work in him" (6:14; cf. 8:28).

- In the historical context, some people confuse Jesus with the Old Testament prophet Elijah, no doubt because of the prophetic expectation that Elijah would return before the "great and dreadful day of the LORD comes" (Mal. 4:5–6). This particular prophecy is fulfilled by the coming of John the Baptist (Mark 1:4; 9:11–12; cf. Matt. 17:10–13). Others venture that Jesus is "one of the prophets" (Mark 8:28b). One commentator suggests that Moses' prophecy in Deuteronomy 18:15 is probably in view here: "The LORD your God will raise up for you a prophet like me from among your own brothers."[5] This specific prophecy is fulfilled with the coming of Jesus Christ (cf. Acts 3:20–22). But the people seem to have in mind just "one of the prophets" (see Matt. 16:14). Jesus considers himself to be a prophet (cf. Mark 6:4), but it is clear from Mark's Gospel that he is far more than merely "one of the prophets" (cf. Mark 1:1).

- Peter confesses that Jesus is "the Christ" (Mark 8:29b). This confession mirrors part of Mark's introduction to Jesus at the outset of his Gospel: Jesus is the "Christ, the Son of God" (Mark 1:1b). In our backward reading of Mark 1:1, we pointed out that *Christ* is not a last name, but a title for God's anointed Deliverer or Messiah (cf. Isa. 42:1; Dan. 9:25–26). Jesus, in response, begins to speak about the suffering, rejection, death, and resurrection of the "Son of Man" (Mark 8:31). It is striking, but hardly surprising in view of Jesus' warning to his disciples in Mark 8:30, that in this saying Jesus refers to himself as the "Son of Man" and not "the Christ" (cf. Mark 14:61–62). By substituting the one title for the other, however, Jesus forges a link between both these titles, and the concept of suffering, rejection, death, and resurrection. Peter's reaction to this teaching reveals that in popular Jewish thinking, this particular connection was not made (see Mark 8:32). The teachers of the law, for example, view "the Christ" as the royal "son of David" (see Mark 12:35), and no doubt would react in the same way as Peter to Jesus' assertions about the sufferings of "the Christ."

  Jesus' preferred use of the "Son of Man" title in the context suggests that it is not subject to the same popular misconceptions

5. Robert H. Stein, *Mark*, Baker Exegetical Commentary on the New Testament (Grand Rapids: Baker Academic, 2008), 399.

as "the Christ." Daniel's portrayal of this "son of man" as a triumphant figure comes most readily to mind whenever a reference is made to him (Dan. 7:13–14; cf. Mark 13:26; 14:62). But Jesus here appears to connect both "the Christ" and the "Son of Man" with the Suffering Servant of Isaiah's prophecy: "He was despised and rejected by men, a man of sorrows, and familiar with suffering. Like one from whom men hide their faces he was despised, and we esteemed him not" (Isa. 53:3). A number of other Old Testament verses paint a similar picture (e.g., Pss. 22:1–21; 118:22; Zech. 12:10; 13:7).

It is evident that Jesus' teaching about a suffering "Son of Man" at this point simply reflects that which "is written about him" in the Old Testament Scriptures (Mark 14:21a): "the Son of Man *must* suffer much and be rejected" (Mark 9:12). But Jesus is apparently the first to connect "the Christ" and the "Son of Man" with the Suffering Servant of Isaiah, and in so doing, he reveals the redemptive nature of the Christ's sufferings: "But he was pierced for our transgressions, he was crushed for our iniquities; the punishment that brought us peace was upon him, and by his wounds we are healed. We all, like sheep, have gone astray, each of us has turned to his own way; and the LORD has laid on him the iniquity of us all" (Isa. 53:5–6, cf. v. 12b).

- Although the focus in the discussions on these verses often revolves around the "suffering" motif, it should be remembered that Jesus also speaks here of the Christ and Son of Man rising from the dead (Mark 8:31b). There are glimpses of this resurrection doctrine in the Old Testament (cf. Hos. 6:2; 1 Cor. 15:4). According to David, "[God] will not abandon me to the grave, nor will [he] let [his] Holy One see decay" (Ps. 16:10), a prophecy that is fulfilled when Christ is raised from the dead (cf. Acts 2:22–32). The prophet Isaiah, speaking of the Suffering Servant, states that "it was the LORD's will to crush him and cause him to suffer, and though the LORD makes his life a guilt offering, *he will see his offspring and prolong his days*, and the will of the LORD will prosper in his hand" (Isa. 53:10). Isaiah here combines the motifs of the suffering and the future glory of the Servant.

- These same motifs are present in our text with the reference to the Son of Man's suffering and resurrection, followed by his coming in glory with "the holy angels" (Mark 8:38). There is a clear allusion at this point to Daniel 7:13–14: "In my vision at night I looked, and there before me was one like a son of man, coming with the clouds of heaven. He approached the Ancient of Days and was led into his presence. He was given authority, glory and sovereign power; all peoples, nations and men of every language worshiped him. His dominion is an everlasting dominion that will not pass away, and his kingdom is one that will never be destroyed." This glorious triumphant Old Testament perspective provides an obvious incentive to Jesus' hearers to follow him, no matter what the cost. It also functions as a reminder to them to look beyond the present life, characterized by the cross, and to embrace Jesus' "words" in the midst of the idolatry of "this adulterous and sinful generation" (Mark 8:38; cf. Isa. 57:3–10; Ezek. 16:32–42), as they look forward to the consummate arrival of "his kingdom . . . that will never be destroyed" (Dan. 7:14b). This will be a time of judgment on the enemies of God and his people (cf. Ps. 110:1–7; Mark 12:35–37).

- As motivation to take up one's cross and lose one's life (Mark 8:34–35), Jesus asks: "What can a man give in exchange for his soul?" (Mark 8:37). According to one commentator, this exchange statement "echoes" Psalm 49:7–9: "No man can redeem the life of another or give to God a ransom for him— the ransom for a life is costly, no payment is ever enough—that he should live on forever and not see decay."[6] In this particular psalm, the psalmist addresses "all who live in this world" (v. 1). He lives in a context where there are "wicked deceivers . . . who trust in their wealth and boast of their great riches" (vv. 5–6). But the psalmist points out that even the rich die: "man, despite his riches, does not endure" (v. 12); "no payment is ever enough—that he should live on forever and not see decay" (vv. 8–9). It is God alone who redeems life from the grave (v. 15a). The psalmist concludes this psalm by reinforcing

---

6. R. T. France, *The Gospel of Mark*, New International Greek Testament Commentary (Grand Rapids: Eerdmans, 2002), 341.

the point that earthly riches cannot prevent death or reach beyond the grave (vv. 16–20).

Caught between the temptation to "save" one's life in the midst of an "adulterous and sinful generation" and the challenge to "lose" one's life for Christ and "the gospel," Jesus reminds his hearers that, paradoxically, only the latter path leads to life. All the wealth in the world can't change that fact: "What good is it for a man to gain the whole world, yet forfeit his soul? Or what can a man give in exchange for his soul?" (Mark 8:35–37). This is the message of Psalm 49.

A FORWARD READING

The teaching of our text is triggered by Jesus' questions directed to his disciples: "Who do people say I am? . . . Who do you say I am?" (Mark 8:27, 29). Peter's response to Jesus reveals some misunderstanding (vv. 32–33). This prompts Jesus to discourse on the true nature of what it means to "come after" or "follow" him (vv. 34–38). There is a discernible parallel between this calling and the ministry of "the Christ"—glory is the end result, but it is attained through suffering (v. 31)! Today there are those who challenge the notion of a Christian discipleship characterized by suffering. As in the case of Peter's view of a suffering Christ, it is anathema to them. It is this particular "suffering" motif that we want to trace in our forward reading of the text.

It is obvious from the pages of the book of Acts that the apostles experience suffering and, on occasion, even death as they follow Jesus (cf. Acts 4:1–3; 5:18; 12:1–4). The apostle Paul is not exempt either. At the time of Paul's conversion and calling, the Lord tells Ananias that "I will show [Paul] how much he must suffer for my name" (Acts 9:16). The subsequent narrative depicts multiple fulfillments of this prediction (see Acts 20:23; 21:11, 27–36; 22:22–29; 23:12–22). Significantly, the Acts narrative ends with Paul in prison (Acts 28:16–31). It is clear from this brief survey of the history of the early church that the leadership of the church of Jesus Christ is not exempt from suffering (cf. 2 Cor. 1:8; 1 Thess. 2:2; 2 Tim. 1:8, 12; 2:9). During one of Paul's missionary journeys, however, Barnabas and Paul point out that suffering of some kind will also be true for all those entering the kingdom of God: "We must go through many hardships to enter the kingdom of God," they tell the disciples at Lystra, Iconium, and Antioch (Acts 14:21–22). Both the church leader and the Christian disciple should expect to suffer for the sake of Christ and the gospel, as Jesus teaches (cf. Mark 8:35b).

We see this truth affirmed in Paul's letters (2 Cor. 1:6; Phil. 1:29; 2 Thess. 1:5; 2 Tim. 3:12). The believer shares in Jesus' sufferings (Phil. 3:10). Elsewhere Paul adopts the imagery of the "sufferings of Christ [overflowing] into our lives" (2 Cor. 1:5a). Thus, when Paul writes to the Roman saints, comprising both Jews and Gentiles, he can refer to "our present sufferings" without fear of contradiction, although at this point he has not yet personally met the saints in Rome (Rom. 8:18). Like Jesus, Paul also links these sufferings to glory: "Now if we are children, then we are heirs—heirs of God and co-heirs with Christ, if indeed we share in his sufferings in order that we may also share in his glory. I consider that our present sufferings are not worth comparing with the glory that will be revealed in us" (Rom. 8:17–18). Present sufferings precede future glory for the believer! This was true for Jesus, and is true for his followers.

We see this same "suffering" motif elsewhere in the New Testament (cf. Heb. 10:32; James 1:2; Rev. 1:9), and this same link between suffering and glory. According to the apostle Peter, "the Spirit of Christ," at work in the Old Testament prophets, "predicted the sufferings of Christ and the glories that would follow" (1 Peter 1:10–11). This prophetic revelation is intended to encourage Peter's readers, "God's elect" (1:1a), who are suffering at the time (1:12; cf. 1:6). Accordingly, Peter instructs his Christian readers "not [to] be surprised at the painful trial you are suffering, as though something strange were happening to you. But rejoice that you participate in the sufferings of Christ, so that you may be overjoyed when his glory is revealed. If you are insulted because of the name of Christ, you are blessed, for the Spirit of glory and of God rests on you" (4:12–14). The Christian who "participate[s] in the sufferings of Christ" will also participate in his glory (4:13; cf. 5:1)! Peter reinforces this link between suffering and glory in his concluding comments in this letter: "And the God of all grace, who called you to his eternal glory in Christ, after you have suffered a little while, will himself restore you and make you strong, firm and steadfast. To him be the power for ever and ever. Amen" (5:10–11). We see this same pattern in the book of Revelation, where John records a letter to the church in Smyrna predicting their suffering, but also promising them glory: "Do not be afraid of what you are about to suffer. I tell you, the devil will put some of you in prison to test you, and you will suffer persecution for ten days. Be faithful, even to the point of death, and I will give you the crown of life" (Rev. 2:10).

Some today insist, however, that when Jesus suffers as a substitute for the sins of his people, he delivers them from physical suffering as well. According to Isaiah, "Surely he took up our infirmities and carried our sorrows . . . and by his wounds we are healed" (Isa. 53:4a, 5b). But although there is comfort in the present for the Christian who suffers and experiences sorrows (cf. 2 Cor. 1:3–7), it is only in glory, when "the old order of things has passed away," that the Christian is promised "no more death or mourning or crying or pain" (cf. Rev. 21:4). Moreover, while the ministry of Jesus confirms that there is a physical dimension to the healing promised by Isaiah (see Matt. 8:16–17), there is no indication in the pages of the New Testament that physical healing is the norm, or is guaranteed, for every Christian in this present age. Indeed, some of God's choicest servants continue to experience physical ailments and the suffering they induce (2 Cor. 12:7–10; 1 Tim. 5:23).

In effect, proponents of this contrary view have collapsed the two stages evident in our text—"suffering now, then glory"—into a single stage to describe the present—glory now! As we have seen in our forward reading of the text, however, the teaching of the New Testament is clear: the suffering of Jesus does not preclude the suffering of his followers! At best, in this life they experience only a foretaste of the glory to come; complete redemption awaits the age to come (cf. Rom. 8:18–25).

SUMMARY

There are two distinct but related sections in our text. Both are important. The first relates to the true identity of Jesus. Jesus asks you: "But what about you? . . . Who do you say I am?" (Mark 8:29). Each reader must confront, and answer, this question in a modern context where various false views of Jesus still abound. But that is only the first step. There is also the call to follow Jesus. That is the theme of the second section (vv. 34–38).

Our downward reading of the text reveals a prominent "suffering" motif in both these sections. According to Jesus, suffering characterizes both the life and ministry of "the Christ" and his followers (Mark 8:31–35). Jesus uses the imagery of the cross to make the point that this suffering may even be unto death for his followers. One commentator states, "The cross is laid on every Christian. . . . When Christ calls a man he bids him come and die."[7] Yet death does not have the last word; after suffering and death comes resurrection glory (vv. 31, 38)!

Our sideways reading of the text reveals Mark's focus on the matter of Jesus' true identity—he does not include Matthew 16:17–19. A backward reading reveals both the necessity of the Christ's sufferings and the redemptive nature of those sufferings. This redemptive picture precedes the call for all followers of Jesus to "take up" their cross (Mark 8:34). God's gift precedes God's demand! To quote the well-known theological dictum, "the indicative precedes the imperative." This is the consistent pattern in Scripture (cf. Rom. 12:1–21). Our forward reading of the account affirms a pattern of suffering in the lives of all followers of Jesus. And like Christ, the Christian's sufferings lead to future glory. But unlike Christ, the Christian's sufferings are not redemptive in nature.

Both the teaching of this text and that of the rest of the New Testament affirm that Christian discipleship is "cross-shaped." Everyone who follows Jesus must take up his or her cross (Mark 8:34). The example of Jesus, "the Christ," in the context, together with the promise of glorious life and the warning of divine rejection, provides the necessary motivation for the reader to heed this call (vv. 31–38).

---

7. Dietrich Bonhoeffer, quoted in Garland, *Mark*, 335.

10

JESUS IS TRANSFIGURED

Mark 9:2–8: After six days Jesus took Peter, James and John with him and led them up a high mountain, where they were all alone. There he was transfigured before them. His clothes became dazzling white, whiter than anyone in the world could bleach them. And there appeared before them Elijah and Moses, who were talking with Jesus.

Peter said to Jesus, "Rabbi, it is good for us to be here. Let us put up three shelters—one for you, one for Moses and one for Elijah." (He did not know what to say, they were so frightened.)

Then a cloud appeared and enveloped them, and a voice came from the cloud: "This is my Son, whom I love. Listen to him!"

Suddenly, when they looked around, they no longer saw anyone with them except Jesus.

A DOWNWARD READING

In our text, Jesus is transfigured. The immediate literary context gives the reader a clue regarding the significance of this incident in Jesus' life: it is a demonstration of the "kingdom of God come with power," intended for the benefit of Jesus' disciples (Mark 9:1; cf. Matt. 16:28).[1] Jesus announces the presence of God's kingdom at the outset of his public ministry (see Mark 1:15). In this transfiguration incident,

---

1. There is some debate about whether Jesus' prediction in Mark 9:1 is fulfilled, partially or fully, in the transfiguration event that follows. In our opinion, this is the most obvious referent in the flow of the narrative.

the disciples are given a glimpse of this kingdom when it comes in its consummate fullness, "with power." This is what Jesus wants his disciples to see in a context in which he has just discoursed on the need for the Son of Man to suffer, be killed, and rise again, before he returns "in his Father's glory with the holy angels" (8:31, 38). It is this "glory" that Jesus' disciples glimpse in the transfiguration event. The impact of the event on the apostolic eyewitnesses is obvious: if the glory of Jesus, just glimpsed, is assured, they should not be discouraged by his sufferings just predicted, or the sufferings that they, in due course, may experience (see 8:34–38).

"After six days," Jesus takes "Peter, James and John with him . . . up a high mountain where they [are] all alone" (Mark 9:2). The time reference connects this action with the predictions in the immediately preceding context, and the three apostles mentioned are the "some" referred to by Jesus (8:31–9:1). They have been handpicked by Jesus no doubt to act as eyewitnesses to the events that will unfold on the mountain. The "mountain" setting is not identified, but given the reference in the preceding context to "the villages around Caesarea Philippi" (8:27a), some commentators would cast their vote in favor of Mount Hermon, a truly "high mountain" nearby, as the site of the transfiguration over against the traditional site, Mount Tabor.[2] According to one commentator, however, "[in the subsequent scene], the presence at the foot of the mountain of a Jewish crowd (including scribes) who are well aware of the reputation of Jesus and his disciples for exorcism (Mark 9:14–18) casts doubt on a location so far north."[3] The gap of "six days" (Mark 9:2a) between the transfiguration and Peter's confession at Caesarea Philippi (8:27–30) would allow Jesus and his disciples the time to travel farther south to reach the traditional site of Mount Tabor. Certainty regarding the location is not possible in the circumstances. Wherever it occurred, it doesn't affect the meaning of the transfiguration event. "For the Gospel writers, it was not where the event took place but rather what took place that was important."[4]

2. See, for example, James R. Edwards, *The Gospel according to Mark*, Pillar New Testament Commentary (Grand Rapids: Eerdmans, 2002), 262–63.

3. R. T. France, *The Gospel of Mark*, New International Greek Testament Commentary (Grand Rapids: Eerdmans, 2002), 350.

4. Robert H. Stein, *Mark*, Baker Exegetical Commentary on the New Testament (Grand Rapids: Baker Academic, 2008), 416.

Jesus is "transfigured before them" (Mark 9:2b). This brief summary statement highlights the fact that Jesus' transfiguration is for the benefit of the trio of eyewitnesses present. It is hidden from the eyes of the crowds, but occurs "before them." The so-called divine passive form of the verb, "was transfigured," implies that it is God who transfigures Jesus. Mark describes what Peter, James, and John see as Jesus is transfigured: "His clothes became dazzling white, whiter than anyone in the world could bleach them" (v. 3). The clear implication of this description is that something supernatural is being witnessed; no one "in the world" is able to do this! The focus shifts from the transfigured Jesus to the appearance before them of Elijah and Moses, two prominent Old Testament figures, who "were talking" with him (v. 4). Their presence adds a definite gravity to the occasion. Mark does not inform the reader how Peter, James, and John are able to identify these two individuals, nor does he divulge the nature of their conversation with Jesus.

Peter responds by making a proposal to Jesus that, according to one commentator, is a rather "bizarre" and "clumsy"[5] attempt on his part to add a sense of occasion to the proceedings: "Rabbi, it is good for us to be here. Let us put up three shelters—one for you, one for Moses and one for Elijah" (Mark 9:5). Peter addresses Jesus as "Rabbi," the Aramaic form of "teacher." This designation is rather surprising, given the occasion and Peter's earlier confession (8:29b). Peter's desire to erect three "tents" (ESV), one each for Jesus, Moses, and Elijah, appears to be motivated by a desire to prolong the experience because "it is good for us to be here" (9:5a). Mark adds a parenthetical observation for the benefit of his readers: "He did not know what to say, they were so frightened" (9:6). Peter is once again the spokesman for his fellow disciples (cf. 8:29). All of them are "terrified" (ESV). This response of fear has connotations of the divine presence (cf. Heb. 12:21). This prompts one scholar to suggest that these tents are intended to protect the eyewitnesses from the radiating divine glory.[6]

A cloud then appears and envelops them, and a voice comes from the cloud: "This is my Son, whom I love. Listen to him!" (Mark 9:7). Clearly, this is the voice of the Lord God, identifying Jesus Christ as

5. France, *The Gospel of Mark*, 353–54.
6. Scott J. Hafemann, "2 Corinthians" (lecture, Bible Teachers Network conference, Cape Town, July 2004).

his "Son." This divine acknowledgment affirms Mark's view of Jesus as "the Son of God" (1:1) and, together with the voice at Jesus' baptism, provides a second divine affirmation of Jesus' divine sonship (see 1:11; 3:11). The difference between these two occasions is that the divine confession at the baptism is directed at Jesus—"You are my Son" (1:11)—whereas on the Mount of Transfiguration, the divine voice is intended for the ears of the disciples who are present—"This is my Son" (9:7b). God commands the disciples, "Listen to him!" This divine injunction relates most immediately to Jesus' teaching on his suffering, death, and resurrection in the preceding context (8:31). Thus, it functions as a divine validation not only of Jesus' sonship, but also of his predicted sufferings, death, and resurrection. "However improbable it may appear, it is the Son of God who will suffer and die."[7] In effect, Jesus is correct and Peter is not (cf. 8:32–33). The divine voice from the cloud vindicates Jesus!

Mark concludes his record of this incident with the observation that it is Jesus alone who remains with the three disciples on the mountain; there is no sign of Elijah and Moses (Mark 9:8). This scenario is probably intended to imply the superiority of Jesus over Moses and Elijah and to keep the focus on Jesus. In no sense, then, should they be understood as equals of Jesus. Indeed, it is striking how Mark's focus remains on Jesus throughout this incident: it is Jesus who takes Peter, James, and John with him (v. 2); it is Jesus who is transfigured (v. 2b); it is Jesus whom Elijah and Moses talk with (v. 4); it is Jesus whom Peter addresses (v. 5); it is Jesus whom the voice from the cloud acknowledges (v. 7); and it is Jesus who remains behind (v. 8)! This Christological focus must be reflected in any interpretation of these verses and indeed, as we have argued elsewhere, in any interpretation of Mark's Gospel narrative.

A SIDEWAYS READING

All three Synoptic Gospel writers record the transfiguration event (Matt. 17:1–8; Mark 9:2–8; Luke 9:28–36). In each account, it follows Peter's so-called confession at Caesarea Philippi (Matt. 16:13–16; Mark 8:27–30; Luke 9:18–20). The most significant differences between Mark and the other accounts may be summarized as follows:

7. France, *The Gospel of Mark*, 347.

- Mark informs the reader that Jesus "was transfigured," but he focuses on the changes to his clothing, rather than his person, probably signifying the all-encompassing nature of the transfiguration: "His clothes became dazzling white, whiter than anyone in the world could bleach them" (Mark 9:2b–3; cf. Matt. 17:2; Luke 9:29). Mark alone records the observation that no one in the world could "bleach" like this (Mark 9:3b), reinforcing the otherworldly, supernatural character of Jesus' transfiguration. It provides a glimpse of heavenly glory, a point made explicit in Luke's account (cf. Luke 9:32).
- All three accounts refer to the appearance of both Moses and Elijah on the mountain with Jesus. Mark lists Elijah before Moses, the reverse order of Matthew and Luke (Mark 9:4; Matt. 17:3; Luke 9:30), thereby giving Elijah prominence in his account of this incident. This reflects Mark's emphasis on Elijah both in this incident (Mark 9:4–5, 11–13) and elsewhere in his Gospel (1:6; 6:15; 8:28; 15:35–36). Peter, in his response to their appearance, reverses Mark's earlier order by listing Moses first, then Elijah (9:5b).
- Luke points out that both Moses and Elijah appear in "glorious splendor" (literally, "in glory," ESV) with Jesus, indicating that they both seem to share a measure of Jesus' transfiguration glory on the mountain (Luke 9:31a; cf. 9:32). This Lukan detail gives credence to the view that Peter wants to erect the three tents to shield himself and his companions from their radiating glory so as to prolong the whole experience (Mark 9:5; cf. Luke 9:32–33). Luke, however, informs his readers that Peter appears rather to be motivated by the fact that Moses and Elijah are about to leave Jesus (Luke 9:33a). Thus, it is an attempt on Peter's part to preserve the status quo (cf. Mark 9:5a).
- Luke informs the reader that Moses and Elijah speak to Jesus about his "departure, which he [is] about to bring to fulfillment at Jerusalem" (Luke 9:31). Commentators often point out that the original Greek word for *departure* transliterated into English is the word *exodus*, alluding to a so-called new exodus event.[8]

8. See, for example, Walter L. Leifeld, "Luke," in *Matthew, Mark, Luke*, vol. 8 of The Expositor's Bible Commentary (Grand Rapids: Zondervan, 1984), 927.

In view, of course, is the deliverance that Jesus will secure in Jerusalem from bondage to sin, effected through his death on a Roman cross! Neither Mark nor Matthew mentions the topic of conversation; it is not important for their purposes.

- On the mountain, Mark alone has Peter address Jesus as "Rabbi" or "teacher" (Mark 9:5a), rather than "Lord" (Matt. 17:4a) or "Master" (Luke 9:33a), as in the parallel accounts. This title is used elsewhere in Mark's narrative, but only where Jesus is directly addressed (see Mark 10:51; 11:21; 14:45). While this is a valid title for Jesus (see 4:38) and reflects the prominence of his teaching ministry (see 4:1; 6:2), in this context it appears to betray an inadequate understanding of Jesus' true identity (see 8:29b). The subsequent "voice . . . from the cloud" rectifies any deficiencies regarding Jesus' true identity; he is God's "Son." It is him alone that the disciples must "listen to" (9:7). Peter should not place Elijah and Moses on a par with Jesus (cf. 9:5).

- Fear among the disciples is a factor in all three transfiguration accounts. In Mark, the fear is directly linked to the transfiguration of Jesus (Mark 9:6), whereas in Luke's account "a cloud appear[s] and envelop[s] them," and the disciples are described as being "afraid as they enter[ ] the cloud" (Luke 9:34). In Matthew's version, the fear is a response to the subsequent "voice from the cloud" (Matt. 17:5–6).

- The "voice . . . from the cloud" in Mark's Gospel describes Jesus as "my Son, whom I love" (Mark 9:7b). In Matthew's account, this confession is expanded to read as follows: "This is my Son, whom I love; with him I am well pleased" (Matt. 17:5), echoing the "voice from heaven" at Jesus' baptism, recorded in all three Synoptic Gospels (Matt. 3:17; Mark 1:11; Luke 3:22). In Luke's narrative, Jesus is simply described as divinely "chosen" (Luke 9:35b).

- In Mark's account, the disappearance of Elijah and Moses from the mountain occurs "suddenly." This particular adverb occurs only here in the New Testament and signals a quick and unexpected transition in the account that leaves the disciples alone with Jesus on the mountain, ensuring that the focus remains on him (Mark 9:8; cf. Matt. 17:8; Luke 9:36).

A BACKWARD READING

A backward reading of this transfiguration incident reveals an account that reverberates with Old Testament links and allusions:

- The parallels with the Old Testament Sinai event in particular are plentiful, as the following comments indicate:

> Underlying Mark's telling of the story are clear echoes of the Old Testament.... The "transformation" of Jesus and the shining of his clothes may recall the shining of Moses' face in Ex. 34:29–35, though Mark offers no verbal echoes or direct parallels to that account. More explicit are the repeated reminders of Moses' experiences at Sinai in Ex. 24. Moses took three named companions (though also seventy others) up onto the high mountain to meet with God (Ex. 24:1, 9), and there they had a vision of divine glory (24:10); subsequently Moses went higher with only Joshua as companion (24:13–14); cloud covered the mountain (24:15), and after "six days" Moses went up into it (24:16); there God spoke to Moses (Ex. 25ff.); when Moses relayed God's words to the people, they promised to obey (24:3, 7). Mark's narrative does not reproduce the Exodus story exactly, but there are enough verbal and conceptual echoes to trigger thoughts of a new Sinai experience, and perhaps of Jesus as a new Moses.[9]

  While the reader may quibble with the conclusion that Jesus is presented in this incident as a "new Moses"—after all, he is explicitly identified as God's "Son" (Mark 9:7b)—the parallels with the Sinai event are numerous. In summary, both Sinai and the so-called Mount of Transfiguration are places of divine revelation and glory, the significance of the latter incident being enhanced by its parallels with the former. Against this Old Testament backdrop, it is hardly surprising that those commentators who detect a "new exodus" motif in Mark's Gospel describe the transfiguration event as a "new Sinai."[10]
- It is noteworthy that Jesus takes "Peter, James and John with him and [leads] them up a high mountain, where they [are] all

9. France, *The Gospel of Mark*, 348.

10. See, for example, Rikk E. Watts, *Mark*, Commentary on the New Testament Use of the Old Testament (Grand Rapids: Baker Academic, 2007), 186.

alone" (Mark 9:2). When the reader is informed that "[Jesus] was transfigured before them" (Mark 9:2), it is apparent that Jesus intends these three disciples to act as eyewitnesses to this incident, in fulfillment of the requirements of Deuteronomy 19:15b: "A matter must be established by the testimony of two or three witnesses." In due course, Peter in his writings duly bears eyewitness testimony to this significant event in the life of Jesus (see 2 Peter 1:16–18).

- As pointed out in our sideways reading of this text, Mark alone refers to the "dazzling white" clothes of Jesus as he is transfigured before his disciples (Mark 9:3). This reference may be an allusion to Daniel's description of "the Ancient of Days," the Lord God, seated on his throne: "As I looked, thrones were set in place, and the Ancient of Days took his seat. His clothing was as white as snow; the hair of his head was white like wool" (Dan. 7:9a). If so, not only does this imply that Jesus shares in the divine glory of the One seated on the throne, but, in keeping with the significance of the transfiguration event, it also anticipates the glory of "one like a son of man," that is, Jesus, depicted in the subsequent Danielic context (cf. Dan. 7:13–14).

- The significance of the appearance of Elijah and Moses—listed in reverse historical order—with Jesus has generated some discussion (Mark 9:4). It is commonly believed that together they represent the Law and the Prophets, which point to Jesus (see Luke 24:27, 44). But according to one commentator:

> This interpretation is inconvenienced by two problems: Elijah was not a writing prophet and seems an unusual choice to represent the prophets, and Mark lists Elijah before Moses. Since Moses was considered the first and greatest of the prophets, why does he come second? The discussion on the way down the mountain (Mark 9:11–13) provides the answer. The disciples recite the scribal expectations about the end, and they maintain that Elijah must play a key role before the restoration of all things. Elijah and Moses are both eschatological figures. Moses was Israel's first deliverer, and people expected a prophet like Moses (Deut. 18:15) to appear and liberate Israel. Elijah was supposed to appear at the dawning of the end time and God's ultimate redemption of Israel. Both

are mentioned in Malachi 4:4-6. . . . Their presence with Jesus on the high mountain, therefore, rouses Jewish hopes about the final redemption of Israel and suggests that the time has been fulfilled. The kingdom of God has drawn near (1:15).[11]

Simply put, the appearance of these two significant Old Testament figures affirms the presence of the messianic age, and its promise of eschatological glory. This makes good sense in a context in which Jesus not only is gloriously transfigured, but has also just been identified as "the Christ," God's Messiah (Mark 8:29b).

- Peter's proposal to erect "tents" (Mark 9:5 ESV) in response to the transfiguration of Jesus, and the subsequent appearance of Elijah and Moses, may have its origins in the Old Testament. Commentators speculate that these "tents" may be associated in Peter's thinking with the "booths," made of branches and leaves, prescribed in the Old Testament Feast of Tabernacles (see Lev. 23:33-43).[12] But if so, the link is not made clear. Others see a connection with the "tent of meeting" or tabernacle in Israel's wilderness wanderings that shielded God's people from the divine presence in their midst (cf. Ex. 29:42-45; 33:7-11).[13] But here three tents, not one, are proposed, suggesting that Peter places Jesus and his Old Testament companions on a par with each other (Mark 9:5). In any discussion of this matter, one should remember that Mark tells his readers that in making this proposal, Peter "did not know what to say" (v. 6a). The implication seems to be that Peter's proposal is a knee-jerk reaction to preserve what he sees on the mountain, rather than a well-thought-out suggestion, because "they were so frightened" (v. 6b).
- The Old Testament is again in view when "a cloud" appears on the mountain and "envelop[s]," or "overshadow[s]" (ESV), them, language reminiscent of the cloud that filled first the tabernacle and then the temple with God's glorious presence (Mark 9:7;

11. David E. Garland, *Mark*, NIV Application Commentary (Grand Rapids: Zondervan, 1996), 344-45.
12. See, for example, France, *The Gospel of Mark*, 354.
13. See, for example, Hafemann, "2 Corinthians"; Craig S. Keener, *The IVP Bible Background Commentary: New Testament* (Downers Grove, IL: InterVarsity Press, 1993), 158.

cf. Ex. 40:35; 1 Kings 8:10–11 LXX). A "voice [emanates] from the cloud" (Mark 9:7). This imagery parallels God's presence and pronouncements on Mount Sinai (cf. Ex. 19:9; 24:16; 24:18–25:1; 34:5), thereby enhancing the significance of the transfiguration event and the divine endorsement of Jesus that follows (Mark 9:7).

- The divine voice "from the cloud" identifies Jesus as "my Son, whom I love" (Mark 9:7b). This filial designation has connotations of divine kingship in the Old Testament. God promises King David that he will "raise up" a descendant to succeed him whose kingdom and throne God will establish forever. Concerning this descendant, God states, "I will be his father, and he will be *my son*" (2 Sam. 7:12–14a). Psalm 2 paints a similar picture of God's "Anointed One," whom he also designates "my Son" (Ps. 2:2, 7). He will "rule" the "ends of the earth" with an "iron scepter" despite opposition from the "kings of the earth" and "rulers" gathered together against him (Ps. 2:2, 8–9).

  No doubt this designation and its Old Testament connotations of universal rule are intended to encourage Jesus' disciples in a context in which Jesus is experiencing intense opposition from the religious and governing authorities that will ultimately end in his death (cf. Mark 3:6; 8:31). Put differently, God intends these disciples to understand that the rule of God's Son, depicted in these Old Testament Scriptures, will be established despite Jesus' present opposition and his predicted sufferings and death (see 8:31). The glory glimpsed in Jesus' transfiguration is a foretaste of "the kingdom of God come with power" (9:1).

- The link between sonship and death is also present with the addition of the words "whom I love." This may be an allusion to Genesis 22:2, where God instructs Abraham, "Take your son, your only son, Isaac, whom you love, and go to the region of Moriah. Sacrifice him there as a burnt offering on one of the mountains I will tell you about." In that ancient context, and in the exact area where the city of Jerusalem would one day be established (see 2 Chron. 3:1), God provides a substitute ram that dies instead of Isaac (Gen. 22:13). This is a picture of God's provision of his own Son, Jesus, as a substitute sacrifice for sinners (see Rom. 8:32). Once again, Mark makes the point that Jesus' predicted death is no ordinary death; it is a sin-sacrifice for the world (cf. Mark 10:45; John 1:29).

But this particular Old Testament allusion is significant for another reason. In Mark's Gospel, Jesus predicts not only his suffering and death, but also his resurrection "after three days" (Mark 8:31b). The notion of resurrection is also present in the Genesis 22 account. On the "third day," Isaac's life is preserved (Gen. 22:4–14). The New Testament writer to the Hebrews interprets this action as a type of resurrection: "By faith Abraham, when God tested him, offered Isaac as a sacrifice. He who had received the promises was about to sacrifice his one and only son, even though God had said to him, 'It is through Isaac that your offspring will be reckoned.' Abraham reasoned that God could raise the dead, and figuratively speaking, he did receive Isaac back from death" (Heb. 11:17–19). Like Isaac, Jesus would rise again after three days (Mark 8:31b), but unlike Isaac, Jesus would literally be raised from the dead by God! The transfiguration of Jesus, God's beloved Son, is an anticipation of that glorious reality. Clearly, death does not have the last word!

- The "voice . . . from the cloud" concludes with a command to "listen to [Jesus]!" (Mark 9:7b). This command no doubt echoes Deuteronomy 18:15, where Moses predicts that "the LORD your God will raise up for you a prophet like me from among your own brothers. You must listen to him." Jesus is the One who fulfills this Old Testament prophecy (see Acts 3:22), although clearly, as God's Son, Jesus is much more than a prophet like Moses. Indeed, Moses and Elijah "suddenly" disappear off the mountain, leaving the disciples alone with Jesus, signifying his superiority (Mark 9:8). Peter, James, and John must therefore heed his prophetic predictions in the context regarding his sufferings, rejection, death, and resurrection (Mark 8:31)!

The heavenly glory glimpsed in the transfiguration, coupled with the divine voice from the cloud, bears powerful testimony to the person of Jesus and his teaching. Our backward reading of this account reveals multiple echoes of the Old Testament Sinai event, which add considerable weight to the significance of this incident in the life of Jesus. It is therefore with merit that one commentator describes the transfiguration event as "a new Sinai and [Jesus'] words as the new Torah"![14]

A FORWARD READING

The rich Old Testament background reflected in Mark's description of the transfiguration incident reinforces the significance of what Jesus' disciples see and hear on the mountain. Both Jesus' person and his teaching are portrayed in their true colors: He is God's glorious Son! Therefore, listen to him (Mark 9:7)! This places both Jesus and his teaching on his suffering, rejection, death, and resurrection, in the immediate context, at center stage (cf. 8:31). Like Peter in the historical context, however, there are those in the church today who reject or disparage the significance of Jesus' death and resurrection so that it is not the heartbeat of the message that is preached (cf. 8:32). We will focus on this particular dimension of the text in our forward reading of these verses. It will become apparent that a mere concordance-type search and analysis of such key words as *death* and *resurrection* will paint an inadequate biblical picture; it needs to be supplemented by more of a conceptual analysis of these motifs in the New Testament.

As one reflects on the preaching and teaching of the early church, it is apparent that the apostles did indeed "listen to [Jesus]" (Mark 9:7b). Jesus, not Moses or Elijah, is at the center of their message, and his death and resurrection prominent in their preaching (see Acts 2:22–36; 3:11–16; 4:8–12; 5:29–32; 8:30–35; 10:34–43; 13:16–37; 17:1–3; 26:1–23). Jesus' death is portrayed as no ordinary death; it effects forgiveness of sins (2:38; 5:31; 10:43). In the Acts narrative, the apostle Paul stresses this truth when he addresses those in the synagogue at Pisidian Antioch: "Therefore, my brothers, I want you to know that through Jesus the forgiveness of sins is proclaimed to you" (13:38). Paul also affirms this truth in his letter to the saints in Rome, linking it explicitly to Jesus' death and resurrection: "He was delivered over to death for our sins and was raised to life for our justification" (Rom. 4:25). Elsewhere in his New Testament correspondence, Paul refers to Jesus' death, using the language of Christ's "[giving] himself for us" to make essentially the same point (Titus 2:14; cf. Gal. 1:4).

The writer to the Hebrews speaks of "Christ, having been offered once to bear the sins of many" (Heb. 9:28 ESV), highlighting the suf-

---

14. Watts, *Mark*, 201.

ficiency of his sacrificial death for sins. The apostle Peter affirms both the sufficiency and significance of Christ's death, using the language of "suffering" and "death" to make the point: "For Christ also suffered once for sins, the righteous for the unrighteous, that he might bring us to God, being put to death in the flesh but made alive in the spirit" (1 Peter 3:18 ESV). Peter here links Jesus' death and resurrection. Earlier in this same letter, Peter describes Jesus' resurrection as giving his Christian readers "a living hope" regarding their heavenly inheritance (1 Peter 1:3–9). The apostle John, for his part, commences the book of Revelation with a Trinitarian doxology that focuses on Christ Jesus: "the faithful witness, the firstborn from the dead, and the ruler of the kings of the earth. To him who loves us and has freed us from our sins by his blood" (Rev. 1:5; cf. 5:9b). John arguably singles out key features of Christ's person and work for praise that include references to his death and resurrection, and once again the significance of Jesus' death is spelled out for John's readers. The New Testament speaks with one voice on this set of events in the life of Christ.

The reader may object that this is a rather slender exegetical base on which to assert the centrality of these truths in the Christian faith. In response, we point out that when Paul writes to the Corinthian Christians, he describes these truths as of "first importance": "For what I received I passed on to you as of first importance: that Christ died for our sins according to the Scriptures, that he was buried, [and] that he was raised on the third day according to the Scriptures" (1 Cor. 15:3–4; cf. Acts 20:24). It is important to notice the sense of continuity that Paul expresses in these verses: these truths that Paul receives he passes on "as of first importance." Neither the content of the message nor its prime importance changes for Paul. The same should remain true for those, like the Corinthian saints, who receive it from Paul. Paul delineates these truths to counter the arguments made by "some" in the historical context "that there is no resurrection of the dead" (1 Cor. 15:12). Paul uses the fact of Christ's resurrection to demonstrate the significance of this doctrine for the believer:

> If there is no resurrection of the dead, then not even Christ has been raised. And if Christ has not been raised, our preaching is useless and so is your faith. More than that, we are then found to be false witnesses

about God, for we have testified about God that he raised Christ from the dead. But he did not raise him if in fact the dead are not raised. For if the dead are not raised, then Christ has not been raised either. And if Christ has not been raised, your faith is futile; you are still in your sins. Then those also who have fallen asleep in Christ are lost. If only for this life we have hope in Christ, we are to be pitied more than all men.

But Christ has indeed been raised from the dead, the firstfruits of those who have fallen asleep. (1 Cor. 15:13–20)

Christ's resurrection is an anticipation of the believer's resurrection (see 2 Cor. 4:14)! Moreover, Paul points out to his Corinthian readers that the reality of the resurrection impacts the believer's perspective on ethics and service, and signifies nothing less than victory over death (1 Cor. 15:32, 54–58)!

In this same New Testament correspondence, Paul discusses the proper practice of the so-called sacrament of the Lord's Supper: "For I received from the Lord what I also passed on to you: The Lord Jesus, on the night he was betrayed, took bread, and when he had given thanks, he broke it and said, 'This is my body, which is for you; do this in remembrance of me.' In the same way, after supper he took the cup, saying, 'This cup is the new covenant in my blood; do this, whenever you drink it, in remembrance of me.' For whenever you eat this bread and drink this cup, you proclaim the Lord's death until he comes" (1 Cor. 11:23–26). While there may be debate in the evangelical church today regarding the proper frequency of the Lord's Supper, whenever it is properly celebrated, by design it places Jesus and his sacrificial death at the center of proceedings; to quote Paul, "[it] proclaim[s] the Lord's death until he comes" (v. 26b).

The impact of Christ's death is evident not only in Paul's preaching, but also in his practice. It is an eminently practical doctrine. This can be clearly seen in Paul's Corinthian model of ministry: "When I came to you, brothers, I did not come with eloquence or superior wisdom as I proclaimed to you the testimony about God. For I resolved to know nothing while I was with you except Jesus Christ and him crucified" (1 Cor. 2:1–2). And when Paul counsels the church at Philippi regarding the steps to spiritual unity, the example of Christ in his death is at the heart of his advice (Phil. 2:5–9). The death of Christ also functions as a model to the Corinthian saints of Christian generosity (2 Cor. 8:9), while both the death and resurrection of Christ feature prominently in the apostle's arguments for righteous living when he writes to the saints in Rome. Paul is worth quoting in full at this point:

> What shall we say, then? Shall we go on sinning so that grace may increase? By no means! We died to sin; how can we live in it any longer? Or don't you know that all of us who were baptized into Christ Jesus were baptized into his death? We were therefore buried with him through baptism into death in order that, just as Christ was raised from the dead through the glory of the Father, we too may live a new life.
>
> If we have been united with him like this in his death, we will certainly also be united with him in his resurrection. For we know that our old self was crucified with him so that the body of sin might be done away with, that we should no longer be slaves to sin—because anyone who has died has been freed from sin.
>
> Now if we died with Christ, we believe that we will also live with him. For we know that since Christ was raised from the dead, he cannot die again; death no longer has mastery over him. The death he died, he died to sin once for all; but the life he lives, he lives to God.
>
> In the same way, count yourselves dead to sin but alive to God in Christ Jesus. Therefore do not let sin reign in your mortal body so that you obey its evil desires. Do not offer the parts of your body to sin, as instruments of wickedness, but rather offer yourselves to God, as those who have been brought from death to life; and offer the parts of your body to him as instruments of righteousness. For sin shall not be your master, because you are not under law, but under grace. (Rom. 6:1–14)

Moreover, without too much difficulty, one can make the argument that the sacrificial death of Christ undergirds Paul's extended exhortation to his Roman readers to live lives that resemble "living sacrifices, holy and pleasing to God," whether in the church or in the world (Rom. 12:1–21). It is hardly an exaggeration, then, to suggest that the theme of Christ's death and resurrection permeates the ethics of this significant New Testament letter.

Few would dispute that the death and resurrection of Jesus are key components of the Synoptic Gospel narratives. Mark's Gospel, in particular, has memorably been dubbed a "Passion narrative with an extended introduction."[15] As Mark develops his portrait of "Jesus Christ, the Son of God" (Mark 1:1), it becomes apparent that "Christ" is a title, and that suffering, death, and resurrection are an integral part of the Christ's calling (see Mark 8:29–33). If this is the case, then it is not too much to assert that every time the New Testament subsequently mentions the "Christ" title, these connotations are present. If this conclusion is warranted, then the true significance of Jesus' death and resurrection is seen in the fact that "Christ" occurs in excess of five hundred times in the pages of the New Testament! Those who are offended by the cross today must repent and, like the writers of the New Testament, heed God's command to "listen"!

SUMMARY

"The heavenly glory of [the Transfiguration] is in striking contrast to the humiliation just predicted in Mark 8:31. The Transfiguration thus serves as a counterbalance to the 'gloom' of the preceding verses."[16] Glory is certain, but it is through the death and resurrection of Jesus. You cannot have the one without the other! This is the lesson of the transfiguration in the flow of Mark's Gospel narrative. Both our downward and sideways readings of the text make this point clear.

Our backward reading of this incident in Mark's Gospel reveals numerous parallels and allusions to the Old Testament Sinai incident, and consequently signals to the reader the significance of the events on the Mount of Transfiguration. Jesus is God's Son; he will usher in God's glorious kingdom—therefore, "Listen to him!" (Mark 9:7). Peter's misgivings about Jesus' predictions regarding his suffering, death, and resurrection are misplaced (8:32). Our forward reading of the text confirms this conclusion.

For the modern reader, the challenge is to continue to listen to the now-glorified Jesus whose voice echoes throughout the pages of the New Testament, reminding the reader of the necessity and importance of his suffering, death, and resurrection "after three days" (Mark 8:31). But more than that, the transfiguration event provides hope and encouragement to the Christian reader that glory awaits those who truly listen to Jesus!

15. Martin Kähler, quoted in Craig L. Blomberg, *Jesus and the Gospels* (Leicester, UK: Apollos, 1997), 116.
16. France, *The Gospel of Mark*, 347.

11

JESUS CHALLENGES A RICH MAN

Mark 10:17-31: As Jesus started on his way, a man ran up to him and fell on his knees before him. "Good teacher," he asked, "what must I do to inherit eternal life?"

"Why do you call me good?" Jesus answered. "No one is good— except God alone. You know the commandments: 'Do not murder, do not commit adultery, do not steal, do not give false testimony, do not defraud, honor your father and mother.'"

"Teacher," he declared, "all these I have kept since I was a boy."

Jesus looked at him and loved him. "One thing you lack," he said. "Go, sell everything you have and give to the poor, and you will have treasure in heaven. Then come, follow me."

At this the man's face fell. He went away sad, because he had great wealth.

Jesus looked around and said to his disciples, "How hard it is for the rich to enter the kingdom of God!"

The disciples were amazed at his words. But Jesus said again, "Children, how hard it is to enter the kingdom of God! It is easier for a camel to go through the eye of a needle than for a rich man to enter the kingdom of God."

The disciples were even more amazed, and said to each other, "Who then can be saved?"

Jesus looked at them and said, "With man this is impossible, but not with God; all things are possible with God."

Peter said to him, "We have left everything to follow you!"

"I tell you the truth," Jesus replied, "no one who has left home or brothers or sisters or mother or father or children or fields for me and the gospel will fail to receive a hundred times as much in this present age (homes, brothers, sisters, mothers, children and fields—and with them, persecutions) and in the age to come, eternal life. But many who are first will be last, and the last first."

A DOWNWARD READING

In this text, Jesus has an encounter with a man who asks him an all-important question: "What must I do to inherit eternal life?" (Mark 10:17b). The immediate literary context prepares the reader for the answer. Jesus uses "little children" as an object lesson to make the point to his disciples that "anyone who will not receive the kingdom of God like a little child will never enter it" (v. 15). Similarly, eternal life must be received, like a gift; it cannot be earned. This truth, as we will see, is verified and explained in this present incident. At the outset of the encounter, Mark does not identify or describe the man. Mark obviously intends him to function as a general example for his readers.

There is an element of urgency about this man: he runs up to Jesus and falls on his knees before him (Mark 10:17a). He asks Jesus a question: "Good teacher, . . . what must I do to inherit eternal life?" (10:17b). Jesus, in earlier teaching, has identified two possible eternal destinies—"life" and "hell" (9:43, 45). This man desperately wants life, eternal life! He is confident that Jesus, a "good teacher," will provide the key to his eternal destiny. While Jesus is elsewhere addressed as "teacher" in Mark's Gospel (4:38; 9:17, 38; 10:35; 12:14, 19, 32; 13:1), it is only here that he is addressed as "good teacher." In his reply, Jesus challenges the man's notion of who is "good": "Why do you call *me* good? . . . *No one* is good—except God alone" (10:18). God is "good" and no one else, asserts Jesus. This reply should not be misconstrued to imply that Jesus, unlike God, is not "good"; rather, Jesus appears to be questioning whether the man understands the implications of calling him "good."

Jesus then recites "the commandments": "You know the commandments." This man, who kneels before Jesus, is obviously Jewish in appearance. Jesus then lists a number of commandments—don't murder, commit adultery, steal, lie, defraud, or dishonor your parents (Mark 10:19). The man responds to the implied duty in the list of commandments: "Teacher, . . . all these I have kept since I was a boy" (v. 20). According to one commentator, "This probably refers to the age of thirteen, when every Jewish boy became [a so-called] 'son of the commandment.'"[1] Jesus does not directly challenge his blanket assertion of obedience. Motivated by love, however, Jesus adds a demand, a deficiency in this man's life that needs to be remedied: "One thing you lack . . . . Go, sell everything you have and give to the poor, and you will have treasure in heaven. Then come, follow me" (v. 21).

The "one thing" that Jesus demands comprises a series of commands: "Go, sell . . . give . . . come, follow me." At the heart of these commands, however, is the singular requirement to surrender all earthly possessions to secure "treasure in heaven" (Mark 10:20). This is a prerequisite to following Jesus (cf. v. 28). One commentator puts it this way: "Jesus' summons in this context means that true obedience to the Law is rendered ultimately in discipleship."[2] It is important to note, however, that in the flow of Jesus' teaching it is the surrender of earthly possessions, and not the command to follow Jesus, that will secure "treasure in heaven" (v. 21).

But this "one thing" he cannot do: "At this the man's face fell. He went away sad, because he had great wealth ["possessions," ESV]" (Mark 10:22). Yet Jesus does not lower the standard by retracting or modifying his challenge in the face of the man's response. Jesus exposes a chink in the man's armor of obedience. In effect, Jesus exposes his lack of goodness; God is good, but he is not (v. 18). His obedience is superficial, not real. His treasure on earth, his "great wealth," prevents him from having "treasure in heaven"! According to one commentator, "He had absolutely everything except eternal life. He wanted it but was unwilling to give up everything else to gain it. . . . So the man went away sad from Jesus and we hear no more of him; he had made his choice."[3]

Jesus then uses the man's response as an object lesson for his disciples about the dangers of wealth; it is a stumbling block that makes it difficult for "the rich to enter the kingdom of God" (Mark 10:23b). The disciples, for their part, are "amazed" at Jesus' words (v. 24a), but Jesus

1. Walter W. Wessel, "Mark," in *Matthew, Mark, Luke*, vol. 8 of The Expositor's Bible Commentary (Grand Rapids: Zondervan, 1984), 715.

2. William Lane, *The Gospel of Mark*, New International Commentary on the New Testament (Grand Rapids: Eerdmans, 1974), 367.

3. R. A. Cole, *Mark*, New Bible Commentary: 21st Century Edition (Downers Grove, IL: IVP Academic, 1994), 966.

reinforces the point and, at first, generalizes it: "Children, how hard it is to enter the kingdom of God! It is easier for a camel to go through the eye of a needle than for a rich man to enter the kingdom of God" (vv. 24–25). Jesus' striking word picture implies that it is, in fact, impossible for the rich to enter the kingdom of God, a truth affirmed by the subsequent interaction between Jesus and his disciples (vv. 26–27).

Jesus' disciples are "exceedingly astonished" (Mark 10:26 ESV) by Jesus' teaching at this point. "The escalation from [difficult to impossible] is matched by a corresponding increase in the disciples' astonishment. . . . In a culture which interpreted wealth as a sign of God's blessing, if the rich cannot be saved, who can be?"[4] And so Jesus' disciples ask, "Who then can be saved?" (v. 26). For the disciples, it is unthinkable that a moral rich man is disqualified from entering the kingdom of God! As an aside, it is worth noting here that Jesus equates "inherit[ing] eternal life" in the "age to come" (vv. 17b, 30b) with "hav[ing] treasure in heaven" (v. 21b), "enter[ing] the kingdom of God" (v. 23b), and "be[ing] saved" (v. 26b). Jesus then uses this encounter to drive home an all-important lesson about salvation: "With man this is impossible, but not with God; all things are possible with God" (v. 27). The man's response to Jesus' earlier injunction to "sell everything" simply proves the point: he found it "impossible" to obey Jesus' commandment (vv. 21–22, 27). Clearly, there is nothing that man can "do to inherit eternal life" (v. 17b). He must receive it "like a little child" (v. 15b).

The apostle Peter, a spokesman for the disciples, suggests that they have done the impossible: "We have left everything to follow you!" (Mark 10:28). They have done what the rich man could not do. Jesus uses Peter's claim as a teaching opportunity: "'I tell you the truth,' Jesus replied, 'no one who has left home or brothers or sisters or mother or father or children or fields for me and the gospel will fail to receive a hundred times as much in this present age (homes, brothers, sisters, mothers, children and fields—and with them, persecutions) and in the age to come, eternal life'" (vv. 29–30). Jesus' response acknowledges the cost of following him, but assures everyone, as one commentator puts it, that "the rewards will far outweigh any sacrifices that we may have made for Christ, even if persecution comes along with them."[5] Jesus' reference

---

4. R. T. France, *The Gospel of Mark*, New International Greek Testament Commentary (Grand Rapids: Eerdmans, 2002), 405.
5. Cole, *Mark*, 966.

to "eternal life" in this context reinforces the link between his teaching at this point and the rich man's initial question (v. 17b). In keeping with Jesus' theology of salvation (v. 27), the motivation for sacrifice here is Jesus "and the gospel" (v. 29), not an attempt to merit eternal life, which must be received as a gift. This truth is affirmed by Jesus' concluding pronouncement: "But many who are first will be last, and the last first" (v. 31). According to one commentator, "they should beware of assuming that their 'sacrifice' has earned them a place of special honor."[6] God does not deal with mankind according to the pattern of this world. According to Jesus, "many" will experience a reversal of fortune; those who, like the rich man, have much in this life will lose everything in the age to come, while those who sacrifice everything now for Christ, like the disciples, will have an abundance both now and in the age to come.

A SIDEWAYS READING

All three Synoptic Gospels record this encounter between Jesus and the man (Matt. 19:16–30; Mark 10:17–31; Luke 18:18–30). Luke alone identifies him as "a certain ruler" (Luke 18:18), while Matthew records that he is "young" (Matt. 19:20a). Both Matthew and Mark refer to his "great possessions" (Matt. 19:22 ESV; Mark 10:22 ESV), while Luke describes him as "extremely rich" (Luke 18:23 ESV). He is therefore commonly referred to as "the rich young ruler." Matthew's account in particular reveals some significant divergences from the parallel account in Mark. At various points, these differences shed light on Mark's account:

- Matthew's version of the man's question to Jesus at the outset of the encounter differs at a significant point, exposing a "works-righteousness" mentality: "What *good thing* must I do to get eternal life?" (Matt. 19:16; cf. Mark 10:17b; Luke 18:18b). Jesus' reply to this question in Matthew's Gospel does not raise the issue of Jesus' goodness, suggesting that this issue is not the focal point of the exchange, even in Mark's and Luke's accounts: "Why do you ask me about what is good? . . . There is only One who is good" (Matt. 19:17). Both Mark and Luke make it clear

6. R. T. France, *Matthew*, New Bible Commentary: 21st Century Edition (Downers Grove, IL: IVP Academic, 1994), 930.

that God's goodness is in view (Mark 10:18; Luke 18:19). Jesus immediately quotes a selection of commandments, with the preface in Matthew's account, "If you want to enter life, obey the commandments" (Matt. 19:17b), providing Jesus' rationale for quoting the commandments in the context (Matt. 19:18; cf. Mark 10:19; Luke 18:20).

- Mark alone mentions the command not to "defraud" (Mark 10:19b). In Matthew's list of commandments, Jesus adds, "Love your neighbor as yourself" (Matt. 19:19b), a commandment that Jesus describes elsewhere as one of the "greatest" commandments on which all the Law and the Prophets "hang" (Matt. 22:37–40). This particular commandment may explain Jesus' subsequent instruction to the young man to "go, sell your possessions and give to the poor" (Matt. 19:21; cf. Mark 10:21) as a challenge to demonstrate love for "your neighbor."

- The man declares his obedience to this list of commandments. In Matthew's account, he places no time frame on this obedience: "All these I have kept" (Matt. 19:20a; cf. Mark 10:20; Luke 18:21). Perhaps sensing that the law cannot save him, however, he raises the question: "What do I still lack?" (Matt. 19:20). This question explains the nature of Jesus' response to the young man in Mark's parallel account: "One thing you lack" (Mark 10:21a; cf. Luke 18:22). In Matthew's account, Jesus prefaces the list of commands that follow with the observation, "If you want to be perfect" (Matt. 19:21a; cf. Mark 10:21a). Jesus' reference to perfection here reinforces the standard for entrance into God's kingdom via obedience to "the commandments" (Matt. 19:17b). It is worth noting here that the only other occurrence of *perfect* in Matthew's Gospel is found in Matthew 5:48, where it refers to God who is merciful to both the "righteous and the unrighteous" (see 5:44–48). It could be that Jesus is saying in effect that if you want to be "good," as God is, then "sell your possessions and give to the poor, and you will have treasure in heaven" (19:21).

- Mark alone records Jesus' love for the young man (Mark 10:21a; cf. Matt. 19:21a; Luke 18:22a), a comment that, according to one commentator, "eliminates any suggestion that the man's profession is insincere and that Jesus has been engaged in unmasking hypocrisy."[7]

- According to Matthew 19:23, Jesus prefaces his pronouncement with the words, "I tell you the truth," to emphasize the point that Jesus makes in all three accounts: "It is hard for a rich man to enter the kingdom of heaven" (cf. Mark 10:23; Luke 18:24). Mark and Luke refer to the "kingdom of God" in this context, demonstrating that the "kingdom of heaven" and the "kingdom of God" are interchangeable (see Matt. 19:24).

- Mark alone records Jesus' words: "Children, how hard it is to enter the kingdom of God!" (Mark 10:24). Mark is intent on making the point that it is not only hard for the rich to enter the kingdom of God, but also hard for anyone else to do so. It is probably for this reason that the man's wealth is not mentioned at the outset of the encounter. Mark intends for him to function as a general example of the truth taught, namely, that it is difficult, humanly speaking, for anyone to enter the kingdom of God.

- Mark's version of Jesus' climactic statement in Mark 10:27 varies slightly from the parallel accounts: "With man this is impossible, but not with God; all things are possible with God" (cf. Matt. 19:26; Luke 18:27). Mark's repeated reference to "God" simply reinforces the essential role of God in the work of salvation.

- In response, Peter tells Jesus, "We have left everything to follow you!" (Mark 10:28). In Matthew's account, Peter adds, "What then will there be for us?" (Matt. 19:27b). This addition explains Jesus' subsequent teaching on rewards that follows in a more expanded form in Mark's account. Most notable is Mark's inclusion of "persecutions" (Mark 10:29–30; cf. Matt. 19:29; Luke 18:29–30).

A sideways reading provides some helpful insights into this encounter between Jesus and this rich young ruler in Mark's Gospel. In particular, Matthew's account sheds light on Jesus' strategy as he responds to the man's initial question, "Teacher, what good thing must I do to get eternal life?" (Matt. 19:16): "If you want to enter life, obey the commandments" (v. 17). "If you want to be perfect . . ." (v. 21). Mark does not include these conditional statements of Jesus because they are not important for his

---

7. France, *The Gospel of Mark*, 403.

purposes. Mark is not seeking to provide a blueprint for evangelism in this incident; rather, he is concerned to make a single overriding point: that man is not "good," and consequently cannot meet the "perfect" standard required to inherit eternal life through obedience to the commandments (cf. Mark 10:18; Matt. 19:21–22). Accordingly, it is impossible for anyone to save himself. But what is impossible for man is possible for God; he alone can save (Mark 10:26–27).

A BACKWARD READING

The reader may recognize that Jesus quotes a selection of the Old Testament Ten Commandments in response to the man's initial question (Mark 10:18–19; cf. Ex. 20:12–16). According to Jesus, obedience to these commandments is the pathway to eternal life (Matt. 19:17b). Jesus hereby refers to the strand of Old Testament teaching whereby God affirms that those who keep his "decrees and laws" will live: "Keep my decrees and laws, for the man who obeys them will live by them. I am the LORD" (Lev. 18:5; cf. Deut 30:15–16; Ezek. 20:11).

Jesus lists the sixth, seventh, eighth, ninth, and fifth commandments, in that order—commandments that focus on man's relationship to man (Mark 10:19; cf. Ex. 20:12–16). There is no mention of the tenth commandment against coveting, but in Mark's Gospel, Jesus adds the command not to "defraud." One commentator views this command as "a substitute for the commandment against coveting, fraud being a manifestation of coveting."[8] Another commentator, however, detects an allusion to this unmentioned commandment in Jesus' subsequent commands to the man to "sell everything . . . and give to the poor" (Mark 10:21). His comments are worth quoting in full:

> To relinquish one's desire [for earthly possessions] was to keep the one commandment Jesus had not heretofore mentioned, "Thou shalt not covet," a part of the second table of the law which dealt with loving one's neighbor as oneself. This commandment was the only part of the second table that put the emphasis on internal righteousness, on the motive and not the external act. Hence, Jesus tested him on his perfect obedience to the commandment, "Thou shalt not covet" . . .

8. Wessel, "Mark," 715.

[However], not only did the [rich young ruler] violate the second table of the law, but he violated the first and greatest commandment, "Love the Lord your God with all your heart, with all your soul and with all your mind" (Matt 22:37). Covetousness is a form of idolatry (Col 3:5). He . . . worshipped the god of money as well as the God of Israel (Exod 20:3). He certainly did not love the Lord with all his heart, soul, and might (Deut 6:5). His love of possessions kept him from a total love for the Lord. The [rich young ruler] made his decision in violation of the law in both love of neighbor and love of God (cf. 1 John 4:20).[9]

Consequently, although the rich man considers himself to be a law-keeper, Jesus exposes his inability to obey the true intent of the law. In a nutshell, Jesus succeeds in verifying that indeed "God alone" is good (Mark 10:18b)!

Jesus is apparently not surprised at the ultimate response of this young man; he knows that God alone is good (cf. Mark 10:18). Yet the young man himself is surprised, to say the least: "At this the man's face fell. He went away sad, because he had great wealth ["possessions," ESV]" (v. 22). According to one lexicon, his facial expression can best be translated as "shocked" or even "appalled" (cf. Ezek. 27:35; 28:19; 32:10 LXX), with the connotation of experiencing "great surprise because of something which appears incredible and alarming."[10] Clearly, he does not expect Jesus' demands. Jesus' disciples, similarly, are "amazed" at his subsequent teaching on the matter: "How hard it is for the rich to enter the kingdom of God!" (Mark 10:23–24). And when Jesus subsequently asserts that "it is easier for a camel to go through the eye of a needle than for a rich man to enter the kingdom of God," his disciples are "even more amazed, and [say] to each other, 'Who then can be saved?'" (vv. 25–26).

A backward reading of the text sheds light on these responses to Jesus' teaching on wealth and salvation. A number of Old Testament texts portray wealth as a sign of divine blessing: "Blessed are all who fear the LORD, who walk in his ways. You will eat the fruit of your labor; blessings and prosperity will be yours" (Ps. 128:1–2). And again: "Praise the LORD. Blessed is the man who fears the LORD, who finds great delight in his

9. Hal. M. Haller, " Did the Rich Young Ruler Hear the Gospel according to Jesus?" *Journal of the Grace Evangelical Society* 13, 2 (2000): 33.

10. J. P. Louw and Eugene A. Nida, *Greek-English Lexicon of the New Testament: Based on Semantic Domains*, vol. 1 (New York: United Bible Societies, 1996), 312.

commands. . . . Wealth and riches are in his house, and his righteousness endures forever" (Ps. 112:1, 3; cf. Deut. 28:1–14; Job 42:10). While it is true that the wicked also prosper and increase in wealth (e.g., Ps. 73:12; Prov. 28:6), this man's wealth, coupled with his track record of obedience to God's law, suggests to the observer that his prosperity is from the hand of God (Mark 10:30). In any event, the shock and amazement in the context indicate that both the man and the disciples share what one commentator calls "the common view of the time that riches were a sign of God's blessing."[11] When Jesus' disciples subsequently ask the question, "Who then can be saved?" (v. 26b), Jesus uses the occasion to drive home the all-important truth regarding salvation: "With man this is impossible, but not with God; all things are possible with God" (v. 27).

A FORWARD READING

Does Jesus command all seekers to sell all and give to the poor in order to secure "treasure in heaven" (Mark 10:21b)? Is this a universal requirement for salvation? This most important question merits a forward reading of the text.

At one point in Luke's Gospel, Jesus challenges his disciples to "sell your possessions and give to the poor. Provide purses for yourselves that will not wear out, a treasure in heaven that will not be exhausted" (Luke 12:33). This set of commands sounds strikingly similar to Jesus' set of instructions to the rich young ruler (cf. Mark 10:21b). But the context is different: Jesus is admonishing his disciples to trust their heavenly Father to meet their basic needs (Luke 12:22–31). Later in Luke's Gospel, Jesus informs the large crowds traveling with him that "any of you who does not give up everything he has cannot be my disciple" (Luke 14:33; cf. 5:11, 28). Certainly Peter interprets Jesus' demand to the rich young ruler in this way (Mark 10:28; cf. 10:21). Clearly, a cost is involved to follow Jesus. In Luke's Gospel, however, the context is the call to discipleship, whereas in his encounter with the rich young ruler, Jesus is responding to the question: "What must I do to inherit eternal life?" (Mark 10:17b). A similar question is asked of Jesus in Luke's Gospel, when an expert in the law stands up to test Jesus: "Teacher, . . . what must I do to inherit eternal life?" (Luke 10:25). As in the case of the rich young ruler, Jesus

11. Donald A. Hagner, *Matthew 14–28*, Word Biblical Commentary 33b (Dallas: Word, 1995), 561.

points the lawyer to God's law (v. 26) and adds, "Do this and you will live" (v. 28; cf. v. 37b). Significantly, however, in this incident there are no specific commands to sell all and give to the poor.

If we survey the remainder of the New Testament, conspicuous by its absence are any similar injunctions. In the life of the early church, believers sell their goods to benefit those in need, but their actions are voluntary and are a response to the work of God's Holy Spirit in the context (see Acts 2:44–45; 4:32–35). Jesus almost certainly has this scenario of communal sharing in view when he encourages his followers with the promise of "a hundred times as much in this present age" if they make sacrifices for him and the gospel in this life (Mark 10:29–30).

Paul commands "those who are rich in this present world . . . to be generous and willing to share" as a means to "lay up treasure for themselves as a firm foundation for the coming age, so that they may take hold of the life that is truly life" (1 Tim. 6:17–19). Only the rich are in view, however, and the standard—"be generous and willing to share" (1 Tim. 6:18)—is not comparable to Jesus' command to "sell everything you have" (Mark 10:21b). Elsewhere Paul encourages, but does not command, generosity among the saints with a number of compelling examples of generosity (2 Cor. 8:1–9). Significantly, according to Paul, sacrificial giving is a reflection of God's grace to the believer (2 Cor. 8:1). When this apostle writes to the Philippian church, he refers to the cost of following Jesus: "for [his] sake [Paul has] lost all things" (Phil. 3:8). In the context, however, the cost appears to refer to a loss of earthly prestige rather than earthly possessions (Phil. 3:4–7; 4:10–13).

If Jesus' command to sell all cannot be universalized, then how does one "inherit eternal life" (Mark 10:17)? In John's Gospel, Jesus makes it clear that "everyone who looks to the Son and believes in him shall have eternal life" (John 6:40). The apostle Paul reflects this same understanding: eternal life is a "gift of God . . . in Christ Jesus our Lord" (Rom. 6:23; cf. John 10:28; 17:2). It is clear that eternal life is by faith in the work of Christ, and not based on the works of man (see Eph. 2:5, 8–9; 2 Tim. 1:9–10; Titus 3:5). The apostle Paul's own conversion experience bears powerful testimony to this truth (1 Tim. 1:16; cf. Acts 9:1–19). Both the apostles Peter and John also affirm it (see Acts 4:12; 1 John 5:11–12).

It is against this biblical background that Paul's teaching in Romans 2:7 should be interpreted: "To those who by persistence in doing good seek glory, honor and immortality, he will give eternal life" (cf. Rom. 2:13, 26–27). While it is possible that Paul is here simply affirming the biblical truth that saving faith produces good deeds (see James 2:14–26; cf. Eph. 2:8–10), Paul cannot be advocating salvation by good works in view of his subsequent conclusion that "all have sinned and fall short of the glory of God" (Rom. 3:23; cf. 3:9–18). Consequently, no one will be saved by the law (see Rom. 3:20; Gal. 2:16; 3:10–12, 18). Therefore, Jesus should not be understood as teaching salvation by works of the law in his encounter with the rich young ruler (Mark 10:17–21).

While it is true that the law of God offers life to those who can obey it (see Lev. 18:5; Matt. 19:17b; Luke 10:25–28; Rom. 10:5), the response of the rich young ruler bears compelling testimony to the truth that natural man cannot obey it (Mark 10:22). To quote Jesus, "no one is good—except God alone" (v. 18). The fact that the man "went away sad, because he had great wealth" (v. 22), simply makes the point that even the rich, contrary to popular theological belief, are not good! At this point, the man disappears from the scene. It is therefore only Jesus' disciples who hear the solution to their dilemma: "Who then can be saved?" Jesus looks at them and says, "With man this is impossible, but not with God; all things are possible with God" (vv. 26–27). It is precisely at this point that we discover Mark's purpose in recording this encounter: to show the Christian reader why the kingdom of God must be received "like a little child" (v. 15). Eternal life is a gift because no one is good enough to merit it (v. 18)! Salvation is possible because of God's intervention in our hopeless circumstances (see v. 27). Herein lies the good news. It is apparent that Mark records this particular incident not because it teaches the gospel, but because it exposes our need for the gospel!

SUMMARY

This incident is triggered by an all-important question that an unnamed man addresses to Jesus: "What must I do to inherit eternal life?" (Mark 10:17). A downward reading of the text identifies the thrust of Jesus' response to this question: eternal life is a gift that must be received from God because no one is good enough to merit it (see Mark 10:15, 18, 27). Our forward reading of the text reveals that this is the consistent teaching of the New Testament Scriptures (see John 6:40; Rom. 3:20; 6:23; Gal. 2:16; 1 John 5:11–12).

Both our sideways and backward readings of the text clarify Jesus' strategy in his encounter with this young man. Jesus quotes the law of God in response to the man's question, not to contradict the concept of salvation as a gift, but rather to verify it: "If you want to enter life, obey the commandments" (Matt. 19:17; cf. Lev. 18:5). The man asserts his obedience to the law of God, but Jesus exposes his inability to do the "one thing" he lacks (Mark 10:21–22; cf. vv. 18–20), demonstrating that salvation is possible only with God's help (vv. 18, 27).

At this point in the narrative, it is revealed that the man has "great wealth," which functions as a barrier to eternal life (Mark 10:22). He is not initially introduced as a rich man, possibly because Mark wants to make the point that wealth is not the only barrier to eternal life. To the utter amazement of his disciples, however, Jesus asserts that, contrary to popular expectation, it is impossible even for the rich to enter the kingdom of God (vv. 25–26). If this is true for the rich, how much more so for others! But salvation is possible with God (v. 27)! Here is the good news of the gospel.

It is in this context that Jesus' concluding pronouncement should be understood: "But many who are first will be last, and the last first" (Mark 10:31). Those who become like "little child[ren]," despised by the world in the context, can enter the kingdom of God, while the moral rich, admired by the world in the context, can't enter (cf. vv. 15, 25)! According to one commentator, this episode is all about the "upside down" values of the kingdom of God that challenge "conventional human values."[12]

We conclude by asking what this particular incident in Mark's Gospel teaches us about Jesus. Significantly, in the context Jesus is addressed and portrayed as a "good teacher" who clearly articulates the way to "inherit eternal life" (Mark 10:17, 20). The call is to follow Jesus, but this pathway is costly and difficult; indeed, it is humanly impossible (vv. 21–25). But according to Jesus, with God's help it is possible (v. 27). The response of Peter and his fellow disciples to the sacrificial call of Jesus is evidence of this truth (v. 28). In a nutshell, Jesus is portrayed as the One who has the words of eternal life (see John 6:68)!

12. France, *The Gospel of Mark*, 399.

12

JESUS CLEARS THE TEMPLE

Mark 11:15–19: On reaching Jerusalem, Jesus entered the temple area and began driving out those who were buying and selling there. He overturned the tables of the money changers and the benches of those selling doves, and would not allow anyone to carry merchandise through the temple courts. And as he taught them, he said, "Is it not written:

"'My house will be called
a house of prayer for all nations'?

But you have made it 'a den of robbers.'"
The chief priests and the teachers of the law heard this and began looking for a way to kill him, for they feared him, because the whole crowd was amazed at his teaching.
When evening came, they went out of the city.

A DOWNWARD READING

After Jesus' so-called triumphal entry (Mark 11:1–10), the setting in Mark's Gospel shifts to the Jerusalem temple, where much of the action occurs in the next few chapters (see 11:11, 15–16, 27; 12:35, 41; 13:1). This is the setting of our text in which Jesus clears the temple (11:15–19). After Jesus enters Jerusalem, he visits the temple and looks around it, but because of the lateness of the hour, he retreats to nearby Bethany with his disciples (v. 11). It is important to note that it is only the next day, after the cursing of a fig tree (v. 21b), that Jesus clears the temple, no doubt responding to what he had seen the evening before (vv. 12–17). This sequence of events suggests that Jesus wants his disciples to see a connection between these two incidents, a connection that Mark reinforces by sandwiching the clearing of the temple with the cursing of the fig tree and its aftermath (vv. 12–21).

There is a clear "judgment" motif in Jesus' words directed against the fig tree: "May no one ever eat fruit from you again" (Mark 11:14). Mark points out that Jesus' "disciples heard him say it," indicating that Jesus intends for them to learn a lesson from the incident. Accordingly, Jesus' act of cursing the fig tree should not be construed as arbitrary or vindictive. Jesus then enters the temple area. One commentator conjures up a rather vivid picture of what greets him: "The smell of the animals entered his nostrils; and the noise from the moneychangers' tables beat on his ears."[1] But Mark's style is terse and devoid of such detail. In quick and dramatic fashion, Jesus clears the temple. A number of commentators suggest that the court of the Gentiles is probably in view, although Mark is nonspecific.[2] Jesus begins to drive out those who both buy and sell in the temple. He overturns "the tables of the money changers and the benches of those selling doves," and does "not allow anyone to carry merchandise through the temple courts" (Mark 11:15–16). All those in view in some way contribute toward the functioning of the sacrificial system in the temple. The temple worshipers in Jerusalem need animals to sacrifice; the visitors to Jerusalem need local currency for this purpose. The commercial activity that caters to these needs is all located in the temple area. Jesus' actions appear intent on shutting down all this activity that supports the sacrificial system in the temple.

Mark then records Jesus' pronouncement in the temple. According to him, the divine purpose of God's "house," the temple, has been perverted: "Is it not written: 'My house will be called a house of prayer for all nations'? But you have made it 'a den of robbers'" (Mark 11:17). The response of the chief priests and teachers of the law who hear Jesus' accusation is to begin to look for a way to "destroy him" (3:6 ESV); they

---

1. Walter W. Wessel, "Mark," in *Matthew, Mark, Luke*, vol. 8 of The Expositor's Bible Commentary (Grand Rapids: Zondervan, 1984), 727.

2. See, for example, James R. Edwards, *The Gospel according to Mark*, Pillar New Testament Commentary (Grand Rapids: Eerdmans, 2002), 342.

fear Jesus "because the whole crowd [is] amazed at his teaching" (11:18; cf. 1:22; 6:2). The response of the religious leaders is instructive; it is uniformly hostile toward Jesus, and violently so. This is in sharp contrast to the adulation directed toward Jesus by the crowds outside Jerusalem the previous day, and the amazement of the crowds at his teaching in the context (cf. Mark 11:8–10, 18b). Jesus threatens the influence of the religious leaders with the crowds; this is the sole motivation for their murderous intent! It simply provides further vindication for Jesus' actions in the temple.

Mark concludes his record of this incident with the comment, "When evening came, they went out of the city" (Mark 11:19). This brief sentence provides a quick transition to a second encounter with the fig tree that Jesus has cursed, reinforcing the connection between this incident and Jesus' actions in the temple (vv. 12–14). The following morning, the disciples see the fig tree that Jesus cursed, withered from the roots. Peter calls attention to it: "Rabbi, look! The fig tree you cursed has withered!" (vv. 20–21). Jesus' earlier word of judgment is pictured as fulfilled; the fig tree is "withered from the roots" (v. 20). Truly, no one will ever eat fruit from it again (see v. 14)!

It is clear from the way in which the narrative is structured that this "judgment" motif in the fig-tree incident provides the key to understanding Mark's portrayal of Jesus' actions in the temple. Jesus does not clear the temple to reform its worship, as some have suggested, but to signal its coming destruction.[3] There is no note of mercy in Jesus' actions or teaching in the temple. There will be no reprieve; the temple will be destroyed (Mark 13:1–2). As one commentator notes, "Jesus does not in any way interpret the [withered tree]. Yet the meaning is obvious: Jesus' predicted judgment on the temple will come to pass as surely as his prediction of the withering of the fig tree."[4]

A SIDEWAYS READING

All three Synoptic Gospels record Jesus' act of clearing the temple (Matt. 21:12–13; Mark 11:15–17; Luke 19:45–46). John's Gospel records a

---

3. See the discussion in David E. Garland, *Mark*, NIV Application Commentary (Grand Rapids: Zondervan, 1996), 434–39.
4. Wessel, "Mark," 729.

MARK BY THE BOOK

similar incident, but this most likely refers to another incident that occurs toward the beginning of Jesus' public ministry (John 2:14–17). Both Matthew and Mark mention Jesus' act of cursing the fig tree in the context (cf. Matt. 21:18–19; Mark 11:12–14), but only in Mark's account is the clearing of the temple sandwiched by this incident. This sideways observation supports our contention that Mark intends the cursing of the fig tree to function as the key to understanding Jesus' purpose in clearing the temple. In this regard, it is worth noting that Mark alone refers to the fact that Jesus did not find fruit on the tree "because it was not the season for figs" (Mark 11:13; cf. Matt. 21:19). One commentator explains the significance of this detail in Mark's narrative:

> This detail is a clue for the reader to look beyond the surface meaning and to see its symbolic meaning. This action is not about a particular unfruitful fig tree; it has to do with the temple. The word "season" (*kairos*) is not the botanical term for the growing season but the religious term found in 1:14–15 denoting the time of the kingdom of God (see 13:33). Moreover, the tenants do not produce the fruits of the vineyard "at harvest time" (12:2; lit., "in season"). The barren fig tree represents the barrenness of temple Judaism.[5]

In both Mark and Matthew, albeit with some variation, Jesus' subsequent curse directed at the fig tree strikes a clear and all-encompassing note of finality: "May no one ever eat fruit from you again" (Mark 11:14; cf. Matt. 21:19). Mark reinforces the sense of finality with the subsequent observation that Jesus' disciples "saw the fig tree withered *from the roots*" (Mark 11:20).

A number of other elements in the narrative are unique to Mark's account. Mark alone mentions the fact that Jesus enters the temple "on reaching Jerusalem" (Mark 11:15). In Mark's Gospel, "Jerusalem" is depicted as the home of Jesus' opponents, the Pharisees and teachers of the law (see 3:22; 7:1), and the place where he will be "betrayed to the chief priests and teachers of the law," condemned to death, and handed "over to the Gentiles" (10:33). Significantly, the adulation directed toward Jesus in the so-called triumphal entry takes place outside Jerusalem, before he enters it (11:8–11). It is clear that Jerusalem is a place where Jesus is not

5. Garland, *Mark*, 440.

venerated (vv. 27–33). This is the location of the temple, a place of worship that reflects its Jerusalem setting (see vv. 17–18). It is possible that Mark's reference to "Jerusalem" in our text alludes to this negative perspective, and is intended to prepare the reader for Jesus' confrontational actions in the temple (vv. 15–17).

In his description of Jesus' actions in the temple, only Mark includes the observation that Jesus "would not allow anyone to carry merchandise through the temple courts" (Mark 11:16), to emphasize the point that Jesus intends to shut down the temple sacrificial system, albeit temporarily and symbolically, rather than reform it. This is an act of judgment, not an appeal for reform! This perspective is reinforced by Jesus' teaching in the context. There is no hint of mercy in Jesus' words of condemnation.

Significantly, Mark alone includes the reference to the "nations": "Is it not written: 'My house will be called a house of prayer *for all nations*'? But you have made it 'a den of robbers'" (Mark 11:17; cf. Matt. 21:13; Luke 19:46). This mention of the "nations" is a rebuke to Jesus' hearers, but would be an encouragement to Mark's Gentile readers. God has always had a heart for the nations; this is evident in Mark's Gospel (see Mark 13:10).

Mark and Luke both refer to the negative response of the religious leaders to Jesus' teaching in the temple, although only Mark identifies the reason for this adverse reaction: "The chief priests and the teachers of the law heard this and began looking for a way to kill him, for they feared him, because the whole crowd was amazed at his teaching" (Mark 11:18; cf. Luke 19:47–48). The amazement of the crowd echoes the reaction of those who had heard Jesus earlier in the synagogue in Capernaum (Mark 1:22; cf. 6:2). It is clear that only the religious authorities are opposed to Jesus at this point. Jesus had predicted this (see 8:31; 10:33–34). It is striking that both Jesus' disciples and the religious leaders hear his words of judgment in the context (see 11:14b, 18); there is a lesson for both of them.

This incident ends with the brief comment, unique to Mark's Gospel, that "when evening came, [Jesus and his disciples] went out of the city" (Mark 11:19). It is unclear whether Jesus' departure has any symbolic intent for Mark. The comment provides a quick transition to the aftermath of the cursing of the fig tree, with its attendant symbolism for the temple (vv. 20–21).

A BACKWARD READING

Jesus' recorded teaching in the temple commences with the words, "Is it not written . . . ?," alerting the reader to the presence of an Old Testament quotation (Mark 11:17). A backward reading of the text reveals a composite quotation drawn from both the prophets Isaiah and Jeremiah. Reading each quotation in its Old Testament context is instructive.

The first Old Testament passage that Jesus quotes is taken from Isaiah 56. In this Old Testament context, the Lord has words of promise for both the foreigner and the eunuch excluded from God's temple (Isa. 56:3–8). Jesus focuses on "the foreigner." According to Isaiah, the Lord will not exclude from his people the foreigner "who has bound himself to the LORD" (Isa. 56:3). According to the Lord, "their burnt offerings and sacrifices will be accepted on my altar; for my house will be called a house of prayer for all nations" (Isa. 56:7). Clearly, as far as Jesus is concerned, based on his observations in the temple (see Mark 11:11), the buying and selling in the court of the Gentiles has functioned to effectively exclude the Gentiles from praying in God's temple. This is a violation of God's intended purposes for his "house" (Mark 11:17), and a stumbling block to his purposes to "gather still others . . . besides those already gathered" (Isa. 56:8).

A second quotation is taken from Jeremiah 7. In the Old Testament context, God calls Jeremiah to stand at the gate of the Lord's house to proclaim a message to all the "people of Judah" (Jer. 7:2). The first segment of this message is worth quoting in full:

> Hear the word of the LORD, all you people of Judah who come through these gates to worship the LORD. This is what the LORD Almighty, the God of Israel, says: Reform your ways and your actions, and I will let you live in this place. Do not trust in deceptive words and say, "This is the temple of the LORD, the temple of the LORD, the temple of the LORD!" If you really change your ways and your actions and deal with each other justly, if you do not oppress the alien, the fatherless or the widow and do not shed innocent blood in this place, and if you do not follow other gods to your own harm, then I will let you live in this place, in the land I gave your forefathers for ever and ever. But look, you are trusting in deceptive words that are worthless.
>
> Will you steal and murder, commit adultery and perjury, burn incense to Baal and follow other gods you have not known, and then

come and stand before me in this house, which bears my Name, and say, "We are safe"—safe to do all these detestable things? Has this house, which bears my Name, become a den of robbers to you? But I have been watching! declares the LORD. (Jer. 7:2–11)

It is apparent that God's people are guilty of all manner of sin, yet they believe they are exempt from divine judgment because of the presence of God's temple in their midst: "We are safe," they say, "safe to do all these detestable things" (Jer. 7:10b). But these are "deceptive words that are worthless," according to the Lord (Jer. 7:8). It is against this background that God questions whether "this house which bears my Name"—"my house" (Mark 11:17)—has "become a den of robbers to [them]" (Jer. 7:11).

In Mark's Gospel, Jesus couches this question as an indictment that he levels against those he encounters in the temple (Mark 11:17). At first glance, it may appear that Jesus is targeting the commercial activity in the temple, and denouncing the robbing of the worshipers there who are being charged excessive prices for sacrificial animals or exorbitant rates to exchange foreign currency (see vv. 15–16). Yet Jeremiah does not include trading in the temple in the catalogue of sins he lists; rather, as we have seen, his message denounces a disobedient and wicked people for their false sense of security in the temple and its sacrificial system. One commentator spells out the implications for understanding Jesus' use of Jeremiah's prophecy:

> The robbers are not swindlers but bandits, and they do not do their robbing in their den. The den is the place where robbers retreat after having committed their crimes. It is their hideout, a place of security and refuge. Calling the temple a robbers' den is therefore not a cry of outrage against any dishonest business practices in the temple. Jesus indirectly attacks them for allowing the temple to degenerate into a safe hiding place where people think that they find forgiveness and fellowship with God no matter how they act on the outside. Jesus' prophetic action and words attack a false trust in the efficacy of the temple sacrificial system.... The sanctuary ... has become a sanctuary for bandits who think that they are protected from God's judgment. The phrase "I have been watching" (Jer. 7:11) matches the description of Jesus' visit to the temple on the previous day, when he "looked around at everything" (Mark 11:11), turning that visit into an inspection. Jesus

shares the purview of God. He has seen what the people are doing and pronounces God's judgment.[6]

This "judgment" motif is reinforced in the next portion of Jeremiah's prophecy. Although the God of Israel will let his people live if they reform their ways and actions (Jer. 7:3), they have a pattern of not listening to his words; now God will not listen to their pleas for mercy:

> Go now to the place in Shiloh where I first made a dwelling for my Name, and see what I did to it because of the wickedness of my people Israel. While you were doing all these things, declares the LORD, I spoke to you again and again, but you did not listen; I called you, but you did not answer. Therefore, what I did to Shiloh I will now do to the house that bears my Name, the temple you trust in, the place I gave to you and your fathers. I will thrust you from my presence, just as I did all your brothers, the people of Ephraim.
>
> So do not pray for this people nor offer any plea or petition for them; do not plead with me, for I will not listen to you. . . .
>
> . . . My anger and my wrath will be poured out on this place, on man and beast, on the trees of the field and on the fruit of the ground, and it will burn and not be quenched. (Jer. 7:12–20)

This same "judgment" motif is evident when Jesus clears the temple (cf. Mal. 3:1–5). What God did to the tabernacle at Shiloh (Ps. 78:60–64) he will do to the temple in Jerusalem (Jer. 7:14); what Jesus does to the fig tree God will do to the temple (Mark 11:12–21; cf. 13:1–2). Judgment is just as certain as the withering of the fig tree in the context, and just as permanent (Mark 11:14, 20–21). But while the "people of Judah" are in view in Jeremiah's prophecy (Jer. 7:2), in Mark's Gospel Jesus targets the religious leaders rather than the entire nation (Mark 11:18; cf. 12:9–12). Like the leafy but barren fig tree that Jesus sees in the distance, these leaders, from a distance, give a false impression of obedience to the Lord. But Jesus is not fooled; they are hypocrites. According to one commentator, "A people which honoured God with their lips but whose heart was all the time far from him (Mark 7:6), was like a tree with abundance of leaves but no fruit."[7] They will be judged along with the destruction of the temple (see Mark 13:1–2).

6. Ibid., 439.
7. C. E. B. Cranfield, quoted in Wessel, "Mark," 726.

A FORWARD READING

A number of different motifs in this text may warrant a forward reading. For example, God intends the temple to function as "a house of prayer for all nations" (Mark 11:17). Both the motifs of prayer and God's heart for the nations, recorded only in Mark's account (cf. Matt. 21:13b; Luke 19:45b), qualify for a forward reading. Alternatively, the "temple" motif can also profitably be traced through the pages of the New Testament, particularly in light of Jesus' actions and teaching that predicted its demise (Mark 11:12–21; 13:1–2). According to apostolic teaching, the temple is redefined (see 1 Cor. 3:16–17; 6:19; Eph. 2:21; Rev. 3:12; 21:22). This new so-called people-temple is built around Jesus Christ, "the capstone" (see Mark 12:10–11). But we will instead focus our forward reading on the "judgment" motif that pervades our text. No doubt Mark wants his readers to clearly grasp this motif by sandwiching the clearing of the temple with Jesus' act of cursing the fig tree (11:12–21). This judgment, symbolically enacted, is directed against the temple and the religious leaders of the day (see 12:9–12). The question we need to grapple with is how this "judgment" motif applies to the Christian reader today.

As we trace this motif through the pages of the New Testament, it is immediately apparent that the motif cannot be limited to the temple and the religious elite of Jesus' day. In the Sermon on the Mount (Matt. 5–7), Jesus concludes his message with a series of striking word pictures that portray the end-of-the-age judgment (Matt. 7:13–27). As in the case of our text, the issue revolves around fruitfulness, a metaphor for obedience to God's Word: "Every tree that does not bear good fruit is cut down and thrown into the fire" (Matt. 7:19; cf. Mark 11:14). And "not everyone who says to me, 'Lord, Lord,' will enter the kingdom of heaven, but only he who does the will of my Father who is in heaven" (Matt. 7:21).

Like Jeremiah's prophecy referred to in our text (Mark 11:17; cf. Jer. 7:9–10), an element of deception is also present in this context: "Many will say to me on that day, 'Lord, Lord, did we not prophesy in your name, and in your name drive out demons and perform many miracles?' Then I will tell them plainly, 'I never knew you. Away from me, you evildoers!'" (Matt. 7:22–23). The same note of judgment is struck in the concluding parable of the wise and foolish builders: "But everyone who hears these words of mine and does not put them into practice is like a foolish man who built his house on sand. The rain came down, the streams rose, and the winds blew and beat against that house, and it fell with a great crash" (Matt. 7:26–27).

Although at various points in this section of the Sermon on the Mount judgment on false prophets is in view (e.g., Matt. 7:15–23), the concluding parable has a broader focus: "everyone who hears these words of mine" (7:24, 26). This includes Jesus' disciples (5:1–2) and the crowds who overhear his message (7:28). Jesus' message to them is clear: it is not sufficient to be a hearer of the Word; only doers of the Word will be able to stand in the judgment. In the parallel account in Luke's Gospel, Jesus paints a rather graphic picture of this judgment: "The moment the torrent struck that house, it collapsed and its destruction was complete" (Luke 6:49b; cf. Matt. 7:27b). We see this same "works" motif in Jesus' parable of the sheep and the goats, a parable about universal judgment (Matt. 25:31–46). In this parable, all the nations are gathered before the Son of Man, Jesus, to give an account to him when he returns in "his glory" (Matt. 25:31–33).

Paul, the writer to the Hebrews, Peter, Jude, and John all make reference to a forthcoming judgment that includes their Christian readers (see 2 Cor. 5:10; Heb. 9:27; 1 Peter 1:17; 4:17; Jude 14–15; Rev. 20:12–13). According to Paul, "we must all appear before the judgment seat of Christ, that each one may receive what is due him for the things done while in the body, whether good or bad" (2 Cor. 5:10). With the reference to "we," Paul makes the point that even he, as an apostle, is not exempt from this judgment. The apostle John, however, makes it clear that there will be differing destinies for believers and unbelievers, or those whose names are "not found written in the book of life":

> And I saw the dead, great and small, standing before the throne, and books were opened. Another book was opened, which is the book of life. The dead were judged according to what they had done as recorded in the books. The sea gave up the dead that were in it, and death and Hades gave up the dead that were in them, and each person was judged according to what he had done. Then death and Hades were thrown into the lake of fire. The lake of fire is the second death. If anyone's name was not found written in the book of life, he was thrown into the lake of fire. (Rev. 20:12–15)

References to the "book of life," described in this vision, are scattered throughout the Old and New Testament Scriptures, with a cluster of references in the book of Revelation (Ps. 69:28; Phil. 4:3; Rev. 3:5; 13:8; 17:8; 20:12, 15; 21:27; cf. Ex. 32:32; Dan. 7:10; 12:1; Mal. 3:16; Luke 10:20; Heb. 12:23). Chosen by God "from the creation of the world" (Rev. 17:8), "those whose names are written in the Lamb's book of life" will experience the glories and eternal blessings of the new heaven and new earth (Rev. 21:27). These names refer to "the church of the firstborn" (Heb. 12:23), "purchased . . . for God from every tribe and language and people and nation" by the blood of the Lamb, Jesus Christ (Rev. 5:9; cf. 1:5). It is apparent that the Jesus who judges is also the Jesus who saves, apart from works!

SUMMARY

In our text, Jesus clears the temple. Our downward and sideways readings of the text highlight the crucial role that Jesus' cursing of the fig tree plays in interpreting this action. The clearing of the temple is an anticipation of divine judgment, symbolized by the cursing of the fig tree and its aftermath that sandwich Jesus' actions in the temple (Mark 11:12–14, 20–21). By these actions, Jesus intends to symbolize the temple's destruction, not call for its reform (Mark 13:2; cf. John 2:16).

Our backward reading of the text clarifies Jesus' indictment of the temple administration. The problem is not that the worshipers are being robbed by the commercialization of the temple worship; rather, the religious elite reject God's rule in their lives and yet view the temple as a secure haven despite their sin. In this sense, it has become "a den of robbers" (Mark 11:17b; cf. Jer. 7:1–11).

Our forward reading of the text highlights the prominent "judgment" motif in the text. It underscores the truth that all mankind, including all believers, not just disobedient Israel, will face judgment one day. But according to the good news of the gospel, the Jesus who judges is also the Jesus who "rescues us from the coming wrath" (1 Thess. 1:10b).

13

JESUS ENDORSES THE COMMANDMENT TO LOVE

Mark 12:28–34: One of the teachers of the law came and heard them debating. Noticing that Jesus had given them a good answer, he asked him, "Of all the commandments, which is the most important?"

"The most important one," answered Jesus, "is this: 'Hear, O Israel, the Lord our God, the Lord is one. Love the Lord your God with all your heart and with all your soul and with all your mind and with all your strength.' The second is this: 'Love your neighbor as yourself.' There is no commandment greater than these."

"Well said, teacher," the man replied. "You are right in saying that God is one and there is no other but him. To love him with all your heart, with all your understanding and with all your strength, and to love your neighbor as yourself is more important than all burnt offerings and sacrifices."

When Jesus saw that he had answered wisely, he said to him, "You are not far from the kingdom of God." And from then on no one dared ask him any more questions.

A DOWNWARD READING

This account occurs in a context of a series of encounters between Jesus and the religious leaders in the Jerusalem temple (Mark 11:27–12:40). They challenge Jesus' "authority" (11:28), look for "a way to arrest

163

him" (12:12), seek "to catch him in his words" (v. 13), and "question" him (v. 18). It becomes clear that Mark records this cluster of so-called controversy stories to expose the sin of the religious leaders, and thereby vindicate Jesus in the historical and religious context of his day. Put differently, Mark wants to make the point that the religious elite reject Jesus not because of any failure on his part; the error lies with those who oppose him. Significantly, this entire section of the narrative culminates with a stark word of judgment on the teachers of the law: "Such men will be punished most severely" (v. 40b). It is therefore striking that in the midst of all this controversy and opposition, Jesus converses with "one of the teachers of the law" who speaks well of him, agrees with him, and, as it turns out, is "not far from the kingdom of God" (vv. 28, 32, 34). Mark no doubt records this incident to vindicate Jesus, significantly through the testimony of one drawn from the ranks of his opponents.

This incident is triggered by "one of the teachers of the law" (NIV) or "one of the scribes" (ESV) who hears Jesus debating with the Sadducees (Mark 12:28). Impressed with Jesus' response to them—Jesus answers them "well" (ESV)—he asks Jesus, "Which commandment is the most important of all?" (v. 28 ESV). It could be that the question is prompted by Jesus' reference to "the book of Moses" in the context (v. 26). In any event, Jesus identifies the command to love Israel's God "with all your heart and with all your soul and with all your mind and with all your strength" as "the most important one" (vv. 29–30). He then quotes a "second" command: "Love your neighbor as yourself." According to Jesus, "There is no commandment greater than these" (v. 31). Jesus' reference to the singular form of *commandment* indicates that he views these two commandments as a unit.

The teacher of the law approves: "Well said, teacher . . . . You are right" (Mark 12:32). He then proceeds to essentially repeat, almost verbatim, Jesus' response to his question, as if to endorse each component of his answer. But he substitutes Jesus' reference to "soul" and "mind" with "understanding," and adds the comparative "[this] is more important than all burnt offerings and sacrifices" (vv. 32–33; cf. v. 30). The net result of this exchange is to emphasize the truth that an all-encompassing love for Israel's God and a love for one's neighbor are at the heart of the commandments, and to elevate this truth above religious ritual.

When Jesus sees that the scribe has answered "wisely," he informs him that he is "not far from the kingdom of God" (Mark 12:34a). Unlike his colleagues, this teacher of the law has a good grasp of the true meaning of the commandments, and so is at least in sight of God's kingdom. At this point, "no one" asks Jesus "any more questions" (v. 34b). To the "delight" of the listening crowd, Jesus then raises a question "in the temple courts" to expose the inadequate understanding of the teachers of the law concerning the true identity of "the Christ" (vv. 35–37). It is as though Mark is informing his readers that while a correct view of the law can bring someone near to God's kingdom, only a true knowledge of "the Christ" qualifies one for entrance into this kingdom.

A SIDEWAYS READING

Mark and Matthew both record this incident (Mark 12:28–34; Matt. 22:34–40). Luke records a similar incident, but the thrust of the text suggests that a different encounter is in view (cf. Luke 10:25–28; Mark 12:34). The parallel accounts in Mark and Matthew occur in a similar literary context in their respective Gospels, but Mark's account is the more detailed of the two, and reveals one or two significant differences:

- In Matthew's account, "an expert in the law" *tests* Jesus with a question, like the religious leaders in the context (Matt. 22:35; cf. 16:1; 19:3; 22:15). Mark's depiction of the scribe, however, appears to be more favorable; he is motivated by "a good answer" that Jesus gives (Mark 12:28; cf. KJV). One Markan commentator suggests that the scribe's failure to address Jesus as "teacher" at the outset, as in Matthew's account (12:28b, 32; cf. Matt. 22:36a), is indicative of a disrespectful attitude toward him.[1] This argument, however, stumbles over the fact that Jesus' opponents, the Pharisees, Herodians, and Sadducees, all address him as "teacher" before testing him in the context (cf. Mark 12:14, 19). In any event, the scribe subsequently addresses Jesus as "teacher," and this goes hand in hand with commending him for a good and "right" answer (12:32).

1. Robert H. Gundry, *Mark: A Commentary on His Apology for the Cross* (Grand Rapids: Eerdmans, 1993), 710–11.

- In Mark's Gospel, the scribe queries the "most important" (literally, "first," KJV) rather than Matthew's "greatest" commandment in the law, although Matthew's account combines these two adjectives in Jesus' reply (Mark 12:28b; cf. Matt. 22:36, 38). Mark's version brings a neater symmetry between the "first" commandment to love God and Jesus' subsequent reference to "the second," to love one's neighbor as oneself (Mark 12:31a).

- In Luke 10:25–28, a lawyer "correctly" summarizes the law with the dual commands to love God and neighbor in response to a question by Jesus. Although, as we suggested above, it is doubtful that this encounter in Luke's Gospel is a parallel tradition to our text, it nevertheless provides evidence that Jesus was not the first or only teacher to link these two love commands. Yet it is important to note that in Luke's Gospel the lawyer asks a different leading question: "Teacher, . . . what must I do to inherit eternal life?" (Luke 10:25b; cf. Mark 12:28b). But Jesus, it appears, is the first teacher to define these two love commands as "the most important" of the commandments (Mark 12:28b; cf. 12:31b), or, for that matter, that "all the Law and the Prophets hang on these two commandments" (Matt. 22:40). To quote one commentator, "Even if some teachers did link these two commandments together before Jesus, the emphasis and centrality that they receive from him is unique and unlike any possible earlier associations."[2]

- Jesus' response to the scribe's question in Mark's Gospel commences with a confession unique to Mark's account: "'The most important one,' answered Jesus, 'is this: "Hear, O Israel, the Lord our God, the Lord is one"'" (Mark 12:29). One commentator suggests that this confession is intended to confirm Jesus' theological orthodoxy as an Israelite, perhaps called into question by his conflict with the religious leaders (see 7:1–23; 12:13–27).[3]

- When Jesus articulates the command to love God, Mark alone includes the requirement to love God with all one's "strength"

2. John Piper, quoted in Robert H. Stein, *Mark*, Baker Exegetical Commentary on the New Testament (Grand Rapids: Baker Academic, 2008), 562.

3. R. T. France, *The Gospel of Mark*, New International Greek Testament Commentary (Grand Rapids: Eerdmans, 2002), 479.

(Mark 12:30; cf. Matt. 22:37). He does not include Matthew's reference to the love command as "the first and greatest commandment" (Matt. 22:38; cf. Mark 12:31), or the concluding pronouncement that "all the Law and the Prophets hang on [the] two commandments" to love God and neighbor (Matt. 22:40). Mark's thrust lies elsewhere, in the scribe's confession that the love commandment is "more important than all burnt offerings and sacrifices" (Mark 12:33b).

• Most notably, only Mark includes the scribe's subsequent approval of Jesus' answer (Mark 12:32–33). This approval, together with his earlier endorsement of Jesus' response to the question of the Sadducees (v. 28)—Jesus answers both "well" (KJV)—suggests that Mark intends to portray this teacher of the law as an ally of Jesus who not only verifies the most important commandment, but also exposes the error of those who, like his fellow scribes, elevate religious ritual over love for God and neighbor.

• Only Mark mentions Jesus' observation that the teacher of the law is "not far from the kingdom of God" (Mark 12:34). Jesus' comments suggest that the door to God's kingdom is not closed to the religious leaders. Perhaps Jesus also intends to alert the scribe to the truth that although a right view of God's commandments is able to bring one near to God's kingdom, it is not sufficient to secure entrance into this kingdom (cf. 10:15–27).

A BACKWARD READING

A backward reading reveals that the Old Testament Scriptures are in view at various points in this text. The teacher of the law raises a question concerning "the commandments": "Which commandment is the most important of all?" (Mark 12:28 ESV). In the context, "commandment" is an obvious reference to the law of God (see Deut. 4:40; 5:31). Given the sheer number of God's commandments recorded by Moses, literally numbering in the hundreds, the teacher of the law's question is hardly surprising.

Jesus responds by quoting Deuteronomy 6:4–5: "Hear, O Israel: The LORD our God, the LORD is one. Love the LORD your God with all your heart and with all your soul and with all your strength." Jesus adds "with all your mind" (Mark 12:30). While the Hebrew mind understood that the "heart" was the center not only of one's emotions, but also of one's thinking (see Gen. 6:5), it could be that Mark includes this additional element for the benefit of his Gentile readers, who would more naturally distinguish between the emotions of the heart and the thoughts of the head. In any event, Mark's addition simply underscores the total allegiance in view.

Deuteronomy 6:4, which Jesus quotes, is not a command, but a confession commonly known as the *Shema*, the Hebrew word for "hear," and the first word in this verse. There is a connection between verses 4 and 5: because God is the "one" and only God, he demands and warrants total allegiance! Mere external compliance is not an option. Moses does not explicitly assert that this command is "the most important one" (Mark 12:29a), but a number of clues in the surrounding verses in the Old Testament context hint at its importance. First, it functions as a masterful summary of the so-called first table of the Decalogue just quoted by Moses (Deut. 5:7–15), and second, it is only after the *Shema*, and not the Decalogue, that Moses informs God's people that "these commandments that I give you today are to be upon your hearts. Impress them on your children. Talk about them when you sit at home and when you walk along the road, when you lie down and when you get up. Tie them as symbols on your hands and bind them on your foreheads. Write them on the doorframes of your houses and on your gates" (Deut. 6:6–9). These instructions appear to underscore the importance of the prior command to love God, and make the point that there is a link between love and the commandments of God. Moreover, the command to love the Lord God is restated by Moses in the chapters that follow (Deut. 10:12; 11:13; cf. 11:1, 22; 13:3; 19:9; 30:6, 16, 20), and is subsequently repeated by Joshua (Josh.22:5; cf. 23:11), indicating its importance for understanding the law of God.

Jesus then quotes a "second" commandment, drawn from the book of Leviticus: "Love your neighbor as yourself" (Lev. 19:18b). This commandment is not a command to love oneself; self-love is implied. Rather, the commandment requires God's people to extend this self-love to their neighbors. Together with love for God, "no commandment [is] greater than these" (Mark 12:31b). In the immediate Old Testament context, *neighbor* is defined as "one of your people" (Lev. 19:18a), although the love commandment is subsequently extended to include the "alien living with you" because God's people "were aliens in Egypt" (vv. 33–34). In the preceding verses, the Lord lists a number of commandments, some of which are obviously drawn from the Decalogue (see vv. 1–13), indicating a link between the love commandment and holiness, the one being an expression of the other. The context also "shows," according to one commentator, "that to love your neighbour as yourself is not a matter of private feelings or interpersonal generosity only, but of practical social ethics in the public arena, including the legal process."[4]

These various laws in Leviticus 19 are introduced with the commandment, "Be holy because I, the LORD your God, am holy" (Lev. 19:2b), followed by the constant refrain, "I am the LORD your God" (vv. 3, 4, 10; cf. vv. 12, 14, 16, 18), suggesting a covenantal God-centered motivation for obedience (see v. 37). Besides these general clues, nothing in Leviticus 19 indicates that the commandment to love one's neighbor should be elevated to one of the two greatest commandments. It should, however, be pointed out that this specific love commandment functions as a useful summary statement of the so-called second table of the law that regulates man's relationship to man (see Deut. 5:16–21).

The scribe affirms Jesus' answer: Jesus is "right in saying that God is one and there is no other but him" (Mark 12:32). He doesn't specifically mention Israel's *Shema* at this point, perhaps hinting at the fact that this truth applies universally, to both Jew and Gentile. But the *Shema* is interpreted to declare not only the oneness of God, but also his uniqueness; "there is no other but him"; the God of Israel is the one and only God! The scribe then repeats the two love commandments, affirming them (v. 33), and asserts that they are "more important than all burnt offerings and sacrifices" (v. 33). Jesus approves (v. 34). By elevating the love commands, the scribe "demotes" the sacrificial system, according to one commentator, echoing the sentiments of the prophet Hosea: "For I desire mercy, not sacrifice, and acknowledgment of God rather than burnt offerings" (Hos. 6:6).[5] Love is more important than sacrificial ritual (cf. Mic. 6:6–8; 1 Sam. 15:22). Hosea prophesies in a context in which God's people have broken his covenant and been unfaithful to

---

4. Christopher J. H. Wright, *Leviticus*, New Bible Commentary: 21st Century Edition (Leicester, England; Downers Grove, IL, USA: Inter-Varsity Press, 1994), 148.
5. Ibid., 481.

him (Hos. 6:7). According to the Lord, "I have seen a horrible thing in the house of Israel. There Ephraim is given to prostitution and Israel is defiled" (Hos. 6:10). A similar scenario is in view in Jesus' day, and so judgment looms for the temple and its leaders (see Mark 11:12–21; 12:9–12; 13:1–2). Mark's inclusion of this prophetic allusion is probably intended as a none-too-subtle reference to the sin of the religious leaders, who elevated religious ritual over true devotion to God (e.g., 7:6–7). But this allusion, recorded on the lips of one drawn from their own ranks, makes the telling point that the teachers of the law should have known better! Their severe judgment is justified (12:40b).

A FORWARD READING

One obvious question that arises out of this text is the matter of the abiding validity of the commandments to love God and neighbor. Do these commands apply to the Christian today? And if so, do they replace the Mosaic law? In Jesus' Sermon on the Mount, he affirms the Law of God and the Prophets; he has not come to "abolish" them, but to "fulfill" them (Matt. 5:17). In the verse that follows, Jesus focuses on the law, and explains what he means: "I tell you the truth, until heaven and earth disappear, not the smallest letter, not the least stroke of a pen, will by any means disappear from the Law until everything is accomplished" (v. 18). This perspective should govern our reading of the sermon that follows. Accordingly, Jesus' antitheses—"You have heard that it was said . . . but I tell you" (vv. 21–22, 27–28, 33–34, 38–39, 43–44; cf. vv. 31–32)—are not a rejection of the law of Moses; rather, they function as a critique of the deficient "righteousness" of "the Pharisees and the teachers of the law" in the context that externalizes and redefines the meaning of this law (vv. 20–48). Therefore, Jesus' subsequent pronouncements in Matthew's Gospel about the love commandments that parallel our text should not be interpreted to mean that love abrogates or replaces the law; rather, "all the Law and the Prophets hang on these two commandments" (22:37–40). In effect, love is the key to correctly understanding the law, a law that is still authoritative for the Christian.

In Jesus' Sermon on the Mount, he refers to the command to "love your neighbor" (Matt. 5:43). Here Jesus expands the distorted definition of *neighbor* in the historical context to include one's enemies (v. 44).

On another occasion, Jesus tells the well-known parable of the good Samaritan to make a similar point regarding the despised Samaritans (Luke 10:29–37).

The apostle Paul, after endorsing the law of God and its commandments for his Christian readers (Rom. 7:12), links love and the law. According to the apostle, love is the "fulfillment" of the law. When he writes to the saints in Rome, he exhorts them to "let no debt remain outstanding, except the continuing debt to love one another, for he who loves his fellowman has fulfilled the law. The commandments, 'Do not commit adultery,' 'Do not murder,' 'Do not steal,' 'Do not covet,' and whatever other commandment there may be, are summed up in this one rule: 'Love your neighbor as yourself.' Love does no harm to its neighbor. Therefore love is the fulfillment of the law" (Rom. 13:8–10). The apostle makes the same point in his letter to the church at Galatia: "The entire law is summed up in a single command: 'Love your neighbor as yourself'" (Gal. 5:14).

Conspicuous by its absence is any reference to the command to love God in Paul's summary statement of the law. But Jesus points in this direction when he quotes the so-called Golden Rule toward the conclusion of his Sermon on the Mount: "So in everything, do to others what you would have them do to you, for this sums up the Law and the Prophets" (Matt. 7:12). James, the brother of Jesus, identifies the command to "love your neighbor" as "the royal law found in Scripture" (James 2:8), and the apostle John points out that love for neighbor is an expression of love for God (1 John 4:20).

In this context, John reminds his readers that "we love because [God] first loved us" (1 John 4:19; cf. 4:10, 21). This truth is reflected in the Decalogue, which commences with the mention of God's rescue of his people from Egypt. The law of God is given to those whom God has already redeemed: "I am the LORD your God, who brought you out of Egypt, out of the land of slavery" (Ex. 20:2; cf. Deut. 5:6). Accordingly, there is no attempt to merit God's love when seeking to obey God's commands to love our neighbor. Love, after all, is a fruit of God's Spirit at work in the believer (Gal. 5:22). We see a similar dynamic in the letter to the Hebrews where the exhortation to "spur one another on toward love and good deeds" (Heb. 10:24; cf. 13:1) is portrayed as an outworking of the new covenant in terms of which the Lord will put his laws in the hearts of his people, and will write them on their minds (10:16). In the context, the Mosaic law must be in view. Once again the link between law and love, or holiness and love, can be seen in these verses, a link reflected in the Old Testament Scriptures (cf. Lev. 19).

Scattered throughout the New Testament letters to the church are also numerous references to the priority of love that reinforce the importance of the command to love one's neighbor. A selection of these verses will make the point. According to Paul, "In Christ Jesus neither circumcision nor uncircumcision has any value. The only thing that counts is faith expressing itself through love" (Gal. 5:6). Paul elsewhere adopts the suggestive imagery of "putting on" love to make the same point: "Therefore, as God's chosen people, holy and dearly loved, clothe yourselves with compassion, kindness, humility, gentleness and patience. Bear with each other and forgive whatever grievances you may have against one another. Forgive as the Lord forgave you. And over all these virtues put on love, which binds them all together in perfect unity" (Col. 3:12–14). And of course there is the oft-quoted 1 Corinthians 13, which highlights the necessity of love in the Christian life: "If I . . . have not love, I am nothing. . . . I gain nothing" (1 Cor. 13:2–3). Other verses in Paul's letters also encourage and commend an increase in love for one another (e.g., 1 Thess. 4:9–10; 2 Thess. 1:3).

The apostle Peter echoes these same sentiments as he writes to "God's elect" (1 Peter 1:1): "Above all, love each other deeply, because love covers over a multitude of sins" (4:8; cf. 1:22). According to the apostle John, love is the mark of the true believer: "Dear friends, let us love one another, for love comes from God. Everyone who loves has been born of God and knows God. Whoever does not love does not know God, because God is love" (1 John 4:7–8; cf. 3:14). At this point, John is simply reflecting the teaching of Jesus: "By this all men will know that you are my disciples, if you love one another" (John 13:35).

It should be obvious from this brief survey of the biblical teaching on love that Jesus' comments on love and the law in our text apply not only to their first-century Jewish context, but also to the Christian reader today.

SUMMARY

In this encounter between Jesus and a teacher of the law or scribe, Mark demonstrates Jesus' orthodoxy regarding the Old Testament's teaching on the law of God. Our downward reading shows that our text occurs at the heart of a series of encounters between Jesus and his opponents in the temple area (Mark 11:27–12:40). The text focuses on the question: "Of all the commandments, which is the most important?" (12:28b). In response, Jesus recites the so-called *Shema* followed by two commands: to love God with one's entire being, and to love one's neighbor as oneself; "there is no commandment greater than these" (12:29–31).

Our sideways reading of the text draws attention to the scribe's subsequent endorsement of Jesus' answer, material not recorded in Matthew's parallel account (Mark 12:32–33; cf. Matt. 22:35–40). This endorsement has the dual function of both vindicating Jesus on a significant point of theology—his view of the law—and, by implication, condemning those who oppose him, significantly through the testimony of one drawn from the ranks of Jesus' opponents.

Our backward reading of the text reveals that Jesus' answer to the scribe's question is drawn from the law of Moses, where a connection between love and law is reflected in the context (cf. Deut. 6:4–5; Lev. 19:18). Our forward reading highlights the abiding priority of the love command for the Christian reader today; it is "more important" than religious ritual (cf. Mark 12:33). Those who grasp this truth are not far from the kingdom of God, according to Jesus (Mark 12:34)!

14

JESUS PREDICTS THE DESTRUCTION OF THE TEMPLE

Mark 13:1–37: As he was leaving the temple, one of his disciples said to him, "Look, Teacher! What massive stones! What magnificent buildings!"

"Do you see all these great buildings?" replied Jesus. "Not one stone here will be left on another; every one will be thrown down."

As Jesus was sitting on the Mount of Olives opposite the temple, Peter, James, John and Andrew asked him privately, "Tell us, when will these things happen? And what will be the sign that they are all about to be fulfilled?"

Jesus said to them: "Watch out that no one deceives you. Many will come in my name, claiming, 'I am he,' and will deceive many. When you hear of wars and rumors of wars, do not be alarmed. Such things must happen, but the end is still to come. Nation will rise against nation, and kingdom against kingdom. There will be earthquakes in various places, and famines. These are the beginning of birth pains.

"You must be on your guard. You will be handed over to the local councils and flogged in the synagogues. On account of me you will stand before governors and kings as witnesses to them. And the gospel must first be preached to all nations. Whenever you are arrested and brought to trial, do not worry beforehand about what to say. Just say whatever is given you at the time, for it is not you speaking, but the Holy Spirit.

175

"Brother will betray brother to death, and a father his child. Children will rebel against their parents and have them put to death. All men will hate you because of me, but he who stands firm to the end will be saved.

"When you see 'the abomination that causes desolation' standing where it does not belong—let the reader understand—then let those who are in Judea flee to the mountains. Let no one on the roof of his house go down or enter the house to take anything out. Let no one in the field go back to get his cloak. How dreadful it will be in those days for pregnant women and nursing mothers! Pray that this will not take place in winter, because those will be days of distress unequaled from the beginning, when God created the world, until now—and never to be equaled again. If the Lord had not cut short those days, no one would survive. But for the sake of the elect, whom he has chosen, he has shortened them. At that time if anyone says to you, 'Look, here is the Christ!' or, 'Look, there he is!' do not believe it. For false Christs and false prophets will appear and perform signs and miracles to deceive the elect—if that were possible. So be on your guard; I have told you everything ahead of time.

"But in those days, following that distress,

"'the sun will be darkened,
    and the moon will not give its light;
the stars will fall from the sky,
    and the heavenly bodies will be shaken.'

"At that time men will see the Son of Man coming in clouds with great power and glory. And he will send his angels and gather his elect from the four winds, from the ends of the earth to the ends of the heavens.

"Now learn this lesson from the fig tree: As soon as its twigs get tender and its leaves come out, you know that summer is near. Even so, when you see these things happening, you know that it is near, right at the door. I tell you the truth, this generation will certainly not pass away until all these things have happened. Heaven and earth will pass away, but my words will never pass away.

"No one knows about that day or hour, not even the angels in heaven, nor the Son, but only the Father. Be on guard! Be alert! You do not know when that time will come. It's like a man going away: He leaves his house and puts his servants in charge, each with his assigned task, and tells the one at the door to keep watch.

"Therefore keep watch because you do not know when the owner of the house will come back—whether in the evening, or at midnight, or when the rooster crows, or at dawn. If he comes suddenly, do not let him find you sleeping. What I say to you, I say to everyone: 'Watch!'"

A DOWNWARD READING

In our text, Jesus predicts the total destruction of the Jerusalem temple (Mark 13:1–2). Significantly, in the preceding context, Mark records Jesus' clearing this temple, symbolizing this impending judgment (11:12–21), followed by a sequence of encounters in the temple area between Jesus and his opponents (11:27–12:40). In Mark's Gospel, the temple is depicted as a place of hostility and opposition toward Jesus. Its days are numbered!

The Jerusalem temple, rebuilt by King Herod, a contemporary of Jesus, was a truly impressive structure. This fact is noted by one of Jesus' disciples in the opening verse of this account: "As he was leaving the temple, one of his disciples said to him, 'Look, Teacher! What massive stones! What magnificent buildings!'" (Mark 13:1). Jesus concurs, pointing to its "great buildings" (v. 2a). He then predicts their destruction in a single sentence: "Not one stone here will be left on another; every one will be thrown down" (v. 2b). With two double negatives in the original Greek text, Jesus' point is emphatic.

It is hardly a surprise that Jesus' prediction elicits a response from his disciples: "As Jesus was sitting on the Mount of Olives opposite the temple, Peter, James, John and Andrew asked him privately, 'Tell us, when will these things happen? And what will be the sign that they are all about to be fulfilled?'" (Mark 13:3–4). These disciples don't question the demise of the temple, but they want to know when it will happen, and "the sign" that will herald its destruction. They are confident that if Jesus can predict this event, he can also supply this information. Jesus' reply to these questions has been dubbed the *Olivet Discourse* because of its Mount of Olives setting. This discourse represents one of only two extended portions of Jesus' teaching material in Mark's Gospel (cf. 4:2–32), and as such, it warrants our close attention. The disciples' question in the context clearly relates to the destruction of the temple (cf. 13:2–4). Accordingly, a number of commentators insist that Jesus' response is limited to this event.[1] Yet other commentators contend that some of the material in the discourse refers more naturally to the end of the age or the *parousia*, that is, Jesus' second coming.[2] It is hoped that our multidirectional hermeneutic will shed some light on this issue.

Jesus commences his discourse with a warning against deception: "Watch out that no one deceives you. Many will come in my name, claiming, 'I am he,' and will deceive many" (Mark 13:5–6). Many will claim to be Christ, the Messiah, and they will deceive many (cf. vv. 21–22). Jesus encourages his disciples not to be "alarmed" by the occurrence of "wars and rumors of wars," nations and kingdoms in turmoil with each other, or earthquakes and famines; "the end is still to come" (v. 7); "these are the beginning of birth pains," according to Jesus (v. 8b). To refer back to the disciples' opening question, none of these events functions as "the sign" of the destruction of the temple, although, to apply Jesus' birth analogy, they are in some way connected to the predicted devastation to come.

Jesus then warns his disciples to "be on . . . guard" (Mark 13:9a) because of the opposition they will encounter. Interspersed with the anticipated struggles they will face, however, Jesus includes numerous encouragements to stand "firm to the end" (v. 13b):

> You will be handed over to the local councils and flogged in the synagogues. On account of me you will stand before governors and kings as witnesses to them. And the gospel must first be preached to all nations. Whenever you are arrested and brought to trial, do not worry beforehand about what to say. Just say whatever is given you at the time, for it is not you speaking, but the Holy Spirit.
>
> Brother will betray brother to death, and a father his child. Children will rebel against their parents and have them put to death. All men will hate you because of me, but he who stands firm to the end will be saved. (Mark 13:9–13)

It is apparent that Jesus' disciples will, on occasion, face a torrid time— floggings, arrest and trial, betrayal and death, and hatred by "all men"— until "the end." Their calling is to be a witness, with the help of the Holy Spirit, and to stand firm. Jesus includes a time marker in this context:

---

1. For a discussion of the various scholarly views of Mark 13, see R. T. France, *The Gospel of Mark*, New International Greek Testament Commentary (Grand Rapids: Eerdmans, 2002), 499–503.

    2. Ibid.

"And the gospel must first be preached to all nations" (Mark 13:10), indicating that some unspecified period must elapse before "the end" occurs (v. 13b). It is possible that "the end" here simply refers to the end of life, but the most obvious referent in the context is the destruction of the temple (cf. vv. 1–2). This conclusion is supported by Jesus' reference, in his next breath, to the region of "Judea" and to a series of related warnings (vv. 14–23). It is evident that Jesus still has this local scenario, and the destruction of the temple, in view:

> When you see "the abomination that causes desolation" standing where it does not belong—let the reader understand—then let those who are in Judea flee to the mountains. Let no one on the roof of his house go down or enter the house to take anything out. Let no one in the field go back to get his cloak. How dreadful it will be in those days for pregnant women and nursing mothers! Pray that this will not take place in winter, because those will be days of distress unequaled from the beginning, when God created the world, until now—and never to be equaled again. If the Lord had not cut short those days, no one would survive. But for the sake of the elect, whom he has chosen, he has shortened them. At that time if anyone says to you, "Look, here is the Christ!" or, "Look, there he is!" do not believe it. For false Christs and false prophets will appear and perform signs and miracles to deceive the elect—if that were possible. So be on your guard; I have told you everything ahead of time. (Mark 13:14–23)

Jesus here mentions "the abomination that causes desolation" without explanation (v. 14), suggesting that its meaning was known to Peter, James, John, and Andrew. Although Jesus doesn't explicitly describe this "abomination" as "the sign" requested by his disciples (cf. v. 4), it seems intended to function that way in Jesus' discourse: "When you see 'the abomination that causes desolation' standing where it does not belong—let the reader understand—then let those who are in Judea flee to the mountains" (v. 14). Jesus' call to "flee" is predicated on the fact that the ensuing events will bring "days of distress unequaled from the beginning . . . and never to be equaled again" (v. 19). Although Jesus does not explicitly mention the destruction of the temple in this context, his assertion of unparalleled "distress" best fits with what we know about the events surrounding the destruction of Jerusalem, including the temple, by the armies of Rome in A.D. 70, as recounted by the first-century Jewish historian Josephus.

There is a clear sense of urgency in Jesus' call to flee (Mark 13:15–16). He singles out "pregnant women and nursing mothers": how "dreadful" it will be for them "in those days," probably because of their inability to flee quickly and easily (v. 17). "Pray that this will not take place in winter," says Jesus (v. 18), because the inclement weather would only add to the misery and distress. Such will be the distress that "if the Lord had not cut short those days, no one would survive. But for the sake of the elect, whom he has chosen, he has shortened them" (v. 20). There is no explicit mention in these verses that this distress is a judgment from the hand of God, but that is the clear implication of Jesus' teaching at this point. Although the distress will be "shortened" for the benefit of the "elect," it is obvious that they will not be spared the distress.

Jesus returns to the motif of deception that introduces this discourse: "false Christs and false prophets will appear and perform signs and miracles to deceive the elect," if possible (Mark 13:22). But here the warning is against believing the false claims that come from the lips of third parties, rather than the claims of the false christs themselves (v. 21; cf. vv. 5–6). Jesus reinforces the warning with an exhortation to his disciples, God's "elect" just referred to, to "be on your guard" (v. 23a). In all likelihood, these false christs are preaching a message of deliverance in the face of God's impending judgment on Jerusalem and the temple, while the false prophets are predicting that there will be no destruction, claims they bolster with "signs and miracles" (v. 22).

There is an element of comprehensiveness about Jesus' concluding statement to this section of the discourse: "I have told you everything ahead of time" (Mark 13:23). It echoes the comprehensive aspect of the disciples' opening question, "And what will be the sign that they are all about to be fulfilled?" (v. 4b), and could therefore act as a concluding summary statement to this question. If this reading of the discourse is correct, it supports the view that in what follows, Jesus shifts his focus to the end of the age:

But in those days, following that distress,

"the sun will be darkened,
    and the moon will not give its light;
the stars will fall from the sky,
    and the heavenly bodies will be shaken."

> At that time men will see the Son of Man coming in clouds with great
> power and glory. And he will send his angels and gather his elect from
> the four winds, from the ends of the earth to the ends of the heavens.
> (Mark 13:24–27)

Jesus' words include another time reference: "in those days, following
that distress" (v. 24a). We have argued that this "distress" refers to the
events surrounding the destruction of Jerusalem and its temple (cf. v. 19).
Accordingly, Jesus' teaching in this portion of the discourse must relate
to a period after the temple's destruction. The vivid imagery that Jesus
now uses includes references to "great power and glory" and the angelic
gathering of the elect "from the four winds, from the ends of the earth
to the ends of the heavens" (vv. 26b–27)—language that most naturally
depicts the end of the age, rather than the destruction of the temple,
when the Son's glory is revealed for all to see (cf. 8:38; 9:1; 14:62). Jesus
then draws a lesson from the fig tree to delineate a time frame for these
events:

> Now learn this lesson from the fig tree: As soon as its twigs get tender
> and its leaves come out, you know that summer is near. Even so, when
> you see these things happening, you know that it is near, right at the
> door. I tell you the truth, this generation will certainly not pass away
> until all these things have happened. Heaven and earth will pass away,
> but my words will never pass away. (Mark 13:28–31)

The lesson from the fig tree is easy enough to understand, but there is less
certainty about the identity of "these things" in the verses that follow (cf.
vv. 29–30). Some commentators simply view "these things" as a reference
to all that has gone before in the discourse, all of which will happen during the lifetime of "this generation," that is, Jesus' contemporaries.[3] But
this reading creates an obvious tension for those commentators who view
verses 24–27 as a reference to the still-future coming of the Son of Man.[4]
To alleviate the tension, some evangelical commentators redefine "this
generation" to refer to this "wicked and adulterous generation" that will

3. Ibid., 540.
4. James R. Edwards, *The Gospel according to Mark*, Pillar New Testament Commentary
(Grand Rapids: Eerdmans, 2002), 402–4.

endure until Jesus returns (cf. 8:38).[5] When Jesus refers to "this genera-tion" in that context (8:11–12), however, he clearly has his contemporaries in view. Others relegate "this generation" to the generation that will be alive when Jesus returns, but that is not a natural reading of the phrase.[6]

In keeping with our analysis of the text, we argue that "these things" in Mark 13:29 refers to the events surrounding the destruction of the temple in A.D. 70. The following observations of the text support this interpretation of these verses: First, the temporal clause, "when you see" (v. 29a), occurs earlier in the discourse on one other occasion, where it is linked to "the abomination" that relates to the "desolation" of the temple (cf. v. 14), suggesting that "these things" relates to the same incident. Second, the phrase "these things" parallels the "these things" in the disciples' question that relates obviously to the destruction of the temple (cf. v. 4). Third, it is possible to draw a distinction in verse 29 between "these things," referring to the destruction of Jerusalem and the temple, and "it," referring to the end of the age, when the Son of Man returns on the clouds in glory. According to this understanding of these verses, Jesus informs his disciples that the destruction of the temple will occur during the lifetime of his contemporaries—"this generation"—and when this destruction occurs, they will know that Jesus' return, the "coming" of the Son of Man, "is near, right at the door" (v. 29b). This interpreta-tion makes good sense of the urgent warnings that Jesus utters in his conclusion to this discourse, warnings appropriate for a cataclysmic event such as the end of the age:

> No one knows about that day or hour, not even the angels in heaven, nor the Son, but only the Father. Be on guard! Be alert! You do not know when that time will come. It's like a man going away: He leaves his house and puts his servants in charge, each with his assigned task, and tells the one at the door to keep watch.
>
> Therefore keep watch because you do not know when the owner of the house will come back—whether in the evening, or at midnight, or when the rooster crows, or at dawn. If he comes suddenly, do not let him find you sleeping. What I say to you, I say to everyone: "Watch!" (Mark 13:32–37)

5. See the various options listed by I. Howard Marshall, *Commentary on Luke*, New Interna-tional Greek Testament Commentary (Grand Rapids: Eerdmans, 1978), 780.

6. Ibid.

These warnings are prefaced by, and based on, the fact that "no one" except God the Father knows the "day" of Jesus' return. Significantly, not even the angels or the incarnate Son of God knows "that day or hour" (v. 32). The emphasis in Jesus' conclusion, however, falls on the fact that his disciples "do not know when that time will come" (v. 33). Jesus tells Peter, James, John, and Andrew a one-line parable to impress on them the implications of this truth. They are like a servant at the door tasked by the owner of a house to "keep watch" for his return (v. 34). They are to "keep watch" because they "do not know when the owner of the house will come back" (v. 35). If he returns "suddenly," he must not find them sleeping (v. 36). The discourse ends with an exhortation to "watch," a command that is extended to "everyone" (v. 37), an indication that this event has broader, if not universal, implications.

Jesus' discourse appears to link, but distinguish, the destruction of the temple and the return of the Son of Man at the end of the age.

A SIDEWAYS READING

Matthew and Luke also record this discourse (cf. Matt. 24:1–51; Luke 21:5–36). It should be noted that elements of Mark's discourse are scattered elsewhere in Matthew's and Luke's Gospels, occurring there in other portions of Jesus' teaching (cf. Matt. 10:17–22; Luke 12:11–12, 37–38). This is evidence that Jesus taught this material on more than one occasion, and in different ways. A sideways reading of the text reveals a number of important differences that shed light on the meaning of the discourse. We will limit our observations to the most salient points:

- In Matthew's account, unlike Mark's and Luke's, the disciples' question that initiates the discourse includes a reference to "the sign of [Jesus'] coming and of the end of the age" (Matt. 24:3; cf. Mark 13:4; Luke 21:7). In the minds of Jesus' disciples, the destruction of the temple, Jesus' coming, and the end of the age are connected in some way. Jesus does not, in a direct way at least, correct their thinking, and in the discourse that follows in Matthew's Gospel, we may safely assume that he answers their questions. Significantly, Mark's account of the discourse is substantially the same as the record in Matthew's Gospel;

therefore, it appears that the reader of the discourse in Mark's Gospel is justified in seeing a reference in Jesus' teaching not only to the destruction of the temple in A.D. 70, but also to matters that relate to the end of the age (Mark 13:32–37; cf. Matt. 24:36). We need to resist the temptation, however, to read back into the plural "these things" in Mark's account of the disciples' question an implied reference to the end of the age (cf. Mark 13:4a). In Mark's account, the subsequent content of the discourse, and not the initial question, suggests that the end of the age is also in view.

- In Mark 13:10, Jesus states that "the gospel must first be preached to all nations." Matthew's version of this saying is more detailed: "And this gospel of the kingdom will be preached in the whole world as a testimony to all nations, and then the end will come" (Matt. 24:14). Matthew makes it clear that this saying envisages a Gentile mission. Jesus' point is that the "whole world" will hear the gospel preached. Whether or not they believe the gospel is not stated. What "must" happen in Mark's account "will" happen in Matthew's account, "and then the end will come" (Matt. 24:14b). In Matthew's account, it is possible that "the end" that Jesus has in view here is "the end of the age" that the disciples refer to in their opening question (see Matt. 24:3b); indeed, some commentators simply assume this understanding of the phrase.[7] Yet it should be noted that Matthew uses two different, albeit related, words in his references to "the end" in Matthew 24:3 and 24:14b. Moreover, in Matthew's Gospel, where "the end of the age" is in view, Matthew tends to be explicit by including the entire phrase, as in the disciples' question (Matt. 24:3; cf. 13:39–40, 49; 28:20). And so in all likelihood "the end" here refers rather to the end of the temple (see Matt. 24:6). If this is correct, all that Jesus is predicting at this point in his discourse is an expanded mission that will include Gentiles before the destruction of the temple (cf. Rom. 16:26; Col. 1:6).

- In Mark 13:14, Jesus makes reference to "the abomination that causes desolation": "When you see 'the abomination . . .' stand-

---

7. See, for example, William Barclay, *The Gospel of Matthew*, vol. 2 of The Daily Study Bible (Edinburgh: St. Andrew Press, 1958), 345.

ing where it does not belong—let the reader understand—then let those who are in Judea flee to the mountains." Matthew's account speaks of the abomination "standing in the holy place," a possible reference to the temple, and links the abomination to "the prophet Daniel" (Matt. 24:15). Possibly, then, the reference to "the reader" in this context is a reference to the reader of Daniel's prophecy, rather than a parenthetical comment by the evangelist directed to the reader of the Olivet Discourse. Luke's account makes no mention of the "abomination," but does include a reference to "desolation": "When you see Jerusalem being surrounded by armies, you will know that its desolation is near" (Luke 21:20). Luke here apparently identifies the cryptic "abomination that causes desolation" for the benefit of his Gentile readers. Whether or not the "armies" are an exact equivalent of "the abomination" is debated; nevertheless, it is evident that the Lukan account grounds these events in A.D. 70, when the armies of Rome surround Jerusalem before destroying it.

- The synoptic parallels to Mark 13:24–27 reinforce the perception that at this point in the discourse the focus shifts from Judea, and the destruction of Jerusalem and the temple, to the nations and the consummation of all things at the end of the age (cf. Matt. 24:29–31; Luke 21:25–28). Jesus now refers in the parallel accounts to "all the nations of the earth" (Matt. 24:30; cf. Luke 21:25) and "what is coming on the world" (Luke 21:26). In Luke's account, Jesus includes an exhortation that relates to the approach of personal "redemption": "When these things begin to take place, stand up and lift up your heads, because your redemption is drawing near" (v. 28). Unlike the events surrounding the destruction of Jerusalem, when escape is still possible—"Then let those who are in Judea flee to the mountains, let those in the city get out, and let those in the country not enter the city" (v. 21)—at this point in redemptive history, all one can do is to "stand up and lift up your heads" while waiting for one's redemption (v. 28); flight is no longer a possibility. Clearly, the consummation of all things is at hand, when God's redemption will be fully revealed.
- This same redemptive scenario is in view in the "lesson from the fig tree" (Mark 13:28–29; cf. Matt. 24:32–33; Luke 21:29–31).

According to Luke's account, "when you see these things happening, you know that the kingdom of God is near" (Luke 21:31). Luke here differentiates between the events surrounding the destruction of Jerusalem and the temple, which they will witness, and the approach of the "kingdom of God" at the consummation (cf. Luke 17:20; 23:51b). The events of A.D. 70 should not be confused with the end of the age, but they do signal that the consummation is near! It is for this reason that Jesus, in Luke's account, concludes his discourse with a warning regarding "that day": "Be careful, or your hearts will be weighed down with dissipation, drunkenness and the anxieties of life, and that day will close on you unexpectedly like a trap. For it will come upon all those who live on the face of the whole earth. Be always on the watch, and pray that you may be able to escape all that is about to happen, and that you may be able to stand before the Son of Man" (Luke 21:34–36). It is evident that, like the destruction of the temple and Jerusalem, the arrival of the Son of Man will also be a "time of punishment in fulfillment of all that has been written" (Luke 21:22).

Our sideways reading of this discourse affirms a dual focus in Jesus' teaching: both the destruction of the temple and the end of the age are in view. Jesus' discourse links them, but also distinguishes them, for the benefit of his disciples, with different sets of instructions related to each event.

A BACKWARD READING

A backward reading of the discourse reveals a distinct Old Testament prophetic background to our text that exposes the so-called apocalyptic or symbolic nature of Jesus' teaching. The discourse also contains a number of Old Testament allusions that we will not dwell on because they don't materially affect our understanding of Jesus' teaching (Isa. 19:2; Dan. 12:1; Mic. 7:6).

- Jesus refers to "the abomination that causes desolation, spoken of through the prophet Daniel" (Matt. 24:15; cf. Mark 13:14). Daniel refers to this "abomination" on three occasions (Dan. 9:27; 11:31; 12:11). The reference in Daniel 9 is part of a rather cryptic prophetic utterance:

> Seventy "sevens" are decreed for your people and your holy city to finish transgression, to put an end to sin, to atone for wickedness, to bring in everlasting righteousness, to seal up vision and prophecy and to anoint the most holy.
>
> Know and understand this: From the issuing of the decree to restore and rebuild Jerusalem until the Anointed One, the ruler, comes, there will be seven "sevens," and sixty-two "sevens." It will be rebuilt with streets and a trench, but in times of trouble. After the sixty-two "sevens," the Anointed One will be cut off and will have nothing. The people of the ruler who will come will destroy the city and the sanctuary. The end will come like a flood: War will continue until the end, and desolations have been decreed. He will confirm a covenant with many for one "seven." In the middle of the "seven" he will put an end to sacrifice and offering. And on a wing *of the temple* he will set up an abomination that causes desolation, until the end that is decreed is poured out on him. (Dan. 9:24–27)

For our purposes, the following observations are relevant to our understanding of Jesus' Olivet Discourse: First, the prophecy draws a connection between the destruction of Jerusalem and its sanctuary and "the end," which will come "like a flood" (Dan. 9:26). It could be for this reason that when Jesus predicts the destruction of the temple, this specific prophecy triggers in the minds of Jesus' disciples their question about the end of the age (Matt. 24:3). According to their understanding of Daniel's prophecy, this cluster of events cannot be separated. If this interpretation of the disciples' question is correct, then we are justified in seeing the Olivet Discourse as Jesus' response to this misunderstanding of Daniel's prophecy. According to Jesus, the destruction of "the sanctuary" and "the end" are linked, yet must be separated in time, much like Jesus' first and second comings.

Second, the prophecy does not identify or describe "the abomination"; it simply predicts that "the ruler" who will "put an end to sacrifice and offering" will "set up an abomination that causes desolation" (Dan. 9:26–27). Some commentators identify this individual as the Antichrist, while others argue for a Christocentric reading of the text, insisting that it is the Messiah who "put an end to sacrifice and offering" through his atoning death on the cross.[8] The NIV supplies "of the temple" in an attempt to bring clarity to the obscure reference to the "wing" as the location of the "abomination."

Jesus sheds some light on these questions in his discourse. In Mark's account, Jesus speaks of the "abomination . . . standing where it does not belong" (Mark 13:14), while the Matthean version records the abomination "standing in the holy place" (Matt. 24:15), a probable reference to the Jerusalem temple. Luke's parallel account makes no mention of the "abomination," but records instead "Jerusalem [being] surrounded by armies," a sign that "its desolation is near" (Luke 21:20). Some commentators view this saying as Luke's editorial comment identifying the otherwise obscure "abomination" for the benefit of his Gentile readers, while others reject the equating of the two. They point out that the subsequent command directed to those in Judea to "flee to the mountains" would no longer be possible once Jerusalem was "surrounded by armies" (Mark 13:14b; Matt. 24:16; Luke 21:20–21a). In their view, the "abomination" must therefore refer to a person—the participle *standing* (Mark 13:14) is masculine—or an incident that occurs before the armies advance on Jerusalem.[9] But this argument is contradicted by the simple fact that even in Luke's account, the command to those in Judea to flee is recorded after Jesus' reference to the "armies" surrounding Jerusalem. Moreover, Luke's account adds, "Let those in the city get out, and let those in the country not enter the city" (Luke 21:20–21); clearly, flight out of Jerusalem and Judea is still a possibility, even in the presence of the opposing armies.

A second prophetic reference to "the abomination" occurs in Daniel 11:31: "His armed forces will rise up to desecrate the temple

8. See, for example, Sinclair Ferguson, *Daniel*, New Bible Commentary: 21st Century Edition (Downers Grove, IL: IVP Academic, 1994), 759.

9. Robert H. Stein, *Mark*, Baker Exegetical Commentary on the New Testament (Grand Rapids: Baker Academic, 2008), 604.

fortress and will abolish the daily sacrifice. Then they will set up the abomination that causes desolation." Most commentators believe this prophecy, in its Danielic context, was fulfilled in 168 B.C. when Antiochus IV Epiphanes, a Syrian king, desecrated the Jerusalem temple by abolishing the "daily sacrifice" and setting up in its stead an altar devoted to the pagan god Zeus (cf. Dan. 12:11; 1 Macc. 1:54).[10] This action therefore functions as an anticipation of the desolation that would occur in A.D. 70, when the armies of Rome destroyed Jerusalem and its holy temple.

- A backward reading of Jesus' teaching in Mark 13:24–27 reveals that it is replete with Old Testament symbolic imagery. These verses signal a change in focus from the unparalleled "distress" surrounding the destruction of Jerusalem and the temple in A.D. 70 (see Mark 13:18–20) to the coming of the Son of Man (v. 26). In this context, Jesus refers to striking cosmic imagery: "But in those days, following that distress, 'the sun will be darkened, and the moon will not give its light; the stars will fall from the sky, and the heavenly bodies will be shaken'" (vv. 24–25). It is immediately noticeable that whereas "men *will see* the Son of Man coming in clouds with great power and glory" (v. 26), there is no indication in the text that this imagery will be visible, at least literally, to the human eye.

This kind of imagery is found in a number of Old Testament prophetic texts. An obvious "judgment" motif links them all together. In Isaiah 13, the prophet records "an oracle concerning Babylon" in which he predicts the coming of the "day of the LORD." The prophet paints a frightful picture of the judgment that will be unleashed:

> See, the day of the LORD is coming
>   —a cruel day, with wrath and fierce anger—
> to make the land desolate
>   and destroy the sinners within it.
> The stars of heaven and their constellations
>   will not show their light.
> The rising sun will be darkened
>   and the moon will not give its light.

10. See, for example, Ferguson, *Daniel*, 761.

I will punish the world for its evil,
　　the wicked for their sins.
I will put an end to the arrogance of the haughty
　　and will humble the pride of the ruthless.
I will make man scarcer than pure gold,
　　more rare than the gold of Ophir.
Therefore I will make the heavens tremble;
　　and the earth will shake from its place
at the wrath of the LORD Almighty,
　　in the day of his burning anger. (Isa. 13:9–13)

Isaiah, once again, and the prophet Ezekiel employ similar imagery in their depiction of God's judgment against the nations and Pharaoh, king of Egypt, respectively (cf. Isa. 34:4; Ezek. 32:7–8), while the prophet Joel describes the coming "day of the LORD" in the same terms (cf. Joel 2:10, 31; 3:15). The judgments predicted in these Old Testament prophecies that historically befell both Babylon and Pharaoh in the distant past caution the reader against taking this cosmic apocalyptic-type imagery literally.

This Old Testament background to Jesus' discourse alerts the reader to an ominous judgment that will accompany the coming of the Son of Man (see Mark 13:24–26), and anticipates the concluding warnings in Jesus' discourse (cf. Matt. 24:45–51; Mark 13:32–37; Luke 21:34–36). The subsequent references in Jesus' discourse to the Son of Man's return "at that time . . . coming in clouds with great power and glory"—a well-recognized allusion to Daniel 7:13–14—accompanied by the gathering of the elect "from the ends of the earth to the ends of the heavens" (Mark 13:26–27; cf. Deut. 30:4), refer most naturally to the end of the age, rather than the destruction of Jerusalem, as some commentators have argued.[11] At the consummation of redemptive history, the Son of Man will be worshiped by "all peoples, nations and men of every language" as his "everlasting dominion" and eternal kingdom are revealed in all their glory (Dan. 7:14).

In the midst of all this eschatological drama is encouragement for Jesus' disciples. With his coming as the Son of Man, "he will send his angels to gather his elect from the four winds" (Mark 13:27a), to preserve them from the judgment to come—a judgment anticipated, and vividly portrayed, in the Old Testament Scriptures. This is the sure hope of all the elect.

11. See, for example, France, *The Gospel of Mark*, 535–36.

A FORWARD READING

The thrust of a discourse is usually located in its conclusion. Jesus' discourse concludes with a clear call to watchfulness that extends beyond his immediate audience: "What I say to you, I say to everyone: 'Watch!'" (Mark 13:37). This concluding exhortation is prompted by the imminence of the coming of the Son of Man (Mark 13:26). According to Jesus, the events of A.D. 70 herald the approach of the Son: "when you see these things happening, you know that it is near, right at the door" (Mark 13:29; cf. Matt. 24:33; Luke 21:31). But "no one knows about that day or hour, not even the angels in heaven, nor the Son, but only the Father" (Mark 13:32). Consequently, Jesus' disciples are to be "on guard" and "alert" because they "do not know when that time will come" (v. 33). The point, of course, is that it could come in their lifetime—hence the warning, "If he comes suddenly, do not let him find you sleeping" (v. 36)!

A forward reading of these motifs reveals that this perspective is the consistent teaching of the New Testament Scriptures. The apostles Paul, Peter, and John affirm the uncertain timing of Jesus' return for their Christian readers (Acts 1:7; 1 Thess. 5:2; 1 Tim. 6:15; 2 Peter 3:10; cf. Rev. 3:3; 16:15). The notes of both imminence and watchfulness in Jesus' discourse also echo in the pages of the rest of the New Testament. Paul informs the saints at Rome that "the hour has come for you to wake up from your slumber, because our salvation is nearer now than when we first believed. The night is nearly over; the day is almost here" (Rom. 13:11b–12a). James and Peter strike the same note of imminence in their General Epistles (James 5:8b; 1 Peter 4:7; cf. Rev. 16:15). In Paul's first letter to the church at Thessalonica, he links the uncertain timing of the Lord's return with the need for vigilance:

> Now, brothers, about times and dates we do not need to write to you, for you know very well that the day of the Lord will come like a thief in the night. While people are saying, "Peace and safety," destruction will come on them suddenly, as labor pains on a pregnant woman, and they will not escape.
>
> But you, brothers, are not in darkness so that this day should surprise you like a thief. You are all sons of the light and sons of the day. We do not belong to the night or to the darkness. So then, let us not be like others, who are asleep, but let us be alert and self-controlled. (1 Thess. 5:1–6)

It is worth noting that in this context Paul employs similar imagery to the Olivet Discourse to describe Jesus' return in glory (Mark 13:26–27; 1 Thess. 4:16–17; cf. Acts 1:9–11; 2:19–20; Rev. 1:7).

Elsewhere Paul is fond of speaking simply of Jesus' "appearing" at the end of the age (1 Tim. 6:14; 2 Tim. 4:1, 8; Titus 2:13). For God's people, this appearing "will bring salvation" (Heb. 9:28; cf. Phil. 3:20), rescue "from the coming wrath" (1 Thess. 1:10), and "relief" from suffering and persecution (2 Thess. 1:5–7). For God's enemies, it will mean punishment "with everlasting destruction" and separation "from the presence of the Lord and from the majesty of his power" (2 Thess. 1:8–10; cf. 1 Thess. 5:3). Accordingly, it is no surprise that the book of Revelation ends with a longing for Jesus' return; it promises those in the church who overcome deliverance from their enemies and from the hardships and temptations of this present evil age, and unimaginable blessing in the age to come (Rev. 22:20; cf. 2–3; 21–22).

Jesus concludes his Olivet Discourse with a series of urgent exhortations related to his return as the Son of Man—"Be on guard! Be alert! . . . Watch!" (Mark 13:33a, 37b)—and if urgent for Jesus' disciples in their first-century historical context, how much more so for the Christian reader two thousand years later!

SUMMARY

The so-called Olivet Discourse, recorded in Mark 13, is Jesus' response to his disciples' questions about when the Jerusalem temple would be destroyed (Mark 13:4). Our downward reading of the discourse, however, reveals a focus not only on the events surrounding the destruction of the temple in A.D. 70, but also on the events associated with the end of the age. In his teaching, Jesus does not disclose a simple timetable of events that lead up to these occurrences in redemptive history; rather, his discussion of these events is interspersed with a series of exhortations aimed at his disciples, to enable them to navigate through deceptive messianic claims and to endure persecution, by foes and even family (vv. 9–13). Prominent is the exhortation to be watchful (cf. vv. 5, 9, 23, 30), indicating the kind of discipleship that Jesus expects of his followers.

Our sideways reading of the text affirms the dual focus of Jesus' discourse on both the destruction of the temple and the end of the age, anticipated by the more extended question of Jesus' disciples in Matthew's account (Matt. 24:3; cf. Mark 13:4). Our backward reading reveals a prophetic Old Testament background to Jesus' teaching, with prominence given to the prophecy of Daniel, particularly regarding "the abomination that causes desolation." In this Old Testament prophecy, a link is drawn between the destruction of "the city and the sanctuary" and "the end," a connection reflected in the Olivet Discourse (cf. Mark 13:14; Dan. 9:26–27). The Old Testament cosmic imagery that accompanies the coming of the Son of Man alerts the reader to a "judgment" motif that is more implicit than explicit in Mark's account of the discourse (cf. Mark 13:24–26; Isa. 13:9–13), but prepares the reader for the series of concluding exhortations (Mark 13:33–37). Our forward reading affirms the uncertain timing of the coming of the Son of Man at the end of the age, and the consequent need for Christian readers to also be alert and watchful as they wait for that day, an obligation reflected in the final exhortation of the discourse: "What I say to you, I say to everyone: 'Watch!'" (Mark 13:37).

Finally, we must ask what this discourse teaches us about Jesus. At an obvious level, Jesus is portrayed as God's true Messiah, and a prophet who knows the future. But at a more significant level, the teaching of the discourse portrays Jesus as the focal point of redemptive history. According to one commentator:

> It is equally important to note what this glorious vision of the future does *not* affirm. There is no mention of a millennium, no new Jerusalem, no rebuilt temple, no restoration of Israel or the State of Israel, no battle of Armageddon, and no hints how and when Christ will return. About all these things the text is silent. All these incidentals yield to the preeminent truth of the power and glory of Jesus' future coming and the promise that his elect will be gathered to him.[12]

Both Jesus' Olivet Discourse and Mark's Gospel place Jesus at the center of God's redemptive purposes, and remind Christian readers to keep their focus firmly on him as they expectantly wait for his return as the Son of Man.

---

12. Edwards, *The Gospel according to Mark*, 404 (emphasis in original).

15

JESUS PREDICTS PETER'S DENIAL

Mark 14:27–31, 66–72: "You will all fall away," Jesus told them, "for it is written:

"'I will strike the shepherd,
and the sheep will be scattered.'

But after I have risen, I will go ahead of you into Galilee."

Peter declared, "Even if all fall away, I will not."

"I tell you the truth," Jesus answered, "today—yes, tonight—before the rooster crows twice you yourself will disown me three times."

But Peter insisted emphatically, "Even if I have to die with you, I will never disown you." And all the others said the same. . . .

While Peter was below in the courtyard, one of the servant girls of the high priest came by. When she saw Peter warming himself, she looked closely at him.

"You also were with that Nazarene, Jesus," she said.

But he denied it. "I don't know or understand what you're talking about," he said, and went out into the entryway.

When the servant girl saw him there, she said again to those standing around, "This fellow is one of them." Again he denied it.

After a little while, those standing near said to Peter, "Surely you are one of them, for you are a Galilean."

He began to call down curses on himself, and he swore to them, "I don't know this man you're talking about."

Immediately the rooster crowed the second time. Then Peter remembered the word Jesus had spoken to him: "Before the rooster crows twice you will disown me three times." And he broke down and wept.

A DOWNWARD READING

Mark records this particular incident in two segments; the first contains Jesus' prediction of Peter's denial (Mark 14:27–31), and the second Peter's actual denial (vv. 66–72). The first segment occurs in the context of Jesus' institution of the Lord's Supper (vv. 12–26), while the second is preceded by Jesus' trial before the Sanhedrin (vv. 53–65).

Peter, it seems, has a penchant for contradicting the predictions of Jesus. When Jesus predicts his rejection, death, and resurrection at the hands of the religious leaders, Peter rebukes him (see Mark 8:31–32). In our text, when Jesus predicts that Peter will "disown" him three times, Peter contradicts him (14:29–31). This time there is a chorus of agreement from all of Peter's fellow disciples; they will "never disown" Jesus (14:31)!

During Jesus' Passover meal with his disciples, on the eve of his death, he predicts that one of them will betray him (Mark 14:18). After the meal, on the Mount of Olives, Jesus makes the bold prediction that all his disciples will desert him: "'You will all fall away,' Jesus told them, 'for it is written: "I will strike the shepherd, and the sheep will be scattered"'" (14:27). The "striking of the shepherd" is no doubt a metaphor for the death of Jesus on the cross, and in the context, the sheep are a reference to his disciples. Jesus predicts that his disciples will literally "stumble" or "turn away." Jesus uses the same word to describe the seed sown on rocky soil in his parable of the sower: "But since they have no root, they last only a short time. When trouble or persecution comes because of the word, they quickly fall away" (4:17). While there is a finality about the fate of the seed sown on rocky soil— "since they have no root, they last only a short time"—the same is not the case with Jesus' disciples. Concerning his disciples, Jesus predicts that "after I have risen, I will go ahead of you into Galilee" (14:28). An adversative, *but*, introduces this prediction, hinting at a reversal of their "fall" after they follow Jesus to Galilee. Unlike the one disciple who will betray Jesus, the rest will stumble, but not without the prospect of recovery (see Matt. 27:5).

Peter ignores Jesus' reference to his resurrection and Galilee, but responds instead to his prediction that all the disciples will "fall away." Peter declares that he will not stumble, even if all the other disciples do (Mark 14:29). Jesus responds to Peter's declaration with a detailed prediction that begins with a solemn note: "'I tell you the truth,' Jesus answered, 'today—yes, tonight—before the rooster crows twice you yourself will disown me three times'" (v. 30). Jesus' prediction is remarkably specific in terms of its time frame, and an obvious challenge to Peter's declaration of fidelity. Peter is unmoved by Jesus' response; he is insistent, "emphatically" so: "Even if I have to die with you, I will never disown you." All the other disciples say the same thing (v. 31). The scene shifts to Gethsemane, but an unresolved issue now hangs in the proverbial air: Whose word will prevail, that of Jesus, or Peter and the rest of the disciples?

The reader is given a hint as to the outcome of this issue as the events in Gethsemane unfold. Jesus asks his disciples Peter, James, and John to "stay here and keep watch" (Mark 14:34b). But on three occasions, Jesus finds them sleeping! One commentator suggests that these three failures are an anticipation of Peter's later threefold denial of Jesus.[1] After the first time, Jesus counsels Peter, "Watch and pray so that you will not fall into temptation. The spirit is willing, but the body is weak" (v. 38). It is this truth that will, in due course, be reflected in Peter's denial of Jesus.

Once Jesus is arrested, Mark tells us that "everyone deserted him and fled" (Mark 14:50). Jesus is vindicated, or so it appears. Yet Peter reappears in the narrative, following Jesus, albeit "at a distance, right into the courtyard of the high priest." Peter sits there with the guards and warms himself at the fire (v. 54). The scene is now set. Peter's declaration "Even if all fall away, I will not" (v. 29; cf. v. 31) will be put to the test. But before this happens, Jesus is also put to the test.

The chief priests and Sanhedrin want to put Jesus to death, but cannot find any evidence to convict him (Mark 14:55); the evidence marshaled against him is riddled with false testimony and disagreement (vv. 56–59). Jesus remains silent throughout the proceedings. But then the high priest asks Jesus a telling question: "Are you the Christ, the Son of the Blessed One?" (v. 61b). Jesus knows that to acknowledge his true identity is a certain death sentence in that setting. He does not hesitate

---

1. James R. Edwards, *The Gospel according to Mark*, Pillar New Testament Commentary (Grand Rapids: Eerdmans, 2002), 435.

to answer: "I am" (v. 62). All those present condemn him "as worthy of death" (Mark 14:64b). Jesus does not fail his test. Like Jesus, Peter will also be tested. Like Jesus, Peter knows that to acknowledge his true identity—a disciple of Jesus—would endanger his life. Jesus' appearance before the Sanhedrin ends with a call to Jesus to "prophesy!" (v. 65). Jesus does not comply with this call, but as the subsequent account of Peter's test unfolds, Jesus' earlier prediction will prove to be prophetic (cf. v. 30)!

The focus now shifts to Peter. A nameless servant girl of the high priest sees him warming himself at the fire in the courtyard below. She looks closely at him and pronounces, "You also were with that Nazarene, Jesus" (Mark 14:66–67). There is an implied threat in this statement. Peter would be declared guilty by association! But Peter denies it: "I don't know or understand what you're talking about." Strike one! Peter attempts to remove himself from further scrutiny by going out into "the entryway" (v. 68). Yet he cannot escape. The same accuser confronts him once again, and with the same outcome: "This fellow is one of them." Again Peter denies it, but this time "those standing around" witness it (vv. 69b–70). Strike two! The group of accusers now expands: "After a little while, those standing near said to Peter, 'Surely you are one of them, for you are a Galilean'" (v. 70b). Peter has an opportunity to redeem himself, but once again he fails, miserably so: "He began to call down curses on himself, and he swore to them, 'I don't know this man you're talking about'" (v. 71). Strike three!

It is important to note how Mark ends this particular episode in his Gospel. The focus shifts back to Jesus' prediction, which is fulfilled to the letter: "Immediately the rooster crowed the second time. Then Peter remembered the word Jesus had spoken to him: 'Before the rooster crows twice you will disown me three times.' And he broke down and wept" (Mark 14:72). Peter is understandably distraught. Jesus remains true to his identity as he faces the onslaught of the Sanhedrin, but Peter's bravado crumbles under the initial scrutiny of a nameless servant girl! Indeed, "the spirit . . . is willing, but the flesh is weak" (v. 38b ESV).

Jesus' predictions in this account are specific, detailed, and extraordinarily bold. Humanly speaking, Jesus has no control over the events that he predicts. Under arrest, Jesus has no influence over the response of his disciples. Yet—and this is an important point to note—even in the face of Peter's most emphatic rejection of Jesus' prediction, his every prediction "immediately" comes true, without delay and to the letter (Mark 14:72)! Jesus' word is trustworthy; this is the point that Mark wants his readers to grasp.

A SIDEWAYS READING

All four Gospels record this incident, and all four record the incident in two segments, although John's Gospel differs; it separates the actual denials into two segments (cf. Matt. 26:31–35, 69–75; Mark 14:27–31, 66–72; Luke 22:31–34, 54–62; John 18:15–18, 25–27). Peter's denials in John's account sandwich Jesus' truthful witness before the high priest (John 18:19–24), drawing a contrast between Peter and Jesus (cf. John 18:15–18; 18:25–27)—a contrast that, as we have seen in our downward reading of the text, is also evident in Mark's account (Mark 14:60–72).

The presence of this incident in the Gospels is sometimes cited as evidence for the historicity of the Gospels. After all, if the Gospels were the fabrication of the disciples or the early church, there would have been a reluctance to include an incident such as this that cast especially Peter, a leader in this church, in such a devastatingly negative light. Be that as it may, there are differences between the four accounts. Our sideways reading will highlight only the most salient differences that affect our understanding of Mark's account:

- In Jesus' more detailed prediction of Peter's denial, Mark alone mentions the rooster crowing "twice" (Mark 14:30; cf. Matt. 26:34; Luke 22:34)—perhaps a reflection, as tradition suggests, of Mark's dependence on Peter's vivid personal recollection of the details of the incident. This detail is repeated in Mark's account "immediately" upon Peter's third denial, reinforcing the exact fulfillment of Jesus' prediction (Mark 14:72). In this regard, however, it should be noted that some early Markan manuscripts lack these details (see NIV footnotes for Mark 14:30, 68, 72).
- In Jesus' detailed prediction of Peter's denial, there is a note of emphasis in Mark's account, lacking in the parallel accounts, in the personal pronoun that Jesus uses to address Peter: "'I tell you the truth,' Jesus answered, 'today—yes, tonight—before the rooster crows twice *you yourself* will disown me three times'"

(Mark 14:30; cf. Matt. 26:34; Luke 22:34). There can be no misunderstanding Jesus' point; it is Peter, and no other, who will disown him in this way.

- Mark alone describes Peter's response to Jesus' prediction in emphatic terms: "But Peter insisted emphatically, 'Even if I have to die with you, I will never disown you.' And all the others said the same" (Mark 14:31; cf. Matt. 26:35; Luke 22:33). Peter's emphatic insistence heightens the issue in the text: will Jesus' prediction come true in the face of such vehement denial? Put differently, can Peter's emphatic word thwart Jesus' word?

- Mark 14:66–70 is largely paralleled in Matthew's account (see Matt. 26:69–73). But Mark's description of the servant girl has some unique details. He describes her as "one of the servant girls of the high priest," as if to underscore her solitary, unthreatening physical profile, yet with links to the high priest, creating a perceived threat from Peter's perspective (Mark 14:66b; cf. Matt. 26:69; Luke 22:56).

- In Mark's account, the servant girl describes Jesus as "that Nazarene" (Mark 14:67b), rather than Matthew's "Jesus of Galilee" (Matt. 26:69b). Although both designations probably have derogatory connotations in the religious-historical context, the former appears to have a more contemptuous note about it, elevating the perceived threat of the accusation (cf. John 1:46).

- Mark, unlike Matthew, Luke, and John, has the same servant girl approaching Peter twice, prompting his first two denials (Mark 14:66–69; cf. Matt. 26:71; Luke 22:58; John 18:25). Perhaps Mark wants to show his readers that Peter cannot escape the girl's scrutiny, because we are told that she "saw him there," in the "entryway" (Mark 14:68b), and approaches him once more with an accusation (v. 69). But once again Peter denies the truth. Mark uses the imperfect tense—literally, "was denying" (v. 70a)—to indicate a series of denials in this encounter, with "those standing around" now also a witness to his failure.

- Before Peter's third denial, "those standing near" Peter identify him as a "Galilean" (Mark 14:70). Matthew's account alerts the reader to the fact that Peter's accent gives him away (cf. Matt. 26:73b).

Perhaps most notable about this sideways reading is the recognition in Mark's account of the increased specificity of Jesus' prediction, and the emphatic nature of Peter's response (Mark 14:30–31), both of which reinforce the concluding lesson of this incident, namely, that Jesus' detailed predictions, even when directly and emphatically challenged, will not fail at any point; they are completely trustworthy!

A BACKWARD READING

Jesus takes the initiative in this incident, predicting that his disciples "will all fall away" (Mark 14:27a). In support of this bold prediction, Jesus quotes the Old Testament Scriptures: "for it is written: 'I will strike the shepherd, and the sheep will be scattered'" (v. 27). Besides the obvious implication that Jesus believes what "is written" in the Old Testament Scriptures, the *for* that introduces the quotation suggests that the events about to unfold in the life of Christ and his disciples are scripted by God in the Old Testament Scriptures: nothing will happen by chance; God is faithfully working out his redemptive purposes through his Son. This truth should not be misinterpreted to mean that Peter and his fellow disciples are not responsible for their "scattering"; Peter instinctively takes responsibility for his subsequent denials by breaking down in sorrow at the conclusion of this episode (v. 72b). He will need restoration, like his fellow disciples (cf. 14:28; 16:7).

Jesus' Old Testament quotation is taken from the prophecy of Zechariah. Zechariah was a postexilic prophet, a contemporary of Haggai, who ministered during the period following the return of the Jewish exiles from Babylon in the sixth century B.C. By the time he records his prophecy, the initial enthusiasm of the returning exiles has dissipated. Both the temple and Jerusalem remain partially rebuilt. According to Zechariah, however, the Lord Almighty promises that the temple will be rebuilt (Zech. 1:16) and that he will "return to Zion and dwell in Jerusalem" (8:3); he will "save" his people and "bring them back to live in Jerusalem" (8:7–8). Jerusalem's enemies will be destroyed (12:1–9; cf. 14:12–13).

The Lord's people and their earthly rulers, however, are not without sin; they reject the Lord's rule. Zechariah uses the metaphor of a shepherd and flock to make the point (cf. Zech. 10:2–3; 11:4–14). But a humble, gentle, righteous king from the house of David will come to

Jerusalem, bringing salvation, proclaiming peace to the nations (9:9–10), and cleansing "the inhabitants of Jerusalem . . . from sin and impurity" (13:1). Quotations from these chapters in Zechariah's prophecy are fulfilled at strategic points in the ministry of Jesus, indicating that he is at the heart of this divine restoration (cf. Zech. 9:9/Matt. 21:5; Zech. 11:12–13/Matt. 27:9–10; Zech. 12:10/John 19:37).

But before this restoration will be a time of divine judgment, and only a remnant will be spared. This is evident from Jesus' quotation in our text taken from Zechariah 13:7: "'Awake, O sword, against my shepherd, against the man who is close to me!' declares the LORD Almighty. 'Strike the shepherd, and the sheep will be scattered, and I will turn my hand against the little ones.'" What is immediately noticeable is that Jesus amends Zechariah's prophecy to explicitly identify the Lord as the One who will strike "the shepherd" (see Mark 14:27). The "shepherd" is described by "the LORD Almighty" in Zechariah's prophecy as "my shepherd, . . . the man who is close to me" (Zech. 13:7a), an obvious allusion to Jesus, his Son. The "striking," in turn, is an allusion to Jesus' death on the cross. The point, of course, is that when Jesus is "struck" at Calvary, it is God's doing; "the LORD Almighty" is at work, judging his Son (cf. Isa. 53:4)! As a consequence, "the sheep will be scattered" (Zech. 13:7). In this Old Testament context, the scattering reflects the Lord's "hand" turned against "the little ones" in judgment (v. 7b). Yet Zechariah's prophecy does not end on a note of judgment:

> "In the whole land," declares the LORD,
>> "two-thirds will be struck down and perish;
>> yet one-third will be left in it.
> This third I will bring into the fire;
>> I will refine them like silver
>> and test them like gold.
> They will call on my name
>> and I will answer them;
> I will say, 'They are my people,'
>> and they will say, 'The LORD is our God.'" (Zech. 13:8–9)

This prophecy has "the whole land" of Israel in view. The majority, two-thirds, will be judged; they "will be struck down and perish" (v. 8). But a third will be left in the land, and will be refined; "they are my people," says the Lord, and they will say, "The LORD is our God," a clear reference to a covenantal promise (Zech. 13:9; cf. Lev. 26:9–12; Ezek. 37:26–27). It could be that Zechariah's prophecy at this point is alluding to the tribulations accompanying the events of A.D. 70 (cf. Mark 13:14–23). In any event, the survival of a remnant, and their restoration as God's people, is possibly in view in Jesus' statement in Mark 14:28 that suggests some kind of reversal: "But after I have risen, I will go ahead of you into Galilee." One commentator observes, "There is a satisfying symmetry in vv. 27 and 28: the 'striking' of the shepherd results in the scattering of the flock, but [Jesus'] resurrection will result in their regathering."[2]

It is evident that Peter's protest, echoed by his fellow disciples, is not just a challenge to Jesus' prediction, but also a rejection of what "is written" in God's prophetic Word (see Mark 14:27–31). Of course, we know the outcome of this saga: not only Jesus but also God's written Word is, in due course, vindicated (cf. vv. 50, 72)!

A FORWARD READING

A forward reading of the text can trace its implications for the Christian reader in a number of different directions. On the one hand is the challenge not to be ashamed of Jesus or his gospel message today, unlike Peter (cf. Mark 8:38; Matt. 10:32–33; Rom. 1:16; 2 Tim. 1:8, 12; 2:13; Heb. 13:13). On the other hand, we could focus on Peter's threefold restoration by Jesus, after his resurrection, as a demonstration of God's grace (John 21:15–19). This is contrary to the pattern of this world. To adopt an analogy from baseball, alluded to earlier: three strikes, but amazingly, you're not out! Paul's conversion experience provides another compelling example of God's mercy and grace toward sinners (cf. 1 Tim. 1:12–17). But because of how our segmented text begins and ends—with Jesus' prophetic prediction, which in due course is fulfilled—it seems more appropriate to focus on the motif of the trustworthiness of the words of Jesus.

As we have seen, Jesus' prediction that all the disciples will "fall away" is based on a prophecy recorded by the prophet Zechariah (cf. Zech. 13:7; Mark 14:27). During the course of Jesus' subsequent arrest, Mark

2. R. T. France, *The Gospel of Mark*, New International Greek Testament Commentary (Grand Rapids: Eerdmans, 2002), 577.

informs us that "everyone deserted [Jesus] and fled" (Mark 14:50). Jesus' confidence in the Old Testament Scriptures is not misplaced. The focus of the text, however, falls on the interaction between Jesus and Peter. Peter insists "emphatically" that he will "never disown" Jesus, despite Jesus' detailed prediction to the contrary (14:31). In the broader flow of the Markan narrative, the outcome of this incident is hardly a surprise. Again and again, the power and authority of Jesus' words have been on display in the Gospel account, as he casts out demons (1:21–28), pronounces the forgiveness of sins (2:1–12), calms "a furious squall" (4:35–41), and even raises the dead (5:35–43)—all with a simple command! Peter duly denies Jesus, but significantly, he does so in exact accordance with Jesus' detailed prediction (cf. 14:30, 72). Jesus' word is tested and demonstrated to be completely trustworthy, like the written Word of God! As Jesus states elsewhere, "heaven and earth will pass away, but my words will never pass away" (Mark 13:31; cf. Isa. 40:8)!

Accordingly, when Jesus challenges the prevailing misinterpretation of the law in the Sermon on the Mount with the words, "You have heard that it was said . . . but I tell you . . . ," we should accept his instruction (cf. Matt. 5:21–22, 27–28, 33–34, 38–39, 43–44; cf. vv. 31–32). When he tells us not to worry because we have a Father in heaven who will take care of us, we should believe him (see 6:25–34). When he defines the "wise man" as the person who hears his words and puts them into practice, we should heed his word (see Matt. 7:24–27). When he commands his disciples to teach the nations to "obey everything I have commanded you," we should obey him (see 28:20a). And when he tells us that he is with us "to the very end of the age," we should depend on it (Matt. 28:20b).

As we trace this motif through the pages of the New Testament, we see the words of Jesus consistently portrayed as trustworthy and authoritative in the book of Acts. The resurrected Jesus predicts the outpouring of the Holy Spirit and the subsequent Spirit-empowered witness of the disciples "to the ends of the earth," both of which come to pass in due course (Acts 1:4, 8; cf. 2:1–41; 8:1–25; 10:1–48). After the apostle Paul's conversion, the "Lord" Jesus tells Ananias in a vision that Paul "is my chosen instrument to carry my name before the Gentiles and their kings and before the people of Israel" (Acts 9:15), all of which clearly transpire in the pages of the book of Acts (cf. 17:1–34; 26:1–32). Moreover, as Jesus predicts, Paul ends up testifying about him in Rome

(23:11; cf. 28:17–31). Neither a ferocious storm nor a deadly snake can derail Jesus' word (see 27:13–28:6)!

In the book of Revelation, the word or "revelation of Jesus Christ" is equated with the Word of God (cf. Rev. 1:1–3; 22:18–19). This truth is reflected in Jesus' authoritative word of revelation to the seven churches in the province of Asia (see 1:11ff.; 2–3). Accordingly, when Jesus tells the reader, "I am coming soon" (22:20a), the Christian should live expectantly! But perhaps more significantly in the historical context, this entire episode should encourage Jesus' disciples to believe his prediction that after he has risen he will go ahead of them into Galilee, a prediction that is reiterated, and affirmed, at the end of Mark's narrative by an angelic witness:

> "Don't be alarmed," he said. "You are looking for Jesus the Nazarene, who was crucified. He has risen! He is not here. See the place where they laid him. But go, tell his disciples and Peter, 'He is going ahead of you into Galilee. There you will see him, *just as he told you*'" (Mark 16:6–7).

SUMMARY

This particular incident in the Gospels, recorded in two segments, is typically referred to as "Peter's denial of Jesus" (Mark 14:27–31, 66–72). But when one recognizes that the two segments are held together by the thread of Jesus' prediction and its subsequent fulfillment, it is more accurate to view the entire incident through this lens. Thus, it is significant that the entire episode ends on this note, with Peter recalling Jesus' detailed prediction (v. 72) and, by implication, testifying to the complete trustworthiness of Jesus' word.

Our downward reading of the text draws attention to Jesus' predictions of denial, first by all his disciples, and then specifically by Peter, both of which are fulfilled in Mark's narrative (see Mark 14:27, 30, 50, 72). Our sideways reading of the text reveals Mark's increased specificity in Jesus' prediction (Mark 14:30; cf. Matt. 26:34; Luke 22:34) and the emphatic nature of Peter's response (Mark 14:31; cf. Matt. 26:35; Luke 22:33). Both of these observations reinforce the concluding lesson of the incident, namely, that Jesus' word will not fail, even when directly and emphatically challenged; it is completely trustworthy!

Our backward reading of the text reveals Jesus' confidence in the prophetic written Word of God, a confidence that, in due course, is vindicated (cf. Mark 14:27, 50) and that, in due course, we can also extend to Jesus' word. Our forward reading of the text affirms the trustworthiness of Jesus' word, with the obvious implication that the Christian reader should not only have confidence in it, but also heed and obey it, to the letter!

16

JESUS LAYS DOWN HIS LIFE ON A CROSS

Mark 15:33–39: At the sixth hour darkness came over the whole land until the ninth hour. And at the ninth hour Jesus cried out in a loud voice, *"Eloi, Eloi, lama sabachthani?"*—which means, "My God, my God, why have you forsaken me?"

When some of those standing near heard this, they said, "Listen, he's calling Elijah."

One man ran, filled a sponge with wine vinegar, put it on a stick, and offered it to Jesus to drink. "Now leave him alone. Let's see if Elijah comes to take him down," he said.

With a loud cry, Jesus breathed his last.

The curtain of the temple was torn in two from top to bottom. And when the centurion, who stood there in front of Jesus, heard his cry and saw how he died, he said, "Surely this man was the Son of God!"

A DOWNWARD READING

Mark's Gospel has been accurately described as a "Passion narrative with an extended introduction,"[1] devoting as it does a disproportionate amount of space to the last week of Jesus' earthly ministry that

1. Martin Kähler, quoted in Craig L. Blomberg, *Jesus and the Gospels* (Leicester, UK: Apollos, 1997), 116.

culminates in his suffering and death. During this week, the energetic pace of Jesus' earlier ministry throughout Galilee progressively slows right down to a crawl, so to speak, as Mark provides the reader with a blow-by-blow account of Jesus' last hours on the cross. These last hours of Jesus are the focus of our text.

Mark informs the reader that Jesus is crucified at "the third hour," that is, at 9:00 AM (Mark 15:25). Crucifixion was not devised by the Roman governing authorities, but it was adopted by them as a public form of capital punishment to deter criminal activity. It is a slow, painful, and shameful way to die. Jesus does not deserve to die on a cross. Pontius Pilate, the Roman governor at the time, knows that it is "out of envy that the chief priests [have] handed Jesus over to him" (v. 10). But Pilate, unwilling to incur the displeasure of the local indigenous population who demand Jesus' crucifixion, eventually has Jesus flogged and hands him over to be crucified (vv. 12–15). According to Mark, "The written notice of the charge against him read: THE KING OF THE JEWS" (v. 26). The derision directed toward Jesus from bystanders and passersby as he hangs on the cross indicates that few, if any, in the vicinity believe it is true (see vv. 25–32).

Our text begins with a reference to "darkness" enveloping "the whole land" from the sixth to the ninth hours, while Jesus hangs on the cross (Mark 15:33). These are the daylight hours of noon to 3:00 PM, indicating that this "darkness" is some kind of supernatural phenomenon. Mark does not elaborate on its significance. At the ninth hour—Jesus has already been on the cross for six hours—he cries out "in a loud voice," as if to rouse heaven: "'Eloi, Eloi, lama sabachthani?'—which means, 'My God, my God, why have you forsaken me?'" (v. 34). The translation of the Aramaic words of Jesus suggests that at least some of Mark's readers are Gentiles. Jesus, unjustly condemned to die on a cross, considers himself "forsaken" by God! One commentator describes Jesus' words as "a cry of dereliction."[2] Yet it is not a cry devoid of faith and hope; after all, although God may have forsaken Jesus at this moment, it is clear from Jesus' cry that he has not forsaken God. Some bystanders, however, misinterpret or distort Jesus' reference to Eloi to be a call to "Elijah," the prophet (v. 35). "One man" responds by filling "a sponge with wine

---

2. C. E. B. Cranfield, quoted in Robert H. Stein, *Mark*, Baker Exegetical Commentary on the New Testament (Grand Rapids: Baker Academic, 2008), 716.

vinegar," placing it "on a stick," and offering it to Jesus "to drink," with the words, "Now leave him alone. Let's see if Elijah comes to take him down" (v. 36). But Elijah does not come to Jesus' rescue: "With a loud cry, Jesus breathed his last" (v. 37).

Mark introduces a change of setting. Without warning, the focus shifts to the Jerusalem temple. Mark informs the reader that the "curtain of the temple was torn in two from top to bottom" (Mark 15:38). One of two possible curtains is in view here—either the outer curtain that separates the sanctuary from the temple courtyard or the inner curtain, sometimes referred to as the "second curtain" (see Heb. 9:3), that separates off the Most Holy Place, with access limited to the high priest once a year.[3] A tear in the outer curtain would be a "more . . . public event," but a tear in the inner curtain would be theologically more significant, according to one commentator.[4] Mark is nonspecific.

Given what we know about the sheer physical dimensions of either curtain, no human being is physically capable of tearing it "in two from top to bottom" (Mark 15:38), nor would anyone with opportunity be inclined to do so. Thus, it is clearly an act of God, alluded to by the so-called divine passive—"was torn." One commentator describes the act as "divine vandalism" of the temple,[5] suggesting that it anticipates the ultimate divine desecration and destruction of the temple sanctuary predicted earlier in Mark's Gospel (see 11:12–17; 13:2; 14:58; 15:29). In favor of this "judgment" motif is the "darkness" that accompanies the crucifixion of Jesus, although "the whole land," rather than just the temple, is in view there (cf. 15:33).

There is another, more positive perspective on the tearing of the curtain, an interpretation that is based on the flow of the narrative in the immediate context. The "curtain of the temple" that is "torn in two" is identified as the one that cordons off the Most Holy Place (Mark 15:38). Mark records Jesus' death on the cross, followed by a Gentile centurion's confession, prompted by the death of Jesus: "Surely this man was the Son of God!" (vv. 37–39). This chronological sequence of events at the cross, however, is interrupted by Mark's reference to the tearing of the curtain

3. James R. Edwards, *The Gospel according to Mark*, Pillar New Testament Commentary (Grand Rapids: Eerdmans, 2002), 477–78.

4. R. T. France, *The Gospel of Mark*, New International Greek Testament Commentary (Grand Rapids: Eerdmans, 2002), 656.

5. Ibid., 657.

in the temple, alerting the reader to the significance of Jesus' death: the way through the curtain into the Most Holy Place and presence of God is no longer reserved for the Jewish high priest; it is now open even to the likes of this Gentile centurion, an enemy of God's people!

It is possible that Mark does not want his readers to choose between these two perspectives on the text; indeed, they are not incompatible. To quote Jesus' earlier teaching in the parable of the tenants: "What then will the owner of the vineyard do? He will come and kill those tenants and give the vineyard to others" (Mark 12:9). Divine judgment and divine blessing go hand in hand in Mark's Gospel.

A SIDEWAYS READING

It is hardly surprising, given the emphasis placed on Jesus' death in the Gospels, that all four Gospels record this incident (cf. Matt. 27:45–54; Mark 15:33–39; Luke 23:44–47; John 19:28–30). John's account is quite different, and so will not detain us in this analysis. Our sideways reading of this account will provide one or two helpful insights into Mark's narrative.

- All three synoptic accounts mention the "darkness" that descends on the whole land from the sixth to the ninth hours (Matt. 27:45; Mark 15:33; Luke 23:44). Luke's account adds that this was because the "sun stopped shining," affirming the perception that this occurrence during the daylight hours was a supernatural event (Luke 23:45a). Interestingly, Luke immediately adds that "the curtain of the temple was torn in two" (v. 45b), forging a link between these two occurrences that supports the view that not only the darkness but also the tearing of the curtain signifies divine judgment.
- All three synoptic accounts record the confession of the Roman centurion, although in Matthew's account the confession is also on the lips of his fellow guards (cf. Matt. 27:54; Mark 15:39; Luke 23:47). Mark alone describes the confession as a response to the way in which Jesus dies: "And when the centurion, who stood there in front of Jesus, heard his cry and saw how he died, he said, 'Surely this man was the Son of God!'" (Mark 15:39). It should

be noted that some Markan manuscripts omit the reference to "heard his cry." The alternative reading is rendered in the ESV: "And when the centurion, who stood facing him, saw that in this way he breathed his last, he said, 'Truly this man was the Son of God!'" Either way, the confession is motivated by the way in which Jesus dies or "breathe[s] his last" (15:37).

What exactly is it about Jesus' death that evokes this confession? Based on Matthew's and Luke's accounts, which attribute the confession more generally to the sight of what "happened" at Jesus' death (cf. Matt. 27:54; Luke 23:47), some commentators suggest that it was a combination of factors that include the supernatural darkness, Jesus' loud cries, the earthquake (in the case of Matthew), and the manner of Jesus' death (cf. Matt. 27:45–54; Luke 23:44–47).[6] Yet Mark appears to place the focus exclusively on the "way [Jesus] breathed his last" (Mark 15:39 ESV). Assuming the accuracy of the NIV reading in Mark's Gospel, it could be that the centurion is inspired to make his confession not by the surprising vigor of Jesus' "loud cry" after six hours on the cross (Mark 15:37), but by the fact that Jesus dies immediately after having the physical strength to utter such a cry. The centurion is witnessing something unnatural. Put differently, he sees Jesus, remarkably in control of events, laying down his life—he "breathed his last"—rather than his life draining out of him from the rigors of the crucifixion (cf. Matt. 27:50b). This conclusion is supported by the fact that Pilate "was surprised to hear that [Jesus] was already dead" (Mark 15:44a). Jesus apparently dies relatively quickly, contrary to normal expectations.

The centurion recognizes "this man" to be "the Son of God" as he lays down his life (Mark 15:39b)! It is astonishing, when one reflects on it, that the sight of a dying man on a cross can evoke such an exalted confession. To fully appreciate the significance of this confession in the broader sweep of Mark's narrative, we need to return to the beginning of this Gospel, where Mark introduces Jesus as both the "Christ" and "the Son of God" (1:1b). Peter will, in due course, identify Jesus as "the Christ," that is, the Messiah, in his so-called confession at Caesarea Philippi (8:29). It is clear from Peter's subsequent rebuke,

---

6. See, for example, D. A. Carson, "Matthew," in *Matthew, Mark, Luke*, vol. 8 of The Expositor's Bible Commentary (Grand Rapids: Zondervan, 1984), 583.

however, that his understanding of Jesus' true identity is "blurred," to borrow the imagery from the first stage of the two-stage healing of the blind man in the preceding incident (see 8:22–24).[7] In Peter's mind, the miracle-working Jesus portrayed in the preceding chapters cannot be reconciled with a suffering, rejected Messiah who will be killed, as predicted by Jesus (see 8:31–33).

But what about Jesus as "the Son of God" (Mark 1:1b)? In Mark's Gospel, God identifies Jesus as his "Son" at two strategic points in his ministry—at Jesus' baptism and transfiguration (see 1:11; 9:7)—an identity reiterated by "the evil spirits" who encounter him (see 3:11; 5:7). Some commentators draw attention to the fact that at Jesus' baptism, the heavens are "torn open," like the temple curtain—the only two occurrences of the word to tear in Mark—both actions being accompanied by the confession of Jesus' divine sonship, suggesting some kind of parallel revelation (cf. 1:10–11; 15:38–39).[8] The centurion's confession, however, is the first time the title "Son of God" is found on the lips of a human being in Mark's narrative (cf. 1:1; 15:39). More than a handful of commentators believe that this is a structural ploy by Mark to make an important point regarding Jesus' identity: only at the cross, as Jesus lays down his life, does the reader see clearly—to borrow the imagery from the second stage of the two-stage healing in Mark 8:22–26—the true identity of Jesus.[9] At the cross, we see the convergence of the ministries of the "Christ" and "the Son of God" predicted by Jesus (see 1:1; 8:29–33; 9:7). The good news about "Jesus Christ, the Son of God," is that he was born to die, so that the likes of a Gentile centurion might be able to experience the blessing of God's kingdom (cf. 1:15; 15:39). This is the picture that Mark paints of Jesus. Any view of Jesus that does not reflect this truth is deficient, according to Mark!

A BACKWARD READING

Elsewhere in the Gospels, Jesus testifies to the truth that the Old Testament Scriptures, rightly understood, predict his suffering and death on a cross (e.g., Luke 24:25–27). We see this truth reflected in Mark's

7. Edwards, The Gospel according to Mark, 245.
8. See, for example, ibid., 478.
9. See, for example, ibid., 244–45.

account of Jesus' death, which simply affirms the point that these events depict the fulfillment of Old Testament prophecy.

- At Jesus' crucifixion, "darkness" descends over "the whole land" from the sixth to the ninth hours, that is, from noon to 3:00 PM (Mark 15:33). For those familiar with the Old Testament Scriptures, the "darkness" motif may bring to mind the exodus account, and the plague of darkness that hovers over the land of Egypt for three days, as a sign of God's displeasure with Pharaoh (see Ex. 10:21–23). In the crucifixion scene, however, the "darkness" lasts only three hours and has shifted to the land of Israel; it is the people of God who will now experience God's wrath!

  Amos, the eighth-century B.C. prophet to the nation of Israel, uses this same imagery to predict just such a judgment: "'In that day,' declares the Sovereign LORD, 'I will make the sun go down at noon and darken the earth in broad daylight'" (Amos 8:9). The "day" is a reference to "the day of the LORD," a time of divine judgment, but the context makes it clear that the target is the nation of Israel, rather than the enemies of God's people (cf. 5:18–27). The Lord shows Amos "a basket of ripe fruit" to make the point that Israel is "ripe" for judgment: "Then the LORD said to me, 'The time is ripe for my people Israel; I will spare them no longer'" because of their many sins (8:2, 4–6). God's judgment on his people will bring "mourning" and "weeping," and "a famine of hearing the words of the LORD" (8:10–12). It is a judgment that "none will escape" (9:1b). The implication for our text is obvious: as Jesus hangs on the cross, the hand of God hovers in judgment, a judgment that will bring both physical suffering and spiritual darkness on "the whole land" of Israel!

- If the "darkness" signifies judgment on Israel, the "loud" cry that follows signifies judgment on Jesus: "And at the ninth hour Jesus cried out in a loud voice, '*Eloi, Eloi, lama sabachthani?*'—which means, 'My God, my God, why have you forsaken me?'" (Mark 15:34). Jesus' words are not a random cry of despair, but a quotation of the opening words of Psalm 22. If, as some commentators believe, Jesus' cry is intended as an allusion to the entire psalm, which includes an expectation of divine deliverance, then clearly the cry is not devoid of hope: "For he has not despised or disdained the suffering of the afflicted one; he has not hidden his face from him but has listened to his cry for help" (Ps. 22:24).[10] One commentator describes this note of deliverance as "a startling reversal" in the psalm, a good description of Jesus' subsequent deliverance through the resurrection (cf. Mark 16:6).[11]

What is remarkable about this psalm, composed by David nearly a millennium before the events depicted, is how accurately it mirrors Jesus' experience on the cross: "All who see me mock me; they hurl insults, shaking their heads: 'He trusts in the LORD; let the LORD rescue him. Let him deliver him, since he delights in him'" (Ps. 22:7–8; cf. Mark 15:29–32). Like the righteous sufferer in the psalm, Jesus is all alone in the midst of a sea of hostility: his disciples have fled; there is no one to help him except God (cf. Ps. 22:11; Mark 14:50). The psalm also contains unmistakable allusions to the physical trauma of crucifixion:

I am poured out like water,
    and all my bones are out of joint.
My heart has turned to wax;
    it has melted away within me.
My strength is dried up like a potsherd,
    and my tongue sticks to the roof of my mouth;
    you lay me in the dust of death.
Dogs have surrounded me;
    a band of evil men has encircled me,
    they have pierced my hands and my feet.
I can count all my bones;
    people stare and gloat over me.
They divide my garments among them
    and cast lots for my clothing. (Ps. 22:14–18; cf. Mark 15:24)

It is important to note, however, that Mark's Gospel, unlike this psalm, does not dwell on the physical aspect of Christ's sufferings on the cross.

10. See, for example, the discussion in Rikk E. Watts, *Mark*, Commentary on the New Testament Use of the Old Testament (Grand Rapids: Baker Academic, 2007), 236–37.
    11. Ibid., 236.

The psalm is also suffused with pockets of hope (Ps. 22:3–5, 9–11, 19–31), but neither Mark nor Jesus quotes from this aspect of the psalm. Of greater consequence in the narrative is Jesus' God-forsakenness: "My God, my God, why have you forsaken me? Why are you so far from saving me, so far from the words of my groaning?" (Ps. 22:1; cf. Mark 15:34). Despite Jesus' cry for help, God does not save him; he hangs on the cross as a substitute, a Passover sacrifice whose blood is shed, who drains the cup of God's wrath on behalf of others, in accordance with God's purposes (cf. Ps. 22:1; Mark 14:22–24, 36).

There is mystery in Jesus' cry on the cross. How can Jesus—the One in whom the Lord "delights" (Ps. 22:8b)—who enjoys perfect intimacy with his Father (see Mark 14:36), experience even for a moment any disruption in this union? But Mark does not pause to address this mystery; he leaves it unexplained. It is enough for his readers to know that Jesus' death was no ordinary death, and that of greater importance than the physical horrors of the crucifixion was the divine displeasure that Jesus absorbed in his body and spirit as a "ransom for many" (Mark 10:45b).

- The crowd at the cross misinterprets Jesus' cry as an appeal to "Elijah," the prophet (Mark 15:35). One man, perhaps motivated by a note of deliverance that he detects in Jesus' cry (cf. Ps. 22:24), runs, "fill[s] a sponge with wine vinegar, put[s] it on a stick, and offer[s] it to Jesus to drink. 'Now leave him alone. Let's see if Elijah comes to take him down,' he said" (Mark 15:36). Some commentators see an allusion at this point to Psalm 69:21: "They put gall in my food and gave me vinegar for my thirst."[12] This connection is strengthened by the addition of "gall" in Matthew's account (Matt. 27:34). In the context of Psalm 69, a psalm that depicts a righteous sufferer also crying out to God for salvation (Ps. 69:1–4), the "gall" and "vinegar" are not, in the words of one commentator, gestures of "mercy," but of "mockery" (Ps. 69:20).[13] If Mark intends the reader to import this perspective from the psalm (and commentators are divided on this question), then the centurion's

12. See, for example, Edwards, *The Gospel according to Mark*, 477.
13. Carson, "Matthew," 579.

215

subsequent confession is the only glimmer of light among the bystanders in this episode (Mark 15:39).[14]

- The centurion confesses Jesus to be "truly . . . the Son of God!" (Mark 15:39b ESV). This title has divine connotations in Mark's Gospel (Mark 1:11; 9:7) and divine kingship connotations in the Old Testament (e.g., 2 Sam. 7:12–14a; Ps. 2:7). According to Psalm 2, God's Son will "rule" the "ends of the earth" with an "iron scepter" despite opposition from the "kings of the earth" and "rulers" gathered together against him (Ps. 2:2, 8, 9). To what extent this full-orbed Old Testament understanding of the title is present in the mind of the confessing centurion is a matter of speculation. But what is astounding, at least from this biblical perspective, is the fact that this divine King dies on a Roman cross, rejected by the religious elite and vilified by men. The centurion's confession, however, hints at better things to come; he is the firstfruits of many Gentiles from the nations of the earth who will in due course also confess Jesus' name, a truth hinted at in Psalm 22: "All the ends of the earth will remember and turn to the LORD, and all the families of the nations will bow down before him" (Ps. 22:27).

A FORWARD READING

We have argued that in Mark's Gospel, Jesus' death on a Roman cross is central to a true understanding of Jesus' identity. But an analysis of our text shows that the significance of Jesus' death is not explicitly spelled out by Mark in the context. Rather, he uses imagery—"darkness . . . over the whole land" and a temple curtain "torn in two" (Mark 15:33, 38)—and Jesus' cry, and a centurion's confession (vv. 34, 39), to make the point that Jesus' death on the cross is no ordinary death. As we trace the significance of Jesus' death in a forward reading of the text, we will see that the writers of the New Testament do not diminish the importance of Jesus' crucifixion and are more explicit in their comments on its purpose.

In the book of Acts, Jesus' death on a cross is recorded as a historical fact in the preaching of the apostles, and is portrayed in a way that reflects some of the distinctives of Mark's depiction of the crucifixion

14. Stein, *Mark*, 716–17.

(cf. Mark 15:16–39; Acts 2:23–24; 5:30; 10:39–40; 13:29–30). These apostles are quick to point out to their audience that Jesus' death was in accordance with God's purposes—that is, in accordance with "all that was written about him" in the Old Testament Scriptures (Acts 13:29a; cf. 2:23a). The mention of "the cross," or Jesus' being hanged on a "tree," is always accompanied by a reference to God's raising Jesus from the dead (see 2:23–24; 5:30; 10:39–40; 13:29–30). It appears that Jesus' cry of God-forsakenness on the cross was justifiably not devoid of hope; in due course, God delivers his Son (Mark 16:6).

Moreover, the death of Jesus is not in vain; according to the teaching of the apostles, it secures the forgiveness of sins for all who repent, both Jews and Gentiles, and even those implicated in the death of Jesus (Acts 2:23, 37–39; 5:30–31; 10:39, 43; 13:27–28, 38–39). Accordingly, whatever the "darkness" and the centurion's confession at the cross signify, they cannot be interpreted to mean that the benefits of Jesus' death are now limited to the Gentiles only. The apostle Paul in his letter to the church at Rome affirms this truth when he writes that the gospel is "the power of God for the salvation of everyone who believes: first for the Jew, then for the Gentile" (Rom. 1:16; cf. 11:22–24), and we see this pattern consistently depicted in Paul's ministry in the book of Acts: it is first to the Jew, then to the Gentile (cf. Acts 9:20, 28–29; 13:4–5, 13–52; 14:1; 17:1–4, 10–12, 17; 18:4–6, 12–13, 19; 19:8–10; 26:19–21; 28:17–28). It is not surprising, therefore, that two of the New Testament's so-called General Epistles—Hebrews and James—are written specifically to Jewish Christians to encourage them in their spiritual pilgrimage.

Speaking of Jew and Gentile, the apostle Paul identifies the cross as God's instrument to effect reconciliation between God and man, and Jew and Gentile. Paul's words are worth quoting in full. The "two" that Paul refers to in the context are Jew and Gentile:

> But now in Christ Jesus you who once were far away have been brought near through the blood of Christ.
>
> For he himself is our peace, who has made the two one and has destroyed the barrier, the dividing wall of hostility, by abolishing in his flesh the law with its commandments and regulations. His purpose was to create in himself one new man out of the two, thus making peace, and in this one body to reconcile both of them to God through

the cross, by which he put to death their hostility. (Eph. 2:13–16; cf. Rom. 5:10; 11:22–24)

The apostle Paul in his letter to the Colossians extends this divine reconciliation, through Jesus' "blood, shed on the cross," to include all things, "whether things on earth or things in heaven" (Col. 1:20). In his letters, Paul reiterates the link between the cross and the forgiveness of sins, while in the same breath attributing the defeat of "the [hostile] powers and authorities" to "the cross" (Col. 2:13–15; cf. Rom. 4:25; Eph. 1:7). The apostle Peter reminds "God's elect" that Jesus "bore [their] sins in his body on the tree" to "bring [them] to God" (1 Peter 1a; 2:24; 3:18), while the apostle John informs his readers that "if we walk in the light, . . . the blood of Jesus, [God's] Son, purifies us from all sin" (1 John 1:7; cf. 2:12).

The writer to the Hebrews mentions "the cross" only once in his letter: Jesus "endured the cross, scorning its shame, and sat down at the right hand of the throne of God" (Heb. 12:2). Here, as in the case of the other New Testament writers, the cross is not the final word—but here Jesus' ascension, rather than his resurrection, is in view. The writer to the Hebrews attaches significance to the death of Jesus: Jesus "shared in [the] humanity [of the children of God] so that by his death he might destroy him who holds the power of death—that is, the devil—and free those who all their lives were held in slavery by their fear of death" (2:14–15; cf. 2:9). Hebrews also teaches that "the blood of Christ . . . cleanse[s] . . . consciences from acts that lead to death" (9:14), and draws a connection between Jesus' death and sin: Jesus dies "as a ransom to set [God's people] free from the sins committed under the first covenant" (9:15). This imagery is taken from the first-century slave market, where a ransom price is paid by the one who is free to purchase the freedom of the slave. The apostles Paul, Peter, and John adopt this same imagery when they speak of Jesus' "blood" that was shed on the cross (cf. Eph. 1:7; 1 Peter 1:19; Rev. 1:5). This blood, John reports, is powerful enough to purchase "men for God from every tribe and language and people and nation" (Rev. 5:9; cf. Acts 20:28). Hebrews also uses the imagery of sacrifice to describe the purpose of Jesus' death: "Christ was sacrificed once to take away the sins of many people" (Heb. 9:28a; cf. 7:27b). The one sacrifice of Jesus is sufficient to "take away" sins (cf. 1 Peter 3:18a). It is no wonder that John the Baptist during his ministry points out Jesus as "the Lamb of God, who takes away the sin of the world!" (John 1:29). And significantly, in the context of our analysis of Jesus' death and the significance of the tearing of the temple curtain (Mark 15:38–39), the writer to the Hebrews adopts this imagery to make the point that Jesus' death—through the tearing of his body on the cross—opens the way for believers to enter God's presence: "Therefore, brothers . . . we have confidence to enter the Most Holy Place by the blood of Jesus, by a new and living way opened for us through the curtain, that is, his body" (Heb. 10:19–20). These verses provide the Christian reader with a striking word-picture to portray one of the most stunning benefits of Christ's death on the cross—direct access to God (cf. Heb.10:21–22).

SUMMARY

In Mark's Gospel, Jesus predicts his death on numerous occasions (e.g., Mark 8:31; 9:31; 10:33–34). It should therefore come as no surprise to the reader of this Gospel, as we discover in our downward reading of the text, that Jesus' death is portrayed as no ordinary death. It is accompanied by supernatural "darkness" (Mark 15:33), an unexpected cry from Jesus (v. 34), the tearing of a curtain in the temple (v. 38), and an exalted confession from a Gentile centurion (v. 39). What is surprising, highlighted by our sideways reading of the text, is the fact that the centurion's confession is prompted by the way in which Jesus dies on the cross, effectively making the point that one cannot truly understand who Jesus is apart from the cross (v. 39).

Our backward reading reveals the presence of a "judgment" motif in the "darkness" that descends over the land (Mark 15:33; cf. Amos 8:9) and a remarkable description of Jesus' crucifixion experience penned by David the psalmist about a thousand years before the event (Ps. 22:1–21). The reader is left with the distinct impression that Jesus' crucifixion is by God's design and represents the fulfillment of a number of Old Testament prophecies.

Our forward reading of the text reinforces the significance of Jesus' death by spelling out its implications for Christian believers—it brings forgiveness of sins, defeats evil, and effects reconciliation of all things, on earth and in heaven; it purifies and redeems God's people! Truly, there is great power in the blood of Jesus! It is this fundamental truth that the Christian reader must grasp and embrace.

17

JESUS RISES FROM THE DEAD

Mark 16:1–20: When the Sabbath was over, Mary Magdalene, Mary the mother of James, and Salome bought spices so that they might go to anoint Jesus' body. Very early on the first day of the week, just after sunrise, they were on their way to the tomb and they asked each other, "Who will roll the stone away from the entrance of the tomb?"

But when they looked up, they saw that the stone, which was very large, had been rolled away. As they entered the tomb, they saw a young man dressed in a white robe sitting on the right side, and they were alarmed.

"Don't be alarmed," he said. "You are looking for Jesus the Nazarene, who was crucified. He has risen! He is not here. See the place where they laid him. But go, tell his disciples and Peter, 'He is going ahead of you into Galilee. There you will see him, just as he told you.'"

Trembling and bewildered, the women went out and fled from the tomb. They said nothing to anyone, because they were afraid.

When Jesus rose early on the first day of the week, he appeared first to Mary Magdalene, out of whom he had driven seven demons. She went and told those who had been with him and who were mourning and weeping. When they heard that Jesus was alive and that she had seen him, they did not believe it.

Afterward Jesus appeared in a different form to two of them while they were walking in the country. These returned and reported it to the rest; but they did not believe them either.

Later Jesus appeared to the Eleven as they were eating; he rebuked them for their lack of faith and their stubborn refusal to believe those who had seen him after he had risen.

He said to them, "Go into all the world and preach the good news to all creation. Whoever believes and is baptized will be saved, but whoever does not believe will be condemned. And these signs will accompany those who believe: In my name they will drive out demons; they will speak in new tongues; they will pick up snakes with their hands; and when they drink deadly poison, it will not hurt them at all; they will place their hands on sick people, and they will get well."

After the Lord Jesus had spoken to them, he was taken up into heaven and he sat at the right hand of God. Then the disciples went out and preached everywhere, and the Lord worked with them and confirmed his word by the signs that accompanied it.

Mark 16 begins with the revelation that Jesus is risen from the dead (Mark 16:1–8). It is unclear, however, how the chapter ends. A number of the major English translations alert the reader to the problem of disputed manuscript evidence with a parenthetical comment inserted between verses 8 and 9 to this effect: "The most reliable early manuscripts and other ancient witnesses do not have Mark 16:9–20" (NIV). Accordingly, some scholars believe that Mark ends his Gospel at verse 8 of chapter 16.[1] The problem is that verse 8 ends on an abrupt and unfinished note. Nevertheless, textual criticism—the discipline of evaluating the variant manuscript readings and attempting to identify the original biblical text—advocates, among other things, a preference for the shorter, more difficult reading, factors that favor the Mark 16:8 ending. But most scholars are not convinced by these arguments. Yet they also reject Mark 16:9–20—the so-called Longer Ending—as non-Markan, and believe there is another original ending to Mark's Gospel that has been lost in the transmission of the Gospel.[2] What is interesting from our perspec-

---

1. See the discussion in R. T. France, *The Gospel of Mark*, New International Greek Testament Commentary (Grand Rapids: Eerdmans, 2002), 670–71.

2. Ibid., 673.

tive is that these scholars adopt elements of our multidirectional hermeneutic to make the point. So rather than engage in exegesis of this chapter, we will implement our model of interpretation to address this textual-critical question.

A DOWNWARD READING

A downward reading of the text identifies factors that, according to one commentator, "weigh heavily against the Longer Ending":[3]

- Twenty percent of words that occur in Mark 16:9–20 are not found elsewhere in Mark's Gospel.
- The transition from verse 8 to verses 9–20 is awkward at best.
- Mary Magdalene, who features fairly prominently in the preceding context (see 15:40, 47; 16:1), is reintroduced to the reader in verse 9.
- The angelic witness to the resurrection affirms Jesus' promise that his disciples would see him in Galilee after his resurrection (16:7; cf. 14:28). In 16:9–20, however, Jesus' post-resurrection appearances among his disciples include appearances in Jerusalem and its vicinity, but with no explicit mention of an appearance in Galilee, leaving Jesus' promise unfulfilled (cf. Mark 16:12–14; Matt. 28:16).

A SIDEWAYS READING

The Longer Ending does not fare much better in a sideways reading of the text. It appears as though a later scribe, familiar with the other Synoptic Gospel accounts and unsettled by the abrupt, unexpected ending of Mark 16:8—the "good news" of Jesus Christ (1:1) ends, inexplicably, on a note of fear (16:8)—cobbles together a pastiche of sayings and traditions borrowed from the other Gospels to provide an ending more compatible with these accounts. For example, Mark 16:12–13 seems to be little more than a brief summary statement of the post-resurrection "road to Emmaus" material recorded in Luke's Gospel (Luke 24:13–23), a Gospel that most scholars believe was written

3. Walter Wessel, *Mark*, The Expositor's Bible Commentary—Abridged Edition: New Testament (Grand Rapids: Zondervan, 1994), 204.

after Mark's.[4] The same problem arises with the material recorded in Mark 16:19, which has an obvious affinity with material reflected in Luke 24:51; both Mark and Luke mention Jesus' being "taken up into heaven." The reference to the sign of speaking "in new tongues," otherwise unknown in the Gospels, may have been imported from the book of Acts (Mark 16:17; cf. Acts 2:4; 10:46).

A FORWARD READING

The material recorded in Mark 16:16–18 is unique to Mark's account. But a forward reading of these verses creates tension with the rest of the New Testament. The mention of baptism as a prerequisite for salvation (16:16) is not reflected elsewhere in the New Testament; the emphasis is on believing only (e.g., John 3:16; Acts 16:31; Rom. 10:9). Some of the "signs," such as driving out demons and miraculous healings, that will accompany those who believe the "good news" are limited to the apostles and their companions in the book of Acts (Mark 16:17–18b; cf. Acts 5:12–16; 8:4–7; 16:18; 19:12; 28:8), while others, such as picking up snakes with one's hands or drinking deadly poison with impunity, are unknown in the New Testament (Mark 16:18; cf. Luke 10:19; Acts 28:3–6—Paul does not intentionally pick up the snake that bites him).

It should be noted that there are actually four different endings to Mark's Gospel in the manuscript evidence—evidence of the discomfort or dissatisfaction not only with the abrupt ending in Mark 16:8, but possibly also with the Longer Ending recorded in Mark 16:9–20. The preacher and teacher today, however, need to show pastoral sensitivity to the men and women in the pew who are largely unaware of textual criticism and its intricacies. To simply "lop off" the Longer Ending in preaching or teaching on this text can have the inadvertent effect of undermining confidence in the Word of God or hindering the ministry of the Word in the context. Accordingly, a better way to proceed is to apply our multidirectional hermeneutic with wisdom and skill as the preacher shows his hearers the echoes of the Longer Ending in the parallel accounts, while cautioning them

---

4. This majority view on Luke's Gospel is evident in discussions regarding a solution to the so-called synoptic problem.

against expecting signs to accompany their ministries that either are limited to the apostles and their companions in the early church or are not found elsewhere in the pages of Scripture.

A BACKWARD READING

Of course, for the sake of completeness, one can add a backward reading on the "resurrection" motif to show the Christian reader that Jesus' resurrection is "according to the Scriptures" (1 Cor. 15:4; cf. Pss. 16:10; 71:20; Isa. 53:10; Ezek. 37:1–14; Dan. 12:2; Hos. 6:2). This approach affirms belief not only in these Old Testament Scriptures, but also in Jesus himself, the focus of these Scriptures, and the One who is magnified as the "good news" of the Synoptic Gospels (see Mark 1:1)!

BiBLiOGRAPHY

Aland, Kurt, ed. *Synopsis of the Four Gospels*. Stuttgart: German Bible Society, 1987.

Barclay, William. *The Gospel of Matthew*. Vol. 2 of The Daily Study Bible. Edinburgh: St. Andrew Press, 1958.

Barker, Kenneth L., and John R. Kohlenberger III. *The Expositor's Bible Commentary—Abridged Edition: New Testament*. Grand Rapids: Zondervan, 1994.

Beasley-Murray, George R. *Preaching the Gospel from the Gospels*. Peabody, MA: Hendrickson, 1996.

Black, David Alan, and David S. Dockery, eds. *Interpreting the New Testament: Essays on Methods and Issues*. Nashville: Broadman & Holman, 2001.

Blomberg, Craig. *The Historical Reliability of the Gospels*. Downers Grove, IL: InterVarsity Press, 1987.

———. *Jesus and the Gospels*. Leicester, UK: Apollos, 1997.

Carson, D. A., R. T. France, J. Alec Motyer, and Gordon J. Wenham, eds. *New Bible Commentary: 21st Century Edition*. Downers Grove, IL: IVP Academic, 1994.

Carson, D. A., and Douglas Moo. *An Introduction to the New Testament*. 2nd ed. Leicester, UK: Apollos, 2005.

Cole, R. A. *Mark*. New Bible Commentary: 21st Century Edition. Downers Grove, IL: IVP Academic, 1994.

Edwards, James R. *The Gospel according to Mark*. Pillar New Testament Commentary. Grand Rapids: Eerdmans, 2002.

Evans, Craig. *Ancient Texts for New Testament Studies*. Peabody, MA: Hendrickson, 2005.

Ferguson, Sinclair. *Daniel*. New Bible Commentary: 21st Century Edition. Downers Grove, IL: IVP Academic, 1994.

Ferguson, Sinclair B., and Packer, J. I. *New Dictionary of Theology*. Electronic ed. Downers Grove, IL: IVP Academic, 2000.

France, R. T. *The Gospel of Mark*. New International Greek Testament Commentary. Grand Rapids: Eerdmans, 2002.

———. *Matthew*. New Bible Commentary: 21st Century Edition. Downers Grove, IL: IVP Academic, 1994.

Gaebelein, Frank E., ed. *Matthew, Mark, Luke*. Vol. 8 of The Expositor's Bible Commentary. Grand Rapids: Zondervan, 1984.

Gaffin, Richard B., Jr. "Sabbath." In *New Dictionary of Theology*. Electronic ed. Downers Grove, IL: IVP Academic, 2000.

Garland, David E. *Mark*. NIV Application Commentary. Grand Rapids: Zondervan, 1996.

Goodrick, Edward W., and John R. Kohlenberger III. *The NIV Complete Concordance*. Grand Rapids: Zondervan, 1981.

Green, Joel B., Scot McKnight, and I. Howard Marshall. *Dictionary of Jesus and the Gospels*. Downers Grove, IL: InterVarsity Press, 1992.

Gundry, Robert H. *Mark: A Commentary on His Apology for the Cross*. Grand Rapids: Eerdmans, 1993.

Hafemann, Scott J. *The God of Promise and the Life of Faith*. Wheaton, IL: Crossway, 2001.

———. "2 Corinthians." Lecture, Bible Teachers Network conference, Cape Town, July 2004.

Hagner, Donald A. *Matthew 14–28*. Word Biblical Commentary 33b. Dallas: Word, 1995.

Haller, Hal M. "Did the Rich Young Ruler Hear the Gospel according to Jesus?" *Journal of the Grace Evangelical Society* 13, 2 (2000): 13–41.

Keener, Craig S. *The IVP Bible Background Commentary: New Testament*. Downers Grove, IL: InterVarsity Press, 1993.

Klein, William W., Craig Blomberg, and Robert L. Hubbard Jr. *Introduction to Biblical Interpretation*. Nashville: Thomas Nelson, 2004.

Koester, Craig R. *Revelation and the End of All Things*. Grand Rapids: Eerdmans, 2001.

Lane, William. *The Gospel of Mark*. New International Commentary on the New Testament. Grand Rapids: Eerdmans, 1974.

Leifeld, Walter L. "Luke." In *Matthew, Mark, Luke*. Vol. 8 of The Expositor's Bible Commentary. Grand Rapids: Zondervan, 1984.

Louw, J. P., and Eugene A. Nida. *Greek-English Lexicon of the New Testament: Based on Semantic Domains*. Vol. 1. New York: United Bible Societies, 1996.

Marshall, I. Howard. *Commentary on Luke*. New International Greek Testament Commentary. Grand Rapids: Eerdmans, 1978.

McCartney, Dan, and Charles Clayton. *Let the Reader Understand: A Guide to Interpreting and Applying the Bible*. Wheaton, IL: Bridgepoint, 1994.

Mounce, Robert H. *The Book of Revelation*. New International Commentary on the New Testament. Grand Rapids: Eerdmans, 1998.

Oswalt, John N. *The Book of Isaiah: Chapters 1–39*. New International Commentary on the Old Testament. Grand Rapids: Eerdmans, 1986.

Richards, Lawrence O. *The Bible Reader's Companion*. Electronic ed. Wheaton, IL: Victor Books, 1991.

Ryle, J. C. *Holiness*. Welwyn, UK: Evangelical Press, 1979.

Stein, Robert H. *Mark*. Baker Exegetical Commentary on the New Testament. Grand Rapids: Baker Academic, 2008.

Torrey, R. A. *The Treasury of Scripture Knowledge*. Peabody, MA: Hendrickson, 1990.

Utley, R. J. D. *The Gospel according to Peter: Mark and I & II Peter*. Vol. 2 of Study Guide Commentary Series. Marshall, TX: Bible Lessons International, 2001.

Wallace, Ronald S. *The Message of Daniel*. The Bible Speaks Today. Downers Grove, IL: InterVarsity Press, 1979.

Watts, Rikk E. *Mark*. Commentary on the New Testament Use of the Old Testament. Grand Rapids: Baker Academic, 2007.

Wessel, Walter W. "Mark." In *Matthew, Mark, Luke*. Vol. 8 of The Expositor's Bible Commentary. Grand Rapids: Zondervan, 1984.

———. *Mark*. The Expositor's Bible Commentary—Abridged Edition: New Testament. Grand Rapids: Zondervan, 1994.

Wintle, Brian. "The New Testament as Tradition." *Evangelical Review of Theology* 19 (1995): 115–30.

Witherington, Ben, III. *The Gospel of Mark*. A Socio-Rhetorical Commentary. Grand Rapids: Eerdmans, 2001.

Wright, Christopher J. H. *Leviticus*, New Bible Commentary: 21st Century Edition. Leicester, England; Downers Grove, IL, USA: Inter-Varsity Press, 1994.

Zerwick, Maximilian. *Biblical Greek Illustrated by Examples*. English ed., adapted from the 4th Latin ed. Rome: Editrice Pontificio Instituto Biblico, 1963.

INDEX OF SCRIPTURE

INDEX OF SUBJECTS AND NAMES